Agricultural Development in Southern Africa

Farm-household economics and the food crisis

Books in African Studies

HISTORY

T. O. Ranger *Peasant Consciousness & Guerrilla War in Zimbabwe* — Cased 0-85255-000-6 / Paper 0-85255-001-4

Robert Shenton *The Development of Capitalism in Northern Nigeria* — Cased 0-85255-002-2 / Paper 0-85255-003-0

Donald Crummey (editor) *Banditry, Rebellion and Social Protest in Africa* — Cased 0-85255-004-9 / Paper 0-85255-005-7

Jan Vansina *Oral Tradition as History* — Cased 0-85255-006-5 / Paper 0-85255-007-3

Ralph Austen *African Economic History** — Cased 0-85255-008-1 / Paper 0-85255-009-X

J. D. Omer-Cooper *History of Southern Africa** — Cased 0-85255-010-3 / Paper 0-85255-011-1

William Beinart & Colin Bundy *Hidden Struggles in Rural South Africa** — Cased 0-85255-012-X / Paper 0-85255-013-8

ECONOMICS

C. George Kahama, T. Luta Maliyamkono & Stuart Wells *The Challenge for Tanzania's Economy* — Cased 0-85255-100-2 / Paper 0-85255-101-0

Allan Low *Agricultural Development in Southern Africa* — Cased 0-85255-102-9

SOCIO-ANTHROPOLOGY

David Lan *Guns & Rain: Guerrillas & Spirit Mediums in Zimbabwe* — Cased 0-85255-200-9 / Paper 0-85255-201-7

GOVERNMENT, POLITICS AND LAW

Roger Tangri *Politics in Sub-Saharan Africa* — Paper 0-85255-300-5

Philip Ndegwa *Africa's Development Crisis* — Paper 0-85255-306-4

Issa G. Shivji *Law, State and the Working Class in Tanzania* — Cased 0-85255-302-1 / Paper 0-85255-303-X

Julie Frederikse *South Africa: A Different Kind of War* — Paper 0-85255-301-3

Peter Lawrence (editor) *World Recession & the Food Crisis in Africa** — Paper 0-85255-304-8

Joseph Hanlon *Apartheid Power in Southern Africa** — Cased 0-85255-307-2 / Paper 0-85255-305-6

LITERARY CRITICISM

Eldred Jones & Eustace Palmer (editors) *Women Writers in African Literature Today** — Paper 0-85255-500-8

Ngugi wa Thiong'o *Decolonising the Mind* — Paper 0-85255-501-6

Georg M. Gugelberger (editor) *Marxism and African Literature* — Paper 0-85255-502-4

*in preparation

James Currey
54b Thornhill Square · Islington · London N1 1BE

Agricultural Development in Southern Africa

*Farm-household economics
and the food crisis*

Allan Low

Southern Africa Regional Economist for CIMMYT the International
Maize and Wheat Improvement Center, Swaziland

James Currey LONDON
Heinemann PORTSMOUTH N.H.
David Philip CAPE TOWN

James Currey Ltd
54b Thornhill Square, Islington, London N1 1BE

David Philip Publishers (Pty) Ltd
P.O. Box 408, Claremont, 7735, Cape

Heinemann Educational Books Inc
70 Court Street, Portsmouth, New Hampshire 03801

© Allan R.C. Low 1986
First published 1986

British Library Cataloguing in Publication Data

Low, Allan
  Agricultural development in Southern Africa: farm-household economics and the food crisis.
    1. Agriculture——Economic aspects——Africa, Southern
    I. Title
  338.1'0968   HD2130

  ISBN 0—85255-102-9

Typeset in 11/11 pt Baskerville by Colset Pte Ltd, Singapore
Printed in Great Britain

Dedication

Anne, Sarah
& Emma

Contents

List of tables	ix
List of figures	xii
Preface	xiii
1 Introduction and summary	1

Part I Household-economics theory and the southern African context — 11

2 Household economics: theory, applications and relevance — 13
  The theory — 13
  Applications in developed societies — 15
  Relevance of the approach in less developed societies — 16
  An early application of household economics in southern Africa — 18

3 Indigenous agriculture in southern African economies — 22

4 A model of the indigenous farm-household in southern Africa — 28
  Chayanov and household economics — 28
  Current farm-household theory and its limitations in southern Africa — 30
  A Z goods approach to subsistence farm production — 35
  Cash cropping and multi-person households — 40
  Observations on the model — 44

5 Historical developments re-examined — 48
  A household-economics interpretation of agricultural development in Botswana and Lesotho — 48
  Contributions to development theory — 53

Part II Field study: regional evidence and analysis — 57

6 Focus on Swaziland — 59
  Geography and climate — 59
  History — 60
  The Swazi rural sector — 62

7 Supporting evidence from Swaziland and elsewhere — 65
  The data base — 65
  Returns to farm labour in crop production — 66
  Cropping patterns — 70
  The domestic development cycle — 75
  Demographic differentiation — 86

8 Adoption of improved crop technology — 90
  Hybrid-maize adoption in Swaziland — 91
  Fertilizer and tractors in Swaziland — 103
  Appropriateness of labour-intensive versus labour-saving technology in southern Africa — 104

viii Contents

9	Non-market benefits of land-use rights and cattle ownership	107
	Land attributes	108
	Cattle attributes	110
10	Labour migration: a comparative-advantage approach	118
	Conventional theories on the development of labour markets in southern Africa	119
	Contradictory evidence	120
	Migration models and analytical concepts	123
	The household-economics argument	123
11	Rural development: towards a broader perspective	134
	Agricultural innovations and development initiatives	136
	Widening the analytical framework	142
	Implications for the evaluation of rural development	151

Part III Wider perspectives — 155

12	Policy implications	157
	Food-price policy	157
	Integrated rural development and rural-urban migration	160
	Land tenure	162
13	Farming-systems research	167
	Characteristics of the approach	167
	Farm-household linkages	169
	Expanding the systems perspective	172
	Evaluation of farming-systems research	176
14	Household economics and agrarian development in other settings	179
	The common circumstances of Peruvian and southern African peasantry	179
	A unifying interpretation of family labour use in farm production	181
	A pan-African perspective	183

Appendix 1	Characteristics of survey areas	192
Appendix 2	Farm management survey data collection and analysis	193
Appendix 3	Statistical supplement	195
References		199
Index		213

List of tables

Table 2.1:	Dean's primitive household-economics framework	19
Table 3.1:	Percentage of GDP and economically active population in agriculture and percentage of population residing in rural areas	22
Table 3.2:	Percentage of land occupied and marketed production supplied by the modern farming sector	23
Table 3.3:	Percentage of cropped area planted to various smallholder crops	23
Table 3.4:	Food aid and commercial maize imports, 1975–9	25
Table 4.1:	Household and farm size in southern Africa and Russia	33
Table 4.2:	Average earnings by sector	34
Table 4.3:	Mean household size and workforce of surplus and non-surplus producers in Zambia, Zimbabwe and Swaziland	35
Table 5.1:	Net maize and wheat exports and gold mining employment: Lesotho 1928–37	51
Table 5.2:	Grain imports and labour migration in Botswana, 1928–38	52
Table 6.1:	Swazi land apportionment (1980)	61
Table 6.2:	Percentage of households growing and area planted to major crops on SNL	62
Table 7.1:	Mean arable areas allocated and cropped per farm by de jure and de facto household workforce (hectares)	67
Table 7.2:	Farms spending less than E10 on power: maize yield and gross margin/hr by labour hours in cropping	67
Table 7.3:	Mean maize gross margins per hour per farm on selected fields	70
Table 7.4:	Reported gross margins per hour for cotton and tobacco	70
Table 7.5:	Output, costs and net value of maize 1977/78	71
Table 7.6:	Mean gross margins per hectare for maize, cotton and tobacco (E/ha)	73
Table 7.7:	Cropping patterns by ecological region	73
Table 7.8:	Household production characteristics by region: 1959/60 sample survey	74
Table 7.9:	Household production characteristics by location: 1980 sample survey	74
Table 7.10:	Farm incomes and the supply of labour: Uganda 1956	75
Table 7.11:	Area cropped and cattle held by household size	76
Table 7.12:	Wage incomes per household and maize deficits per head (lbs) (1959/60)	77
Table 7.13:	Maize deficit/surplus by household size (1959/60)	78

List of tables

Table 7.14:	Correlation coefficient significance levels: household size with crop production and wage income	78
Table 7.15:	Relationship between household size, maize sales and off-farm income in Zimbabwe	79
Table 7.16:	Types of Swazi household grouping	80
Table 7.17:	Domestic development groups: criteria for classification and basic characteristics (5 RDAs)	82
Table 7.18:	Net voluntary cattle disposals by domestic development group (Cattle Marketing Survey 1980)	83
Table 7.19:	Domestic development groups: resource structures and production characteristics	84
Table 7.20:	Farm-household characteristics in Zambia	87
Table 8.1:	Local-maize and hybrid-maize yields (kg/hectare) (1980/81)	90
Table 8.2:	Local-maize and hybrid-maize returns per hectare (1977/78)	91
Table 8.3:	Local-maize and hybrid-maize returns to labour (1977/78)	92
Table 8.4:	Derived cost and return parameters for local maize and hybrid maize	92
Table 8.5:	Calculation of full maize subsistence procurement cost for households with different wage potentials (cents per hour)	97
Table 8.6:	Percentage of households selling maize and reporting regular selling (1977/78)	98
Table 8.7:	Hybrid-seed uptake in four RDAs (tonnes)	99
Table 8.8:	Hybrid-maize adoption compared with surplus production and off-farm employment	99
Table 8.9:	Household size related to cash cropping, maize selling, and hybrid-maize adoption	101
Table 8.10:	Mean household sizes and adoption rates for deficit and surplus producers (Group B households with wage earners)	101
Table 8.11:	Proportion of households selling maize: hybrid-maize adopters compared with non-adopters	102
Table 8.12:	Proportion of households adopting hybrid maize: domestic development cycle groupings compared	102
Table 8.13:	Fertilizer and tractor uptake in four RDAs	103
Table 9.1:	Cattle sales and slaughter rates by herd size	112
Table 9.2:	Cattle sales rates by ecological region	113
Tabler 9.3:	Reasons for cattle sales by ecological region	114
Table 10.1:	Employment rates and educational levels in Swaziland (percentage of 25–64 resident age cohort in employment, 1976)	124
Table 10.2:	Age-specific migration and employment rates for Lesotho and Swaziland	125
Table 10.3:	Comparative age distribution of male workers (1970, except Swaziland = 1976)	125
Table 10.4:	Percentage rural household income distribution by income source: Lesotho, 1976	130

Table 10.5: Estimates of area planted and percentage composition of rural household income in Lesotho — 130
Table 10.6: Crop yields recorded by uniform crop cutting field surveys in Lesotho (kg/ha) — 132
Table 11.1: RDAP (1977/8–1982/3): financial performance — 140
Table 11.2: Percentage of de facto working-age population in wage employment — 143
Table 11.3: Employment and wage rates (1971–82) — 144
Table 11.4: Aggregate areas cropped and planted to maize on Swazi Nation Land, 1972–82 — 146
Table 11.5: Average Swazi Nation Land maize yields (kg/ha) — 147
Table 11.6: Simple correlation coefficients of fertilizer with maize yields and gross margins in Lesotho and Swaziland — 148
Table 11.7: Cereal production and capital equipment in South African reserves 1930–69 — 149
Table 11.8: Percentage of households mentioning particular development needs — 150
Table 12.1: Wheat and maize imports and utilization: percentage annual growth rates 1971–9 — 158
Table 12.2: Kg of maize per day's wage employment (1982/83) — 161
Table 13.1: Characteristics of two recommendation domains in Mangwende, Zimbabwe — 170
Table 13.2: Farm-based partial budget analysis — 175
Table 13.3: Household-economics time-efficiency analysis — 176
Table A1.1: Details of the Swaziland Rural Development Areas covered by the Farm Management Surveys — 192
Table A7.1: Standard errors of the means: arable areas allocated and cropped per farm by de jure and de facto household workforce — 195
Table A7.2: Standard errors of the means: farms spending less than E10 on power, maize yield and gross margin/hr by labour hours in cropping — 195
Table A7.11: Standard errors of the means: area cropped and cattle held by household size — 196
Table A7.14: Correlation coefficients and number of observations: household size with crop production and wage income — 196
Table A7.18: Standard errors of the means: net voluntary cattle disposals by domestic development group (Cattle Marketing Survey 1980) — 197
Table A7.19: Standard errors of the means: domestic development groups – resource structures and production characteristics — 198

List of figures

Figure 4.1:   The standard neo-classical farm-household model   31
Figure 4.2:   Household-economics farm-household model: the two-person household – subsistence cropping versus wage employment   38
Figure 4.3:   Household-economics farm-household model: the multi-person household – subsistence and cash cropping versus wage employment   43
Figure 6.1:   Ecological regions in Swaziland   60
Figure 8.1:   Household-economics farm-household model: hybrid-maize technology alternatives   94
Figure 11.1:   Mahlangatsha RDA: physical and financial performance   138
Figure 11.2:   Mahlangatsha RDA: input uptake and production performance   139
Figure 11.3:   Rural development areas programme (1977/8–82/3)   141
Figure 11.4:   Movements in wage rates and maize prices 1972–82   143
Figure 11.5:   Effects of increased wages and hybrid maize on household labour allocation   145

Preface

The concepts presented in this book originate from an attempt to understand the reasons for the poor production performance of a well-executed rural development programme in Swaziland, where the agro-climatic and infrastructural environment are very favourable. Conventional assessments on the difficulties of rural development in Africa caused by a harsh environment, dispersed rural populations, poor infrastructure and limited implementation capacity simply did not hold water in the Swaziland case. Neither did conventional farm-household models, based on the Asian labour surplus situation, provide much help in understanding the response of Swazi farm-households to rural development initiatives including supply of inputs, extension advice and improved infrastructure.

An understanding of what was happening in the Swazi rural areas and why came out of many hours of discussion among colleagues in the economics department of the Ministry of Agriculture and Cooperatives and at the University of Swaziland. The main contributors to these formative debates were: E.V. Dlamini, Nomathemba Dlamini, Martin Doran, Martin Fowler, Harriet Sibisi and Fion de Vletter. I owe much to their stimulating comment, observations and knowledge of the Swazi rural scene. The ideas developed in this forum in relation to Swaziland were further developed at Reading University in the course of my Ph.D. research and extended to cover most of the other countries of southern Africa. At Reading John McInerney introduced me to the new theory of household economics, which provided a theoretical framework that I was able to use to refine the ideas and empirical models I had developed.

My subsequent work with CIMMYT's Eastern and Southern Africa Economics Programme has given me the opportunity to work with small farmers in all the southern Africa countries I write about and has confirmed the general applicability of the concepts developed in the Swaziland context. The outcome is a new perspective on the basic causes of poor agricultural productivity in the region. It is a perspective that comes out of development experience in the region and seems to provide a better explanation of much of this experience than conventional theory and analysis.

I do not attempt to provide answers to Africa's food production problem in this book. My aim is to contribute to a better understanding of why it is a particularly African problem, different from the Asian food crisis of the 1960s, and to offer researchers, planners and aid agencies addressing the problem an analytical framework of practical value based on the socio-economic realities of Africa.

Allan Low

1 Introduction and summary

Introduction

> Africa's inability to feed itself amid vast amounts of unused land and record levels of foreign aid is, on the surface, one of the major paradoxes of Third World development (Eicher, 1982, p. 163).

In 1984 and 1985 Africa's food production problems came to the forefront of world attention. Yet the tragic and monumental famines in north-eastern Africa and the Sahel zone of West Africa are in many ways more readily comprehensible than the general malaise of agriculture elsewhere in Africa which has so far thankfully taken a less critical form. Even in the famine areas, although drought and destructive cultivation practices may be paramount, there are also underlying social and economic causes of production shortfalls which are not reflections of ecological constraints. Elsewhere in Africa, where natural conditions may have deteriorated less drastically, or may remain favourable to agriculture, food production has also failed to keep pace with population expansion, despite an abundance of land and substantial foreign aid and inputs of new technology.

In this book the new household-economics theory of consumer choice is used to throw light on the apparent paradox pointed to by Eicher, with particular reference to southern Africa. It will be argued that the new household-economics approach, which has provided a number of insights into the behaviour of modern households in North America, Japan and Israel, enables the behaviour of subsistence farm-households in southern Africa, and their response to development initiatives, to be seen in a new perspective. This new perspective has particular relevance at a time when agricultural development in Africa is beginning to take centre stage in international development thinking.

It has been widely noted that sub-Saharan Africa is the world's only region where food production through the 1970s did not keep pace with population expansion (IBRD, 1981, p. 3; OECD, 1980, p. 34; USDA, 1981, p. 1; Eicher, 1982, p. 154). While declining agricultural (especially food) production is generally recognized to be at the core of the development problem in Africa, economic development in broad terms has been less of a problem in southern Africa. Of the six former British colonies and High Commission Territories in southern Africa (Zambia, Malawi, Zimbabwe, Botswana, Swaziland and Lesotho), and South Africa, five countries had annual per capita growth rates of gross national product in excess of 2.5 per cent between 1960 and 1979. This was the case for only four of the remaining thirty-three countries in sub-Saharan Africa (IBRD, 1981, Table 1). Nevertheless, the performance of indigenous agriculture in southern Africa has been typical of the general sub-Saharan trend. While rapid growth has taken place in the modern sectors of the southern African economies, in the indigenous agricultural sectors, where over half the populations continue to live, production per person has stagnated or declined (Gulhati, 1980, p. 2).

The common interpretations of the underdevelopment of the indigenous sectors in southern Africa stress either historical neglect and policy discrimination or the current institutional biases that have favoured and continue to favour large-scale modern, urban and capital-intensive production over small-scale peasant farming. Development strategies have therefore concentrated on compensating for previous neglect and correcting the sectoral biases. These strategies have been implemented through various rural-development projects, aimed at increasing the agricultural production of small family farms. Rural infrastructure has been constructed, marketing organizations established, credit facilities made available, extension services strengthened and new crop and livestock production technology has been developed, extended and utilized. The results, in common with those elsewhere in Africa, have, on the whole, been disappointing and production figures per hectare and per person in indigenous farm sectors have continued to fall, even in areas where agro-climatic conditions are particularly favourable and over a decade in which the problem of drought was not a factor.

In this book, we present a view of farm-household production in the southern African context, which sees present production patterns and output trends as resulting not only from historical neglect and sectoral biases or drought, but also from the nature of the peasant farm-household production unit and the indigenous environment in which it operates. This view provides an explanation for the general lack of production response to agricultural development efforts and provides a new perspective on the link between the development of the modern sector and the underdevelopment of the indigenous sector in southern Africa. The perspective that emerges also contributes to an understanding of why development strategies and technologies that have dramatically reduced food imports in most Asian countries do not appear to be having any impact on today's African food crisis.

The new household-economics theory of consumer behaviour forms the basis of the analytical approach used in this study, which is divided into three parts. In Part I the relevance of the household-economics approach to agricultural development in the southern Africa setting is established. The applicability of conventional farm-household models developed in the Asian context is challenged and an alternative analytical model is presented which fits more closely the circumstances faced by African farm families. In Part II this analytical framework is used to explain farm-household behaviour in the region and to throw new light on a number of development issues. Part III discusses some of the implications of the foregoing analysis for agricultural research and development policy, and considers to what extent, and with what caveats, the approach adopted in this book is applicable to the study of agrarian development in other countries of the Third World.

Summary

The origins and applications of the new household-economics theory are discussed in Chapter 2. The theory has been applied to the analysis of the consumption behaviour of modern households in Western industrialized societies and represents a reformulation of the traditional theory of consumer choice, in which the household rather than the individual is taken as the basic analytical unit. Consumption is viewed as a process which involves the allocation of both money expenditure and the time of household members. In this formulation, time, rather than a budget limit, becomes the basic constraint. Household members' time may be spent in market production (e.g. wage employment) or in the non-market production of consumption goods within the household. The non-market production processes may involve the use of varying proportions of purchased inputs and time. Thus clean clothes may be produced within the household using a time-intensive technology, such as hand-washing, or an inputs-intensive technology, such as the utilization of a laundry service. The technology chosen will depend on the relative costs of the purchased inputs and the opportunity cost of the household members' time in other market or non-market activities.

In this approach the household is seen as a production/consumption unit, which attempts to combine market inputs with the time of its members so as to produce its consumption requirements as cheaply as possible. It is suggested that this approach is as relevant to the indigenous farm-household in southern Africa as it has been shown to be for modern households in America, Israel and Japan. An early analysis of farm-household behaviour in Malawi, for example, provides evidence that part of the secular increase in tobacco production between 1920 and 1960 was due to the introduction of superior, and increasingly cheaper, consumer goods, which encouraged farm-households to allocate more time to market production of tobacco. Due to both the increasing value of time in market (tobacco) production and reduced costs of market consumer goods, it became cheaper to grow tobacco and purchase consumption requirements, such as clothes, building materials and household utensils, in the retail market, than to produce them with more time-intensive technology within the farm-household.

In Chapter 3 we show that the stagnation of traditional agriculture in southern African countries has proceeded alongside rapid expansion in modern agriculture and industrial development. Modern-sector development in these countries has resulted in the introduction of market consumer goods and the simultaneous provision of wage employment opportunities. African farm-households have taken up these market opportunities but have also retained their rural home bases for the provision of non-market consumption goods. Conventional neo-classical models of the farm-household (e.g. Nakajima, 1970) do not allow an explicit analysis of such non-market production aspects of farm-household behaviour, and, for a number of reasons, are shown to be of limited applicability in southern Africa. The market/non-market interaction is, however, central to household-economics theory and, in Chapter 4, household-economics concepts are used to develop a model of the farm-household, in which the relationships between market and non-market production can be analyzed.

In order to illustrate how the household-economics approach can contribute to a better understanding of agricultural development in the region, a household-economics interpretation of the historical development of two southern African countries with markedly different agro-climatic characteristics is presented in Chapter 5. While Botswana is flat, semi-arid and poorly watered with annual rainfall of less than 600 mm, Lesotho is mountainous, temperate and well watered with annual rainfall in excess of 1000 mm. Despite such marked agro-climatic differences, the historical development of agriculture in these two countries has followed a very similar pattern which has been determined by economic rather than agro-climatic factors. The major influence on agricultural production in these two countries was the simultaneous introduction of market consumer goods and off-farm wage employment opportunities, which encouraged farm-households to engage in market production through wage employment rather than commercial farming. However, migration to wage employment in mining and industrial centres did not reduce population (human and cattle) pressures on the land, since most migrants retained their rural home base. Under traditional land-use rights, this necessitated only the continued presence of some household members on the land. Also, by maintaining a rural home base, farm-households retained access to a wide range of household necessities, such as food, shelter, water, fuel, grazing and security, which could be procured more cheaply through non-market 'own production' by household members with low wage potentials, than by their purchase in the marketplace. The market/non-market interactions have encouraged an oscillating pattern of migration by adult male farm-household members between their rural home base and places of work, which has adversely affected farm production and resulted in low levels of productivity per worker and per hectare.

The foregoing analysis of farm-household behaviour in terms of the relative costs of procuring consumption goods through the market (via market production and retail purchases), compared to own production, has a number of implications for agricultural production and development which are examined empirically in the second part of this study. Subsequent analysis is based largely, although not exclusively, on data from Swaziland. Chapter 6 presents a brief profile of that country, which has good agricultural potential and which through the 1970s enjoyed both political and climatic stability, together with substantial development of the modern market sector and stagnation of the subsistence sector. In Chapter 7, the prevalence of subsistence-crop production and lack of cash cropping in Swaziland are explained in terms of the costs of procuring household food requirements and the relatively high opportunity costs of some farm-household members in wage employment. A key implication of the farm-household model developed in Chapter 4 is that the time of members with the lowest off-farm wage earning potential will be allocated to subsistence production first, followed by members with increasingly higher wage potentials. Household members with low wage-employment prospects will often be used to produce subsistence food crops in preference to non-food cash crops, because they can produce more food than could be purchased with the proceeds of the cash crops they might otherwise grow. Although cash crops may be more profitable than the production of surplus food crops for sale, after household subsistence needs have been met (or before in many cases), the employment opportunities of household members not needed to produce food requirements will often be more attractive than cash cropping. This implies that cash crops need to provide better returns to labour than either subsistence crops valued at retail prices, or than the wage employment opportunities of the better-qualified household members. Neither of these conditions seems to apply to most farm-households in Swaziland. However, the latter does apply to some farm-households, which have relatively few consumers per producer and thus have more low-potential wage earners remaining after food requirements have been met, or who operate in situations where wage employment opportunities are scarce. Empirical evidence from Swaziland and elsewhere indicates that commercial crop production is more prevalent in regions where wage opportunities are limited and is more common among households which have low consumer/worker ratios.

The last observation suggests that the structure of the farm-household has an important influence on the pattern of production. The influence of the domestic development cycle on farm production was first stressed by Chayanov (1966) in respect of Russian peasants in the 1920s. More recently Murray (1980) and Spiegel (1981) have re-emphasized its importance in accounting for production differences between farm-households in the southern African context. In Chapters 7 and 8 we relate (theoretically and empirically) the adoption of certain crop production technologies to the stages of the domestic development cycle, and show that households with relatively high consumer/worker ratios and high wage-earning potentials have demonstrated a greater propensity to adopt time-saving techniques in the production of subsistence crops.

The different rates of adoption of hybrid maize in Swaziland between geographical areas, and between farm-households within regions, can also be explained in terms of the time-saving properties of hybrid maize. Farm management studies show that hybrid maize increases yields per unit of time by about 50 per cent. The increased input costs associated with hybrid-maize adoption result in net commercial returns being no better than lower cost local varieties. Nevertheless, hybrid maize has been rapidly adopted in areas where wage employment opportunities are good and by households with high consumer/worker ratios and relatively good wage employment prospects. In those areas and for these households, the value of time saved in subsistence production is relatively high and this increases the incentive to adopt the time-saving hybrid-maize technology.

In the light of these findings the question of the appropriateness of crop technology for indigenous farm-households in southern Africa takes on a new complexion. Increasing population densities and low levels of production have led most observers to advocate the introduction of labour-intensive, yield-increasing (land-augmenting) crop technologies. However, from the farm-household's point of view, labour-intensive technologies are not appropriate unless they result in a reduction in the time required to produce a unit of food.[1] Labour-intensive crop inputs that do not save labour time per unit of output are about as appropriate to most subsistence farm-households in southern Africa as a costly new domestic appliance, which consumes rather than saves time, would be to most Western households.

In Chapter 9 the non-market benefits of land-use rights and cattle ownership are analyzed in household-economic terms. Sociological analysis is presented which suggests that, in southern Africa, land has many socio-economic roles and farm production is by no means the most important one. Commercial farm production is shown to conflict with the other roles of land, and with its role as a social pension fund in particular. The possibility of engaging in wage employment to earn income removes this potential source of conflict, but results in residual farm labour forces whose household responsibilities compete directly with the demands of high-productivity crop farming. Child care and domestic duties are essential household production activities and are also highly time-intensive, so they inevitably compromise the needs of good crop husbandry.

The damaging effect of overgrazing and overstocking on both livestock production and soil conservation in southern Africa has been repeatedly documented. Like land, cattle have numerous social and economic roles. In particular they represent both productive assets and consumption goods. The reluctance to sell cattle that are surplus to productive needs can be understood in terms of their consumption attributes, which include luxury characteristics such as prestige, security, bridewealth and status. Such luxury consumption in the form of unsold cattle may be sacrificed in times of need, and empirical evidence is presented which accounts for differing rates of cattle sales between years, regions and farm-households on the basis of this 'sale for specific cash needs' hypothesis. One implication of this hypothesis is that attempts to reduce overstocking by introducing private ownership of rangelands, on the assumption that the maintenance of excessive numbers of cattle is a direct consequence of 'the tragedy of the commons', will be unsuccessful. This appears to have been borne out in Botswana. Of the newly developed private ranches there, most are overstocked and many were seriously overgrazed within two or three years of their establishment. Solutions to the overgrazing problem in southern Africa need to recognize the consumption roles as well as the production roles of cattle. Action on the production side alone has been and, under prevailing socio-economic conditions, is likely to continue to be counter-productive.

The causes and effects of labour migration in southern Africa, which have been the subject of much debate in recent years, are addressed in Chapter 10. Orthodox neo-classical economists suggest that rural Africans choose temporary migration and subsistence farming in preference to commercial agriculture, because they maximize their total incomes in this way. The more radical Marxist view is that coercion and discrimination (through asset confiscation, taxation and trade restrictions) have forced the Africans from the land, and that the pattern of oscillating migration occurs because wages paid by capitalist employers are not sufficient to support whole families at places of work.

The household-economics approach provides a new neo-classical perspective on this issue. Labour-force participation by indigenous farm-households in southern Africa may be explained in terms of the comparative-advantage analysis, which is based on the household-economics approach and has been used to analyze labour-force participation in Western households. According to this analysis, indigenous farm-household members do not enter the labour market because the marginal returns to labour on the family farm fall below the prevailing wage rate, but rather because some household members have a comparative advantage in wage employment compared with farm-household production. This comparative-advantage concept of labour migration helps to resolve the empirical paradox of under-utilization of arable land in areas where population pressures and migration rates are high. The under-utilization of land is exacerbated by the indigenous tenure arrangements and is encouraged by relatively high off-farm wage rates, which not only draw labour from the land but also increase the value of household members' time and encourage the search for subsistence production methods that save on high-value labour time. Thus increasing wage opportunities, which encourage labour-extensive methods of farm production (implying lower productivity per hectare), combined with a residual work force of women and children, lead directly to reduced productivity per hectare and per worker. This reverses the generally accepted direction of causation and provides a direct link between migration and low farm productivity at the micro-level, without involving the land sufficiency question. At the macro-level the maintenance of land-use rights by most farm-households means that, as populations expand over time, each household will tend to be allocated smaller and more marginal arable areas. While potential farm production per household is thereby reduced, other non-market advantages of maintaining a rural home are not necessarily reduced to the same extent. Temporary migration therefore persists.

The forgoing household-economics perspective of agricultural development in southern Africa has implications for the concept and evaluation of rural development in the region (Chapter 11). Rural development projects have been appraised and justified on the basis of incremental farm production which, in most cases, has not been forthcoming. The failure of rural development efforts in Africa has been attributed to the difficulties of delivering project inputs to large numbers of farmers in sparsely populated and institutionally underdeveloped countries (Lele, 1979). These reasons do not fit with experience in southern Africa where, even when inputs have been successfully delivered and taken up by farmers, production has not been significantly increased. The lack of production impact resulting from the introduction of farm technology is related to the purposes for which this technology has been adopted by farm-households. Since wage employment opportunities have continued to be available, market production has tended to take place off the farm and production-increasing crop technology has been adopted to save time in own production of farm-household consumption requirements, rather than to increase farm production and produce surpluses for the market.

Other infrastructural inputs, such as the supply of piped water, have had exactly the same effect of saving labour in non-market household production and been much in demand for this reason. Yet other developments, such as fencing of grazing areas, have been welcomed because they have made it easier for farm-households to send children to school, who would otherwise be required to herd cattle. In terms of farm-household production, investment in children's education is as potentially productive as investment in land improvement or crop production. Thus, while rural development projects in southern African have been conceived, appraised, justified and evaluated in terms of increased farm production, farm-households have viewed such projects and responded to their inputs in much broader terms. Donors and planners should follow suit if they wish to be more effective in matching rural development initiatives with policy objectives.

Part III of the book looks at some more general implications of the analyses presented in previous chapters for agrarian development in the region as well in other settings, particularly the rest of sub-Saharan Africa.

The issue of food-price policy is discussed in Chapter 12. From a household-economics perspective it becomes clear that food-price policy per se can be expected to have a substantial influence on food production in the region.

However, to be effective, this price policy must address retail prices of indigenous and non-indigenous foods in conjunction with producer prices. Furthermore, food-price policy in general needs to be related to urban wage levels.

This last observation leads us to consider the nature of the relationship between rural development and rural–urban migration. Our analyses of the experiences in Lesotho and Swaziland, as well as evidence from Latin America and Nigeria, indicate that there does not exist a simple one-way relationship between rural development and reduced rural–urban migration. The success of rural development in Malawi compared with elsewhere in the region, for example, has probably less to do with the way in which rural development projects have been managed and implemented than to the strict and deliberate wage policy in Malawi that has kept real urban wages there well below those in neighbouring countries.

Lastly in Chapter 12 the issue of land tenure is examined in terms of how productively land is likely to be used under freehold and traditional tenure. The differences are seen not so much in terms of the security of tenure that an individual has, as in the costs and methods of maintaining land rights, as well as the extent of supplementary benefits associated with traditional land ownership. Under traditional tenure, maintenance costs are low and are not related to the potential productivity of the land. Neither is the extent of associated supplementary benefits related in any way to how productively arable land is utilized. These aspects of traditional tenure encourage all households to maintain use rights even though many concentrate on non-farm activities and are not capable of or interested in using their land very productively. In contrast, under freehold tenure, the costs of keeping land under-utilized are relatively high and are related to the potential productivity of the land through the opportunity to rent or sell. The implication is that freehold tenure is more likely to result in land being distributed to those in the community who are most willing and able to use it productively. From a household-economics perspective, then, the distinction between freehold and traditional tenure rests on the objectives and capacity of those in the community who get to use land, rather than what can or cannot be done by any single owner.

In Chapter 13 the new farming-systems research approach to generating technology appropriate to the needs of small farmers is assessed in the light of both the research experiences gained to date in the region and our household-economics analysis. This assessment suggests a need to widen the systems perspective of the approach from the farm to the farm-household. It also suggests that expectations of the impact of the approach should be based more in terms of a general improvement in farmer–extension–researcher relationships giving rise to more effective research and extension over time and less in terms of substantial short-term production improvements.

The book ends with a discussion on how the general analytical framework, developed and illustrated in a southern African context, relates to situations in other parts of the Third World and to the rest of sub-Saharan Africa in particular. The new perspective that this book gives on the relationship between modern-sector development and the stagnation of indigenous agriculture in southern Africa is shown to be applicable elsewhere and contributes to an understanding of why the food crisis persists in sub-Saharan Africa despite the delivery of 'green revolution' technology and large aid inflows to the small farm sectors. At the macro-level, Aboyade (1983, p. 14) sees the African problem in terms of the inherent tendency for the marginal productivity of labour in non-agriculture to rise above average income from agriculture and for the latter sector to experience both out-migration and production decline. Mellor (1985) attributes Africa's poor record on food production to the labour constraint combined with rapid urbanization, rising urban incomes, and rising remittances to rural areas, all of which serve to reduce labour input into agriculture and slow the expansion of area cultivated as well as yields per acre. Hyden (1984) refers to this process as 'premature urbanization'[2] which he sees as being associated with three special characteristics of the socio-economic environment in which African farm-households operate:

1) universal access to land by all members of society;
2) a lack of agricultural surplus labour;
3) the maintenance of strong rural links by urban migrants.

From our farm-household analysis perspective we can see that these characteristics are closely linked. Universal access to land results in specialization taking place *within* rather than *between* households. Where wage employment or other non-farm production opportunities exist this means that farm-households are often not solely or primarily farmers. Some members specialize in non-farm or wage employment, while those who remain on the farm have other household maintenance activities to see to besides farming. As there are no landless families, it is not possible to hire labour to substitute for alternatively occupied family labour especially where other job opportunities exist. Farm production thus suffers from a lack of individuals who are able to devote most of their time and attention to farming.

Even where most income is earned off the farm, households maintain a rural base for social and security reasons and because, within the indigenous social systems, households can procure a number of important subsistence goods cheaply by non-market production in the rural areas. Thus overall household welfare is maximized by maintaining a rural base even though it may be associated with reduced farm production due to outmigration and labour shortages at the farm-household.

This household-economics perspective provides some insights into the causes of the inherent tendency for food production per person to decline and why it should be more of a problem in Africa than in other parts of the Third World.

Notes

1 While this may seem to be an obvious point, it needs making because of the tendency to advocate labour-intensive technologies on the basis of their capacity to increase yields per hectare, without considering their effects on production per unit of labour time.
2 Premature in relation to conventional expectations based on Lewis's (1954) model of structural, change and development.

Part I
Household-economics theory and the southern African context

Part 1

2 Household economics: theory, applications and relevance

The theory

The modern theory of household economics originated with the work of Becker (1965), Lancaster (1966) and Muth (1966). The approach adopted by these economists represented a fundamental reformulation of the theory of consumer choice. The essence of this reformulation is that consumers do not directly maximize their utility by consuming the best combination of goods, but that a two-stage process is involved. In the first stage the household uses goods as inputs in a production process to generate more basic commodities (Z goods). In the second stage consumers choose the best combination of these basic commodities in the conventional way by maximizing a utility function.

In the traditional theory of consumer behaviour, the individual attempts to maximize utility which he obtains directly from the services of goods, Xi, purchased in the marketplace:

$$U = U(X1, X2 \ldots Xn) \qquad (1)$$

subject to the resource constraint:

$$I = \sum_i PiXi = W + V \qquad (2)$$

where Pi are the prices of goods purchased in the market, I is money income, W is earnings and V is other income.

In the new household-economics approach the household's utility function becomes:

$$U = U(Z1, Z2 \ldots Zn) \qquad (3)$$

The Zi are produced by the household using a vector of market goods and a vector of quantities of its own time, Ti:

$$Zi = Fi(Xi, Ti) \qquad (4)$$

The utility function is maximized subject to the production-function constraints, equation (4), and a constraint on the household's available time:

$$\sum_j Hj = \sum_j Tjw + \sum_{ji} Tji \qquad (5)$$

13

as well as the usual income constraint:

$$I = \sum_i PiXi \tag{6}$$

where Hj is the total time available to the jth household member, Tjw and Tji are the time spent by household member j in the labour market and in producing Zi respectively. Pi and Xi are respectively the price and quantity of the market-good input used in producing Zi.

If we call Ej the market-earning potential of member j per unit of time, and substitute equation (5) into the definition of money income equation (2),

$$I = \sum_j EjTjw + V = \sum_j Ej(Hj - \sum_i Tji) + V \tag{7}$$

and by adding the value of time spent in producing Zi, we obtain the 'full-income' constraint, S:

$$I + \sum_j Ej \sum_i Tji = \sum_i PiXi + \sum_j Ej \sum_i Tji = \sum_j EjHj + V = S \tag{8}$$

This full income then embodies both money income and the household-time constraint and its magnitude is independent of the fraction of time that the household chooses to allocate to income-earning activities. It simply states that the value of labour plus other non-labour earnings must equal the value of market goods plus the value of time spent in procuring non-market consumption commodities, including leisure.

In this formulation the time that is allocated by household members to income-earning activities or to non-income-earning activities (production of Z goods) becomes an integral part of the analysis. Thus as Michael and Becker (1973) say, this approach 'expands the applicability of the economist's theory of choice into the non-market sector and hence makes the theory more useful in analysing household behaviour in its many dimensions' (p. 147).

The concepts embodied in this reformulation of the theory of consumer choice are not new in themselves but taken together they have formed a new framework for thinking about aspects of behaviour, especially non-market aspects, which had previously been less amenable to economic analysis. In his critique of household economics, Nerlove (1974) identifies four basic elements of this framework:

1) a utility function with arguments that are not physical commodities, but home-produced bundles of more basic commodities or attributes;

2) a household production technology;

3) an external labour market environment providing the means for transforming household resources into market commodities; and

4) a set of household resource constraints – most notably the time of household members.

The first element involves the concept that goods as such are not the immediate objects of preference or utility or welfare, but have associated with them attributes which are directly relevant to the consumer (Lancaster, 1966). Thus, for example, an apple is not desired for its own sake but for the attributes it provides when time is taken out to eat it: flavour, texture, juiciness. These attributes must be produced within the household and physical goods or purchasable services are viewed as inputs in a production process in which the desired attributes are the outputs. This household production-function framework emphasizes the parallel services performed by firms and households as organizational units and leads to the use of the household, rather than the individual, as the basic unit of analysis.

The second element in household-economics theory is the technology of household production. Typically the inputs are time, distinguished by household member and market purchasable inputs (Becker, 1965). Households will respond to prices and productivities of factors of production as they attempt to minimize their costs of production and maximize their utility. Thus a reduction in the price of a factor of production will shift the production process towards techniques that are more intensive in the use of that factor as well as towards consumption activities that use the factor relatively intensively. For example, a reduction in the value of a wife's time through the loss of a part-time job would likely result in a change in the quality of household meals (e.g. more fresh and less frozen, tinned and pre-cooked food) as well as more time being spent on household maintenance (decorating, gardening, cleaning etc.).

The third element is related to the second and recognizes that household resources, principally time, can be transformed into market purchasable inputs to be used in the household production process. Thus it is recognized that consumers may not only sell their leisure time in labour markets, but may also buy time in the form of certain consumer goods and services (Sharir, 1975). In purchasing child-care services a housewife is buying time. This may be worth doing if this time can be sold on the labour market for more than the cost of buying it (including the costs involved in terms of child distress, extra travel etc).

The final element of the household-economics theory distinguished by Nerlove (1974) is the resource constraints facing the household in its production and optimizing decisions. These are generally taken to be the time of household members and other non-wage income, e.g. property income.

Applications in developed societies

These elements of the theory emphasize the central role of human time as a factor input and as the basic scarce household resource. Schultz (1974, p. 7) notes that the central principle of the new theory is that in reality each consumer service has two prices attached to it: 1) a money price, as in the traditional theory of consumer choice and, 2) a time cost of acquiring the consumer goods, and processing them in the household; and the time that is involved in consuming the services obtained from this household activity. It is the recognition of the importance of human time that has given rise to much of the empirical application of the household production-function approach.

A major implication of the theory is that the incentive to economize on time increases as its relative cost does. This throws light on the apparent paradox that people in high-income countries are much more conscious of time compared with those in poorer countries, even though it might be expected that those with higher incomes could afford to spend less time in work and lead a more leisurely life. Yet, as Becker (1965) notes, Americans in particular keep track of time continuously, make (and keep) appointments for specific minutes, rush about a great deal, and cook convenience and pre-prepared foods (i.e. the pace of life is hectic). At the same time they are supposed to be wasteful of food, oil and other goods. But this behaviour may be explained in terms of the high value of market time relative to the price of goods in America compared with elsewhere, which encourages Americans to be simultaneously economical with time and lavish with goods.

The growing human-capital literature has been supplemented with applications of household economics. The effect of human capital on the efficiency of non-market production is seen as part of the returns from investment in education and health. Human-capital investments can raise full income, S, by raising the market value of time and can also reduce a household's cost of living through the more efficient production of Z goods, and thus raise full real income.

Another area in which household economics has been applied is in the analysis of the labour-force participation of women (Gronau, 1973). Since husbands' wage rates as a rule exceed those of wives, it is observed in general that husbands tend to specialize in the market, while wives specialize in the production of household goods. However, as household economics predicts, highly educated married women participate to a greater extent in the labour force than married women with less schooling and lower earning potentials. The composition of a woman's family has also been shown to be strongly associated with her labour-force participation: married women as a group tend to withdraw from the labour force when they have children. This is an implication of household economics, if it is assumed that children are more time-intensive than other commodities produced within the home.

Finally, marriage and fertility are further aspects of behaviour that have been analyzed using the household-economics framework. The analysis of fertility in particular depends largely on the time-intensity of the bearing and rearing of children. Nerlove (1974) suggests that declining rates of population growth and infant mortality, which are a feature of demographic transition in developed countries, may be viewed in terms of the household-economics approach, with the value of human time providing the link between the household and the economy. As the value of human time increases over time, fewer children are reared per household (since child rearing is time-intensive), but each child embodies greater investments in human capital, which results in lower mortality and greater productivity in the economically active years. This in turn further raises the value of a unit of time and income in the subsequent generation and enables persons of that generation to make efficient use of new knowledge and new physical capital. As long as investment occurs which increases the amount of human capital per individual, the value of a unit of human time must continue to increase and fertility and child mortality to decrease.

Relevance of the approach in less developed societies

While household-economics theory has been applied to a wide range of activities in the settings of the United States, Israel and Japan, it has hardly been applied at all in less developed country situations.[1] And yet as Schultz (1974, pp. 20-21) argues, its potential for the analysis of household activities in less developed countries is probably greater than in advanced ones, since households in low-income countries perform a substantially larger economic role than they do in high-income countries:

> The value of home production is not only large relative to the total family income, it is also produced predominantly by family labor and only in small part by purchased inputs, because in low-income countries the purchased material goods that households can acquire are very high in price relative to the economic value of the time of members of the household.

Furthermore the size and composition of families are more directly related to household production in low-income countries, where children are valued less in terms of adding to the quality of life and more in terms of their contribution to production. For example, Cain (1980, p. 218) calculates that male children in Bangladesh compensate for their own cumulative consumption by the age of 15. Nag, White and Peet (1980, p. 270) conclude that the addition of children to rural households' labour forces in Java and Nepal increases the opportunity for adults to engage in productive activity and enhances the efficiency of their work. We can therefore expect the life cycle to affect household production behaviour not only in terms of changes in the values of human time of household members over time, but also in terms of the numbers of members in a household and their potential to contribute to production.

Another characteristic of traditional households in low-income countries is that much of their production is for own consumption and does not enter the market. As we have seen, household economics is particularly suitable for the analysis of non-market production at the household level. And in traditional societies the relevant production unit is often the household (or peasant farm-household), albeit an extended one, but a household nevertheless, with its members working towards a common objective, or having a single utility function. Hyden (1980, p. 17) argues that the peasant mode of production is pre-eminent in Africa and that in this mode 'the family is the basic work unit and commerce is undertaken in the context of familial principles of organization and orientation. The individual remains subordinate to the corporate household.'

The household-economics approach can also contribute to an understanding of the behaviour of households in the very different socio-economic environments that exist in traditional compared with modern societies. Behavioural differences may often be related to differences in the socio-economic environment within which households operate, which imply differences in the opportunity and costs of producing consumption goods. For example the traditional 'value' placed on cattle numbers rather than quality by many of the peoples of southern Africa may have much to do with the attributes that cattle confer as consumption goods in these societies: meat, milk, draughtpower, savings with interest, security, bridewealth and prestige. Moreover there is only a small cost involved in obtaining these attributes through cattle, where grazing is communal and herding is done by young boys with little alternative earning potential. Thus cattle represent very powerful goods and are also relatively cheap, so there is a high derived demand for them. By increasing the quality and reducing the number of cattle the income obtainable from a household's herd may be raised. However this extra cash income may not be able to purchase alternative goods in the marketplace that fully compensate for the loss of attributes that having a smaller herd entails. In this case it would not be irrational to purchase more cattle with any extra income obtained from the sale of better-quality cattle.

Since its origins in 1965, the household-economics approach has provided new insights and new economic interpretations of observed behaviour of modern households in the industrial developed countries. These insights have been gained by taking the view that consumption involves a production process at the household level. In this book it will be argued that the new household-economics theory of consumption can also contribute to our understanding of the production and consumption behaviour of traditional farm-households in southern Africa. These households can be more obviously and directly described as production/consumption units than their modern counterparts in America or Japan. In particular, it will be argued that a household-economics perspective can throw light on the relationship between market and non-market production and the important bearing that this has on the response of formerly self-sufficient subsistence households to 'modernization' and the introduction of new market opportunities.

An early application of household economics in southern Africa

It is significant to note that Dean's (1966) enquiry into the allocation of time by Malawi farmers between subsistence work and market participation in response to the opportunities of tobacco cash cropping and wage employment, provided part of the stimulus that led Becker (1965) to formulate his theory of the allocation of time, upon which most of the subsequent applications of household economics have been based. In a sense then, this book takes household economics back to a setting 'where some of it began'.

By way of introduction to the application of household economics in the southern African setting, it will be instructive to consider Dean's approach to analyzing the determinants of tobacco sales by Malawian farm-households. Dean (1966, pp. 22–4) describes farm-households in the Central Region of Malawi in 1960 in terms that remain typical of traditional farming in southern Africa. These farm-households:

> attempt to attain self sufficiency in the basic foodstuffs, so a large portion of family labor is devoted to the production of corn, which is the staple grain in most of Malawi . . . In addition family labor is engaged in many other tasks connected with running a farming household. Thus, the labor devoted to tobacco production is in most cases a small part of total family labor. Only rarely do trust land tobacco growers use hired labor.

Food crops are the responsibility of the women, although men help with the more arduous tasks such as preparing the garden and harvesting. 'The woman also has housekeeping chores, such as the pounding of grain into flour, the preparation of food, cleaning the house, fetching water and washing clothes. She may also manufacture pots or brooms or sell produce at a nearby market'. Men grow tobacco with the assistance of women and do the household construction work. Men may also work for wages on a monthly basis on a nearby European farm or by migrating for one to two years to Zimbabwe,

Zambia or South Africa. (It is now more common for Malawi men to work in the expanding estate sector within Malawi than to seek work outside Malawi.)

Under the customary tenure arrangements, 'all families must be allocated land by one means or another, so there is no rural landless class in Malawi'. Hand cultivation with the hoe is the norm and negligible cash expenditure is used in the cultivation of tobacco. Dean (1966, p. 28) summarizes his description of the tobacco-growing areas in Malawi thus:

> Africans expend effort to produce non-market goods such as foodstuffs, buildings and various services, and they expend effort to earn cash to spend on goods. It has also been shown that they consume leisure. Tobacco growing is one of the ways in which they expend effort in order to earn cash. By these choices, they have revealed a desire for leisure, for non-market goods, and for goods which are purchased with cash.

Dean developed a primitive[2] household-economics framework which he depicts in a form shown in Table 2.1. The amounts of leisure and home goods consumed are assumed to be uniquely determined by the inputs of time and land. Cash goods may be obtained by the production of tobacco or other cash-earning activities, including wage employment. Dean uses this framework to explore the implications of changes in prices and incomes on the amount of tobacco that a farm-household will plan to grow on the assumption that a grower will wish to consume relatively large amounts of cash goods, other things including income being equal, if the amount of resources necessary to obtain them is relatively small.

TABLE 2.1 *Dean's primitive household-economics framework*

OUTPUTS:	*leisure*	*home goods*		*cash goods*
INPUTS:	leisure	home goods production	tobacco production	other cash production e.g. wage employment

Subsequent development of household-economics theory allows us to enlarge on Dean's interpretation of Malawi farm-households' behaviour patterns. The farm-household allocates the time of its members to either home production of Z goods and leisure (subsistence production) or to earning income through tobacco production or wage employment (market participation). The amount of time that is spent in market participation by different household members will depend on the value of their time in market production compared with that of their and other household members' time spent in subsistence activities. Thus men migrate (rather than women) because the available wage work (mostly on mines) in South Africa, Zambia and Zimbabwe is male-specific and men therefore have a comparative advantage over women in wage employment. On the other hand, of those family members remaining at the homestead, it is the men who see to the relatively time-intensive tasks of tobacco production (compared with maize growing), because women have a comparative advantage in other time-intensive household tasks such as child care.

The demand for market goods will determine how much of the household's human time is devoted to market production and this demand will depend on the quantity and quality of goods that can be purchased with the earnings from this time-expenditure. Goods available in the market, which have superior attributes to those produced at home and cost less in terms of time to obtain, will tend to replace traditional own-produced goods. Dean presents evidence which suggests that the secular increase in tobacco production in the Central Region of Malawi between 1920 and 1960 was partially due to the introduction of European consumer goods and improved transport which made them available in the rural areas at reasonable prices. Dean argued that the introduction of European consumer goods caused a change in the tastes of Malawians from home-produced goods to market goods, which raised the marginal rate of substitution between home-produced goods and market goods and resulted in an increased allocation of household time to tobacco production relative to subsistence production and/or leisure.

However, if we examine the nature of the consumer goods most commonly purchased, many of these 'changes in tastes' can be explained in terms of the superior and time-saving attributes of the European goods over local products. Cotton cloth replaced bark cloth and animal skins as wearing apparel. Apart from the superior attributes of cotton cloth over the home-produced materials, it is likely that, at an early stage, the time required to earn enough to purchase a pair of cotton trousers became less than that needed to hunt, kill, skin and tan the skins of the rapidly decreasing wild game population in the locality. Bicycles were another major purchase item whose time-saving and anti-drudgery attributes are obvious. Dean (1966, p. 98) notes that the 'increase in the number of bicycles also had the effect of reducing the costs of the individual in getting from his home to a store (and since bicycles were used to transport tobacco, in getting his tobacco to the market)'. Expenditures on human capital such as European drugs and especially schooling represented behavioural patterns, which suggest that the 'tastes' of subsistence farm-households in Malawi in the 1920s were not that different from those of modern Western households of today.

Dean used his 'primitive' household-economics framework to account for the annual variations in tobacco production and its secular increase in Malawi between 1920 and 1960. In this book the 'more mature' household-economics approach will be used to explore some of the reasons behind the rather unsuccessful attempts to develop and commercialize traditional farming in southern Africa, despite the considerable efforts that have been made in this regard since the 1960s.

Notes

1 A number of household studies have been carried out, particularly in Asia (see Binswanger et al., eds, 1980), but few have been based explicitly on the new household-economics school. The exception is Evenson, Popkin and Quizon (1980, p. 336), who find that, in

rural Philippine households, the economic value of children is rather high when valued in terms of full income instead of market income. They also examine the question of fertility and investment in children in rural households in the Philippines using the full-income concept.
2 Dean's framework is termed primitive because market production is seen as a residual activity after home goods requirements have been met, and is undertaken if spare time and land is available and the effort required is not too great. Modern household-economics theory assumes a greater degree of substitutability between market and non-market production and also integrates the consumption and production aspects of household behaviour. Households are assumed to combine market and non-market production so as to minimize the 'full' cost (market plus time costs) of producing household goods, and thereby maximize the utility of consumption.

3 Indigenous agriculture in southern African economies

As in the rest of sub-Saharan Africa, agriculture occupies a prominent place in the economies of southern Africa. Apart from South Africa with its highly diversified economy, over half the economically active population is estimated to be employed in the agricultural sector and over 60 per cent of the population reside in rural areas. This applies even in Zambia and Zimbabwe where the share of agriculture in the gross domestic product is below 20 per cent (see Table 3.1).

TABLE 3.1 *Percentage of GDP and economically active population in agriculture and percentage of population residing in rural areas*

	Percentage of GDP in agriculture[a]	Percentage of economically active population in agriculture[b]		Percentage of population residing in rural areas
		1970	1980	
Botswana	24 (1976)	87	80	82[f]
Lesotho	38 (1974)	90	84	95[c]
Malawi	49 (1973)	89	84	90[c]
Swaziland	32 (1973)	81	73	85[e]
Zambia	16 (1978)	73	67	62[c]
Zimbabwe	15 (1977)	64	59	77[c]
South Africa	8 (1978)	31	29	52[d]

Sources:
- a) Yearbook of National Accounts Statistics, 1979, Vol. II
- b) FAO Production Yearbook, 1980
- c) IBRD, 1981, Table 36
- d) United Nations, 1980, p. 648. Within the homelands 91 per cent of the population is rural.
- e) Swaziland Government, 1979, Table XII.3
- f) Botswana Government estimate for 1976

Accurate data on the indigenous farm sector are hard to come by. Despite this it is clear that a considerable disparity exists between the production and performance of the indigenous farm sector and that of the modern sector of the economy, both in agriculture and non-agriculture. Dualism is a marked feature of agriculture in most of southern Africa. In Botswana, Malawi, South

Africa, Swaziland, Zambia and Zimbabwe commercial farms are operated (generally by European farmers or international companies) on a relatively large scale, employing wage labour on a regular basis and applying relatively modern techniques of production. As Table 3.2 indicates, these enterprises account for a disproportionate share of marketed agricultural production. In contrast African farming is predominantly subsistence-based and is carried out by individual families on small plots of 1 to 5 ha, using mostly own-family labour and relatively low levels of material inputs.

TABLE 3.2 *Percentage of land occupied and marketed production supplied by the modern farming sector*

	Year	Percentage of land occupied	Percentage of marketed production supplied
Zimbabwe[a]	1973	42	95.6
Malawi[b]	1967	2	30.0
Zambia[d]	1973	4	55.0
Swaziland[c]	1974	33	86.9
Botswana[e]	1982	8	37.1

Sources:
 a) Berg, 1980
 b) Brand, 1974
 c) Refers to cropland and crop production only. Annual Statistical Bulletin 1976, Swaziland Government, Mbabane
 d) IBRD 1975(b)
 e) Central Statistics Office, Gaberone

Another notable feature is the predominance of the major staple, maize, throughout the region as indicated by the aggregate cropping pattern data in Table 3.3.

TABLE 3.3 *Percentage of cropped area planted to various smallholder crops*

	Maize	Sorghum	Roots and tubers	Pulses	Cotton	Tobacco
Botswana	21	59	—	14	—	—
Lesotho	48	—	—	11	—	—
Malawi	64	8	3	18	—	5
Swaziland	76	2	6	2	12	—
Zambia	77	6	5	1	—	—
Zimbabwe	61	7	1	3	3	3

Source: FAO Production Yearbook (1980)

The dualism within agriculture, between traditional African farming on the one hand and the modern European farms and estates on the other, mirrors the overall economic dualism in all southern African economies between the indigenous subsistence sector and the modern monetary sector. In Botswana and Lesotho, where a modern agricultural sector hardly exists, this dualism is reflected in the disparity between high per capita GNP growth rates and negative growth rates in the agricultural sector. In Botswana recent rapid growth in infrastructure and the mining sector is partially responsible for the high per capita growth rates. However in Botswana, as in Lesotho, much of this increase is attributable to increased numbers and earnings of temporary migrants to South Africa since the late 1960s. For Lesotho it has been estimated that nearly three-quarters of the growth in gross national income during the 1970s was provided by migrant remittances (Eckert and Wykstra, 1980, p. 8).

In Swaziland there have been similar increases in migrant income, but modern-sector growth within the country has included expansion in sugar, forestry and citrus production as well as considerable infrastructural development. In Zambia, formal modern-sector jobs increased from 200 000 in 1960 to over 400 000 in 1970. Mine wages also increased substantially so that in 1971 a miner's average wage was not far short of £1000 sterling per annum (Roberts, 1976, p. 236). This expansion in modern-sector activity in Zambia was accompanied by rising food imports, which doubled between 1964 and 1974. In the South African homelands farm output per head has fallen since 1920, while total income per head remained static as income from migrant labour increased in importance (Knight and Lenta, 1980, Tables 1 and 2).

Perhaps the most dramatic contrast between the growth of the modern sector and the relative stagnation of the indigenous subsistence sector is seen in Zimbabwe. In the communal areas (formerly tribal trust lands or TTL), which contain 76 per cent of the African population, per capita production of maize fell from 140 kg in 1962 to 92 kg in 1977 (Simson, 1979, p. 30). However, for the country as a whole, agricultural performance was reported to be particularly favourable:

> Between 1965 and 1974 Rhodesia achieved near self sufficiency in wheat production . . . cattle and milk production doubled, maize output increased sixfold, wheat twenty six times, groundnuts four times, tea three times, soya beans sixty times, cotton ten times, sugar production doubled, while tobacco output fell by a quarter (cited in Berg, 1980, pp. 4–5).

While the TTL farmers contributed to the increase in cotton production to some extent, they apparently did not do so in respect of maize. Nor did they for other crops such as sugar, wheat, soya beans and tea, which are not produced on communal areas. Over this same period (1964–74) manufacturing and mining output doubled.

While the indigenous agricultural sector continues to play an important, even dominant, role in the economies of southern Africa in terms of employment and residential base, its direct contribution to production has declined in relative terms, and even absolutely in some cases. Productivity and production data on the subsistence sector are scarce and are often unreliable, but circumstantial evidence on grain imports, such as that given in Table 3.4, indicates that per capita production is falling in indigenous agriculture.[1]

In many respects the indigenous agricultural sectors of southern African countries are no different from those of sub-Saharan Africa as a whole. The World Bank (IBRD, 1981, p. 41) summarizes the 'crisis in African agriculture' in terms of the following five trends:

TABLE 3.4 *Food aid and commercial maize imports, 1975-9*

	Food aid imports[a] (thousands of tonnes grain equivalent)				Commercial maize imports (thousands of tonnes)
	Malawi	Lesotho	Zambia	Botswana	Swaziland[b]
1975	0.2	13.9	1.0	5.4	21
1976	0.8	18.5	5.3	3.4	22
1977	3.4	11.5	28.6	3.4	31
1978	3.2	23.6	31.2	8.4	34
1979	2.2	37.8	49.9	8.8	43

Sources:
 a) IBRD, 1981, Table 24
 b) Fowler, 1980, Appendix 6

1) In the 1970s the growth rate of agricultural production was less than the population growth rate almost everywhere;
2) agricultural exports stagnated;
3) food production per capita fell in the 1970s;
4) commercial imports of food grains grew more than three times as fast as population and food aid increased substantially; and
5) more of the population shifted its consumption to imported wheat and rice.

Apart from 5), which is less apparent in southern Africa, where maize remains the basic staple, these trends are characteristic of indigenous agriculture in all countries in the region, with the possible exception of Malawi. The World Bank argues that falling levels of food production per head of the rural population indicate that labour productivity fell in the 1970s and makes the significant point that this decline occurred over a period when various governments and external sources of finance focused more strongly on food production projects than ever before. This is an aspect we will examine more closely in Chapter 11, which deals with the production performance of rural development projects in southern Africa. Here we may note that the rural and food development programmes that have been funded and implemented in Lesotho, Swaziland, Zambia and even Malawi have had little success in raising production per hectare or per head.

The reasons enumerated by the World Bank for the stagnation of agricultural production in sub-Saharan Africa are equally applicable to indigenous agriculture in southern Africa. These include disruptions caused by war and civil strife (e.g. in Zimbabwe), rapid population growth pushing cultivation into less productive areas, previous neglect by government and donors, economic policies reducing producer prices, and poor input supply and marketing systems. In southern Africa we need to take account of another important factor: the growth of the modern sector both within individual countries and in the region as a whole. This is a factor that has been given little attention by donors, policy-makers or academics, even in southern Africa. For example referring to Zimbabwe, Berg (1980, p. 19) says:

> It is also true that per capita TTL (Tribal Trust Land) production of foodstuffs may have stagnated or declined during these decades of rapid economic growth. But the long history of discriminatory policies and lack of attention are not irrelevant to this outcome.

Neither is the rapid rate of modern-sector growth itself irrelevant to the outcome. As Simson (1979, p. 77) argues, the development of the modern sector in Zimbabwe has been directly related to the underdevelopment of the peasant sector. A major argument of this book is that growth of the modern sector, which introduces new consumer goods and new employment opportunities, tends, under the socio-economic conditions prevailing in Africa, to reduce the attraction of and, over time, the returns to indigenous farming.[2] This effect is not confined to southern Africa, but is most noticeable there because of the distinctive nature and sustained growth of the modern sector in the region and because, in some cases, many of the other constraints on the development of indigenous agriculture are less dominant.

In Chapter 2 we noted that increases in the availability of consumer goods and the opportunity to obtain them appear to have stimulated the production of tobacco in Malawi between 1920 and 1960. But the introduction of a modern monetary sector can also have contrary effects as Pike (1968, p. 190) observes:

> The production of cash crops [in Malawi], while being controlled by such ecological factors as soil and climate, is limited by the effort devoted to subsistence needs and the demand for labour in the near by towns. In areas surrounding major towns and European-owned estates, no interest is shown in the production of cash crops, the main aim being to produce as much food as possible (chiefly maize) on small gardens which are cultivated by dependents and the part time efforts of the worker himself.

Recent surveys (1982/83) in Blantyre Agricultural Development Division in Malawi indicate that the value of farm production from crops and livestock amounts to only 54 per cent of total household income, the balance coming from off-farm activities and remittances (Umphawi, 1984).

The opportunity to earn incomes outside agriculture also affects the production impact of rural development projects. According to the World Bank (IBRD, 1981, p. 76n), in Malawi it was found that 'the main income effect of agricultural projects resulted from the returns to labour in activities outside the sector, made possible by the labour releasing effect of innovations'. These observations relate to an economy in which 15–20 per cent of the adult male work force is engaged in wage employment and where real wages rose by less than 3 per cent per annum during the 1960s and the 1970s. In the South African homelands, in most communal areas of Zimbabwe and in Lesotho, Botswana, Swaziland and some regions of Zambia, 50–60 per cent of the adult male work force is engaged in wage employment. And in these countries real wage rates have increased faster than in Malawi. Between 1960 and 1970 the real average earnings of African workers increased by 10 per cent per annum in Zambia (Fry, 1980, Table 7). In Zimbabwe African real wages rose by 6.5 per cent per annum between 1956 and 1977 (Simson, 1979, Tables 8 and 23). In the 1970s South African mine wages, and thus the earnings of most Basotho and a large proportion of Batswana, Ciskei and Transkei off-farm workers, rose by 13 per cent per annum in real terms. Clearly the development of indigenous, subsistence-orientated agriculture in southern Africa cannot be realistically planned or assessed without regard to the influence of the modern monetary sector, which forms such an important part of the overall environment in which indigenous farming takes place, and has provided increasing opportunities for, and rewards to wage employment in the past two decades.

In a post-independence sector review of Zimbabwean agriculture the World Bank shows that most communal area families have members working and living away from home. It is estimated that on average half of rural incomes come from the sale of crops and the other half from migrant remittances. The study contrasts the low level of rural incomes with the impressive development of the modern sector. However, it is also noted that rural incomes have now started to rise and 'that it is the rapid increase in cash in the hands of rural farm families of the usually male migrants in the towns buying food for their spouses that has induced the explosive growth in wholesale and retail trade aimed at rural African families' (IBRD, 1983).

It is with the influence of the modern market sector on indigenous farm-households, their agricultural production and their response to development initiatives that subsequent chapters are primarily concerned. We will start by employing the new household-economics concept to develop an analytical model of the African farm-household.

Notes

1 These statistics do not reflect the extent of food deficits in some countries. For example in 1979 the maize deficit in Zambia was around 300 000 tonnes. In Botswana the average annual cereals deficit was 30 000 tonnes in the 1960s and has certainly risen in the 1970s. Lesotho now imports half its food and Swaziland 40 per cent of its maize requirements. In 1971–3 Kwazulu produced about 30 per cent of its cereal requirements (Lenta, 1978).
2 This implies a fall in marketed surpluses, which might be expected to cause a rise in food prices and hence improve the terms of trade for agriculture. But in southern Africa, as elsewhere on the continent, food shortages have been met from imports and modern sector agriculture.

4 A model of the indigenous farm-household in southern Africa

The indigenous farm-household model developed in this chapter draws on two areas of behavioural theory: household economics and the subjective equilibrium theory of the farm-household. It will be argued that, as recently developed, the subjective equilibrium theory of the farm-household (e.g. Nakajima, 1970) is not very appropriate under southern Africa conditions. However the original theory as presented by Chayanov (1966) has been shown to have particular relevance elsewhere in Africa[1] and would appear to be equally valid in southern Africa. Parts of Chayanov's original theory of peasant economy will therefore be employed in conjunction with household-economics thinking to develop a model of the farm-household that is more appropriate than current models in the southern African context.

Chayanov and household economics

The household-economics approach outlined in Chapter 2 has many of the same characteristics as the subjective equilibrium theory of peasant economies originally put forward by Chayanov in the 1920s. Chayanov held that a peasant household, using its own labour, would apply it to farming according to its internal equilibrium. This was determined not in terms of maximizing monetary profit, but in terms of equating family demands and needs with the drudgery involved in meeting them. If we substitute human time for drudgery, Chayanov's theory comes close to that of household economics, which implies that households are concerned to minimize the cost (ultimately in terms of their members' time) of meeting their sets of consumption needs, so that they maximize the utility of consumption.

In common with household-economics theory, Chayanov viewed the entire family as a single economic unit and insisted that the returns to family activities could not therefore be broken down into its components of wages and other factor payments. Non-market aspects of production and consumption were stressed and household decisions were assumed to be based on use values rather than exchange values. Also in common with household economics, Chayanov emphasized the importance of labour effort and argued that family farms would be organized so that family labour was employed as efficiently as possible. However, Chayanov did not consider the implications of this in terms of the allocation of tasks between household members and the possibility that some of them may have a comparative advantage over others in certain tasks. Hunt (1979, p. 278) considers this to be one of the deficiencies of Chayanov's model.

Again in common with household economics, Chayanov recognized the importance of family size and composition on household activity. However, Chayanov concentrated on the effect of household structure in respect of its capacity to meet the household's demand for consumption goods. In household economics, on the other hand, the effects of changing household structure have been analyzed in terms of *relative* changes in the demand for time-intensive versus goods-intensive commodities through the life cycle of a household (Becker, 1976).

Chayanov introduced the concept of consumer/producer ratio to analyze the effect of changing household structure on production and income over the life cycle of a peasant household. A newly established household, with only a husband and wife, has a relatively low consumer/worker ratio. This ratio increases as children are added to the family. Over time, as the children grow up and begin to contribute to production as well as consumption, the consumer/worker ratio decreases again. Chayanov showed that, at any given level of income, the days worked per worker increased as the consumer/worker ratio and thus the absolute level of family demands per worker increased. This led Chayanov to state that the 'volume of the family's activities depends entirely on the number of consumers and not at all on the number of workers' (Chayanov, 1966, Chapter 2).

In household-economics terms, non-working members (e.g. children) are assumed to have a zero time value, since they contribute nothing to production. They affect the pattern of consumption though, since they are assumed to be time-intensive (relative to other consumption goods) and cause a household's relative consumption of goods-intensive commodities to fall. The effect of changing absolute demands per worker as the household structure (consumer/worker ratio) changes and children become older and more productive has not been incorporated into household-economics analysis. For subsistence farm-households this absolute effect may be more important than the relative shifts in consumption emphasized by the household-economics approach. On the other hand, the simple consumer/worker ratio does not take into account differences in current and future productive potential of household members over time. While a young household with husband and wife may have the same consumer/worker ratio as a lone couple in old age, the values of their time, in wage employment as well as household production, will be greater than that of the old couple. As a result the young couple can be expected to exhibit a relatively greater consumption of goods-intensive commodities.

Chayanov recognized another relationship between household structure and farm production that has not featured in household-economics analyses. He stated that attention should be given to 'the increase, as it [the farm-household] matures, of the numbers of working hands; this gives the chance of applying the principles of complex cooperation and, thus, increases the power of each of them' (Chayanov, p. 60). Complex cooperation implies that production efficiency increases as more hands become available and according to household-economics thinking this would increase the value of household members' time and encourage a relative shift from time-intensive to goods-intensive commodities.

The principle of complex cooperation can operate in a more general way as household studies in Asia have indicated. In Java it was observed that expansion of the household labour force gives poor rural households a greater margin of income over food consumption and greater savings. This is attributed in part to the ability of large families to displace adults from household maintenance tasks into productive work in order to increase overall labour efficiency:

> Whereas the smallest households devoted up to 52 per cent of their total working time to household maintenance tasks and thus had little left in which to obtain income, larger households were able to spend up to 81 per cent of their working time directly in the acquisition of income; these substantial differences in the efficiency of the household labour unit are significantly related, at the .01 level, to the amount of children's labour input (Nag, White and Peet, 1980, p. 284).

To summarize then, both Chayanov and household economics view the household as a single production/consumption unit engaged in non-market as well as market activities. Both stress the paramount importance of family labour effort, but household economics goes further and recognizes that different household members have different relative time values in market and non-market activities. Both also recognize the influence of household structure on production and consumption. While Chayanov concentrates on how the structure of a household affects its capacity to supply a household's consumption requirements, household economics emphasizes changes in the value over time of household members' time and the effect that this has on the pattern of demand for time-intensive versus goods-intensive commodities.

Current farm-household theory and its limitations in southern Africa

Current farm-household theory (Nakajima, 1970; Krishna, 1970; Barnum and Squire, 1979; Strauss, 1982) represents a development of Chayanov's subjective equilibrium analysis. Chayanov argued that each peasant farm-household works to the point where the household's subjective evaluation of the marginal disutility of work equals its estimate of the marginal utility of output gained. This is the basis of Nakajima's model of the commercial farm-household presented in Figure 4.1. The quantity of family income is measured on the vertical axis OM. Labour availability is given by OA' on the horizontal axis. The curve OL is the production response curve for the family farm. The competitively determined wage rate is given by the line WW'. If we introduce the indifference curve representing the marginal rate of substitution of family labour for money UU' (Chayanov's utility/disutility schedule), we can see that at the family's subjective equilibrium, OAf units of its labour will be employed in farm production, $AfAw$ units will be allocated to wage employment and the balance, AwA', will be consumed as leisure.

Introduction of the indifference curve, UU', enables the productivity of labour to be considered separately from its disutility. A consequence of this is that as soon as any part of family labour is marketable at all, the amount of it used on the farm (Af) is determined by the equality of its value of marginal product (VMP) with the wage rate (W), i.e. $W = VMPa$. Thus we do not need to know anything about the utility function to determine the amount of family labour that is used on the farm.

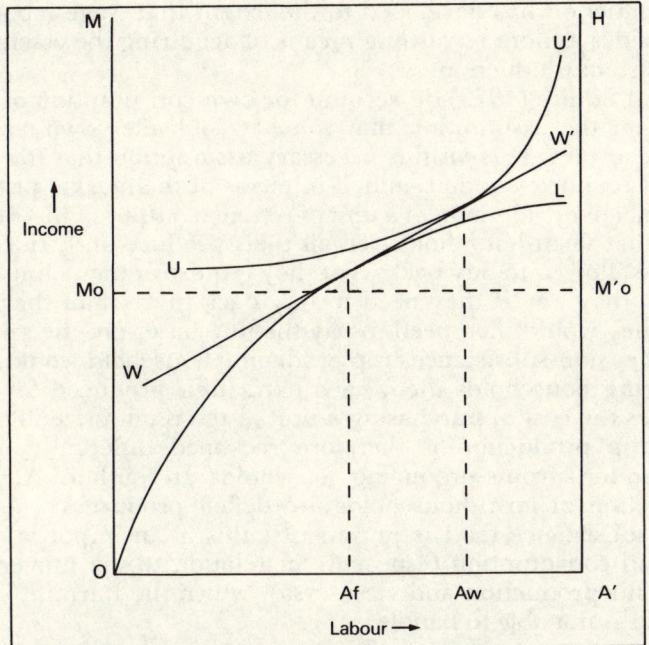

FIGURE 4.1: *The standard neo-classical farm-household model*

Given a declining production possibility curve for labour on the farm and a straight wage line, the total labour input on the farm (a') is determined by the equality of the marginal (subjective) valuation of family labour with the wage rate: $-Ua'/Um = W$.

Nakajima presents this model for a pure commercial farm, where all farm production is sold. Krishna (1970) shows that the possibility of ov consumption can be incorporated within the same framework as long as part of the farm output is marketed. If this is the case, the amount of output retained (x) is determined by the equality of the marginal (subjective) valuation of retained output with its market price (P): $Ux/Um = P$.

Barnum and Squire (1979) quantified Krishna's version of the Nakajima model in respect of Malaysian farm-households.[2] They showed that the signs of the response elasticities for own consumption of farm production, consumption of market goods and consumption of leisure all changed when consumption was examined alone, compared to when the production and consumption parts of the model were allowed to interact. This was a useful analysis because it demonstrated the importance of considering the production and consumption aspects of farm-household behavior simultaneously. However, it is based on a model which is not entirely appropriate to indigenous farming in southern Africa.

First, the model analyzes production and consumption activities in purely monetary terms and Fisk (1975) has questioned whether a single model of this type is applicable where, as in southern Africa, a considerable proportion of a farm-household's time is taken up with non-market activities. Fisk suggests that a single model of the Nakajima type is only applicable once specialization in market production has developed to the extent that wage labour or cash cropping provides a more rewarding means of acquiring the essentials of life than self-subsistent production.

Barnum and Squire (1979) do account for own-consumption of farm production, but on the assumption that some is sold after own-consumption needs have been met. It is on this necessary assumption that the quantities marketed and retained are determined in terms of the market price and the marginal (subjective) valuation of a unit of retained output. This is equivalent to assuming that farm-households sell all their produce and, since they are producers, are allowed to buy back what they require at the selling price. But what price do they pay if they need to buy back more than they produce? Presumably they would then need to pay the purchase, not the selling price, just as any other non-subsistence crop producing household would. For these deficit-producing households then, each extra unit produced for own consumption saves the cost of purchasing a unit at the retail price. The value of subsistence crop production is therefore reckoned differently for deficit-producing than for surplus-producing households. In southern Africa, where a high proportion of farm-households are deficit producers who purchase part of their subsistence food requirements, this is an important aspect of production and consumption (especially in relation to the movement from deficit to surplus production and vice-versa), which the Barnum and Squire type of analysis is not able to handle.

Second, in common with most subjective evaluation analyses of the farm-household (e.g. Mellor, 1963; Sen, 1966; Sumner, 1982), Nakajima makes the assumption that land area is fixed at the farm-household level and that this results in declining returns as more labour is applied on the family farm. In southern Africa, as well as in Russia in the 1920s, the assumption that the household has a fixed area of land available to it is not supported by empirical evidence. Chayanov showed that the area sown by peasant households increased as household size did and he established the direction of causation from household to farm size with time-series data on the change in area sown by households between 1882 and 1911. Likewise in southern Africa the available evidence indicates that farm sizes increase as household size does (see Table 4.1).[3] Indeed the indigenous land-tenure system is designed to enable this to happen. It is therefore questionable whether, over a certain range at least, the returns to labour do decline as more labour is added to the farm-household.[4] The assumption of declining returns is however an essential part of most subjective equilibrium models: since it is also invariably assumed that the wage rate is fixed and constant, the participation in off-farm wage employment by part of a farm-household's labour force can only be explained in terms of decreasing returns to labour on the farm.

The assumption that households face a fixed and constant wage rate for all their members is also questionable. Table 4.2 indicates that wage rates facing (male) members of farm-households vary considerably in southern Africa, as elsewhere. Male/female wage rates are even more disparate and the job opportunities open to males, especially young adult ones eligible for mine employment, are much more numerous than those available to females (or older men). The assumption of a fixed and constant wage rate applying to all working household members is therefore unrealistic. The need to assume diminishing returns to labour on the farm and constant returns in wage employment clearly limits the relevance of the Nakajima-type model in indigenous agriculture in southern Africa, where there is reason to question both these assumptions.

TABLE 4.1 *Household and farm size in southern Africa and Russia*

	Average household size	Average farm size/area cultivated (ha)
Zambia (Mpika)[a]		
Group 1 (n = 24)	5.5	1.1
Group 2 (n = 28)	6.6	2.2
Group 3 (n = 22)	8.4	5.4
Zimbabwe (Chibi)[b]		
Group 1 (n = 50)	6.5	2.4
Group 2 (n = 46)	9.0	3.2
Swaziland (Rural Development Areas)[c]		
Group 1 (n = 39)	5.0	0.7
Group 2 (n = 72)	8.2	1.1
Group 3 (n = 86)	14.5	2.0
Lesotho (census data)[d]		
Bottom quartile	4.8	0.6
2nd quartile	4.9	1.2
3rd quartile	5.5	1.7
Top quartile	6.0	4.4
Malawi (Rukuru Rural Development Area)[e]		
Group 1 (n = 102)	4.0	1.8
Group 2 (n = 34)	7.2	3.2
Russia (Suratov, 1927)[f]		
Group 1	5.0	7.1
Group 2	6.6	12.3
Group 3	7.4	16.9

Sources:
a) Bwalya, 1980, Tables 3 & 4 (crop area cultivated)
b) CIMMYT, 1982, Table 2.2.1 (crop area cultivated)
c) Chapter 7, Tables 7.17 and 7.18 (crop area cultivated)
d) IBRD, 1980b, Annex 1, Appendix Table 1.9 (arable area held)
e) Dorward, 1982 (crop area cultivated), personal communication
f) Shanin, 1972, Table 4.III (crop area held)

A third limitation of the Nakajima model in the southern African context concerns its implications for the effect of changes in household size and structure on the farm production and consumption situation. Nakajima introduces the basic consumption requirement concept by drawing the horizontal line $MoM'o$ (see Figure 4.1). An increase in the number of producers in a household would result in this $MoM'o$ line moving upwards as well as the $A'H$ line moving to the right. Neither of these movements would affect the level of family farm labour applied, since this is determined by the equality of the marginal value product with the wage rate, and neither the wage rate nor the production possibility curve will have been affected by the change in household size.[5] The right-hand shift of the $A'H$ line is expected by Nakajima to result in a reduction in the slope of the indifference curves in the area

MMoM'oH and this will cause an increase in the amount of labour utilized in wage employment. Since farm production has not changed, but the basic consumption requirement will have risen, the ratio of farm production to the basic consumption requirement will fall as a result of an increase in the size of the household.

TABLE 4.2 *Average earnings by sector*

	Agriculture	Mining	Administration or commerce	Construction
Malawi (Kw/annum)[a]				
1964	41	52	63	62
Zambia (Kw/annum)[b]				
1970	348	1543	795	609
Zimbabwe (Z$/annum)[c]				
1977	232	659	1099	739
South Africa (R/annum)[d]				
1977	221	1203	n.a.	n.a.
Swaziland (E/month)[e]				
1975	29	60	n.a.	31

Sources:
    a) Malawi Government, 1970, Table 7.2
    b) Fry, 1980, Table 7
    c) Simson, 1979, Table 20
    d) Knight & Lenta, 1980, Table 3
    e) Swaziland Government, 1976, Table K7

The implication of the Nakajima-type model is that as the sizes of farm-households increase, farm production surpluses above consumption requirements decrease (or deficits increase). This implication does not fit with empirical observation in many southern African countries, where farm-households with larger labour forces and populations tend to produce greater crop surpluses. In Lesotho, Guma and Gay (1978) classified farmers into 'ordinary' and 'better', and found that the 'better' farmers had larger maize surpluses and labour forces (as well as populations) than 'ordinary' farmers. A similar pattern has been observed in Zambia, Zimbabwe and Swaziland (see Table 4.3).

Chayanov observed the same positive relationship between household size and composition on the one hand, and peasant farm-household production on the other. He introduced the concepts of consumer/worker ratio and 'complex co-operation' to account for his observations. Since these concepts are not compatible with current farm-household models, based on the assumption of declining returns to labour on the family farm, they have not been considered in subsequent subjective equilibrium analyses of the farm-household.

Thus the current subjective equilibrium theory of the farm-household as expounded by Nakajima and quantified by Barnum and Squire and others is of limited applicability in southern Africa because:
    1) it represents commercial farmers, who consume part of their produce, whereas in southern Africa the production of many farmers never enters the market at all;

TABLE 4.3 *Mean household size and workforce of surplus and non-surplus producers in Zambia, Zimbabwe and Swaziland*

	Household size	No. of 15–55 years olds
Western Province, Zambia[a]		
Subsistence producers (n = 50)	3.9	1.9
Surplus producers (n = 50)	5.7	2.8
Chibi South, Zimbabwe[b]		
Subsistence producers (n = 46)	6.5	3.2
Surplus producers (n = 50)	9.0	4.5
Swaziland, Rural Development Areas[c]		
Never selling maize (n = 377)	7.2	n.a.
Selling maize regularly (n = 179)	8.1	n.a.

Sources:
  a) Marter, 1978, Table 2.2. Subsistence producers classified as those selling less than K50 worth of farm production per year
  b) CIMMYT, 1982, Table 2.2.1 and 3.1.1
  c) RDA Monitoring and Evaluation Unit (1980), Table 4a

2) it assumes constant returns to family labour in wage employment and diminishing returns on the farm, neither of which are observed to apply; and

3) the assumptions under 2) lead to implications about the effects of changing farm size and composition that are at variance with the observed facts.

Adoption of the household-economics approach can help to overcome these deficiencies by: 1) enabling market and non-market activities to be analyzed within the same framework; 2) avoiding the need to assume diminishing returns to farm labour in order to account for participation in off-farm wage employment; and 3) allowing a more explicit account of Chayanov's neglected consumer/worker ratio and complex co-operation concepts.

We will begin the construction of our model by applying Becker's Z goods analysis to subsistence farming in southern Africa (see also Low, 1982a, 1984b).

A Z goods approach to subsistence farm production

According to Becker's (1965) theory of the allocation of time, households combine time and market goods in the production of basic commodities, Z goods, which are not marketable and enter directly into their utility functions. Maximizing income subject to Becker's full-income constraint implies that the household acts as a cost-minimizing firm in the production of household goods. Multi-person households also allocate the time of different members so that the required Z goods are produced as cheaply as possible (Evenson, 1978; Gronau, 1973). Assuming that inputs vary proportionately with the amount of the Z good produced, the marginal cost of producing a unit of the Z good in a two-person household is:

$$C_z = P_x.X_i + W_i.T_i \qquad i = 1,2 \qquad (1)$$

where: Cz is the full cost of producing a unit of Z

Px is the price of input x

Xi is the amount of input x required by member i to produce a unit of Z

Wi is the wage rate of member i

Ti is the amount of time required by member i to produce a unit of Z.

The cost-minimizing household will turn for its supply of the Z good to the cheaper of the two producers. Each of the members' marginal costs of producing the Z good will depend on his marginal productivity ($1/Xi$ and $1/Ti$) and his wage rate. In general the member with the lowest potential wage rate will be allocated to the production of the Z good, unless the higher wage earner is also more efficient in the production of Z goods by an amount that offsets the difference in wages.

Suppose, for example, that the marginal productivity of market inputs is the same for both members, but that member A has twice the wage-earning potential and requires 25 per cent less time to produce a unit of Z compared with member B. From equation (1), we can see that even though A is more efficient than B in the production of Z, B is the cheaper producer because his lower wage rate more than offsets his lower efficiency. It therefore pays the household for A to specialize in wage employment, because that is where his comparative advantage lies.

The subsistence crop as a Z good

It is possible to think of the semi-subsistence farm in the same terms. These households will make decisions about the allocation of the labour of their members to produce income, through wage employment, or to combine market inputs and time on the farm to produce subsistence goods. Thus a subsistence crop produced on the farm for own consumption is equivalent to a Z good. The household members with the greatest comparative disadvantage in wage employment will be allocated to subsistence production, so that labour with a greater comparative advantage in wage employment can specialize in generating income.

Given the additional possibility of obtaining the subsistence good through direct purchase in the retail market, the household is faced with an alternative method of obtaining its requirement of the subsistence Z good. Compared with growing the crop, the time required for purchase is negligible and can be ignored for simplicity. Thus the purchase alternative involves only market input costs, Pz, i.e. the price of a unit of Z in the retail market. In purchasing a unit of the subsistence Z good, the household saves on the cost of producing it. Thus when:

$$Pz < Px.Xi + Wi.Ti \qquad i = 1, n \qquad (2)$$

the subsistence requirement will be purchased rather than grown by member i.

Dividing equation (2) through by Ti and isolating Wi we get:

$$\frac{Pz - Px.Xi}{Ti} < Wi \qquad i = 1, n \qquad (3)$$

We can call the left-hand side of equation (3) the *opportunity cost of purchase* for member i, since it is the net cost (or benefit forgone) of not applying a unit of the time of member i to own production of food.[6] Where this is less than the returns to a unit of the time of member i in market production (e.g. Wi), the time of member i will be allocated to wage employment and food will be purchased rather than grown by member i.

Thus, where there are opportunities for wage employment and it is possible to purchase subsistence requirements as well as grow them, we can say that:

The time of household members with the greatest comparative disadvantage in wage employment will be allocated to subsistence production first, followed by members with increasing comparative advantage in wage employment until, either the household's requirement for the subsistence Z good is satisfied, or the next member's wage rate becomes greater than his opportunity cost of purchase, in which case the balance of requirements will be purchased.

This can also be shown geometrically. Consider a two-person farm-household, where the production activity possibilities are either subsistence crop production on the farm or wage employment in the market. We will assume that the two members are equally efficient in the production of the subsistence crop and that the returns to their labour in subsistence production are constant since land availability is flexible. However, we will assume that one member (m) has a higher wage potential than the other member (n). In Figure 4.2 the OA axis measures labour applied to the farm and, on the assumption that returns are constant, it also represents the amount of subsistence crop produce obtained. The segment On represents the amount of farm labour supplied by member n as well as the amount of the subsistence crop that member n could produce. The Om-On segment represents the labour input of member m and also his/her potential contribution to subsistence production. The OY axis measures market input costs and the PX line represents the market costs of growing the subsistence crop. Its slope (vx/t) also represents the market input costs incurred per unit of time used in subsistence production.

The WH axis is the corollary of the OA axis and measures the amount of labour applied to wage employment. The wage-earning potential of each household member is represented by the slope of the WWn curve. The segment WWm representing the wage of member M (em/t) and the $WmWn$ segment representing that of member n (en/t).

We can now consider the costs of subsistence production. For member n the full cost of producing a unit of the subsistence crop on the farm is ($vx + en$), i.e. market input cost per unit of time plus forgone wage earnings. This is less than the full cost for member m ($vx + em$) who has higher forgone wage earnings. The time of member n would therefore be preferentially allocated to farm production of the subsistence crop. However, if the household's subsistence crop requirement was greater than member n could produce alone, say OR, then part of the time of member m would need to be allocated to farm production and the overall (as well as marginal) unit cost of procuring the household's subsistence crop requirement would increase.

38 A model of the indigenous farm-household in southern Africa

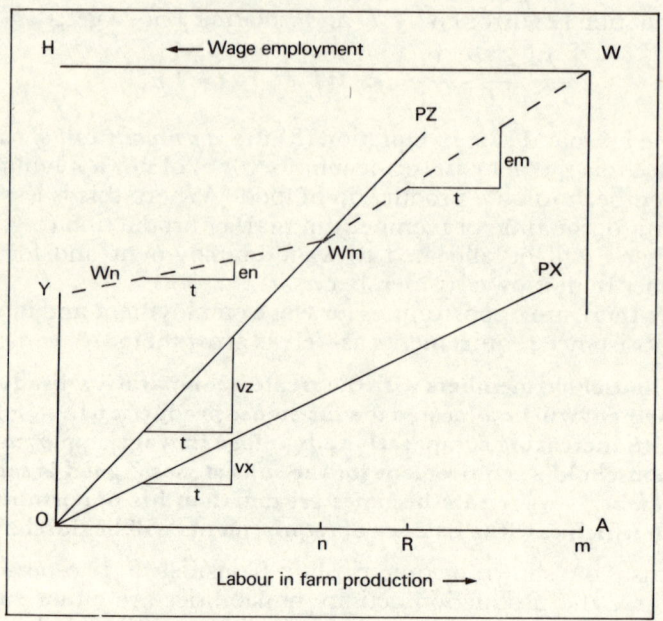

FIGURE 4.2: *Household-economics farm-household model: the two-person household – subsistence cropping versus wage employment*

We can consider the alternative possibility of purchasing the subsistence requirement on the retail market by introducing the retail price line *PZ*. Assuming again negligible time costs in purchasing compared with growing, this alternative saves all the time (*t*) required to grow a unit of the subsistence crop. Thus the slope of the *PZ* line (*vz/t*) represents the full cost of obtaining a unit of the subsistence crop through the purchase option.

When it costs less to purchase a unit of the subsistence crop (and save a unit of a member's time in doing so) than to grow it at the full cost of production for that member, the household requirement will be met more cheaply by direct purchase than by farm production.

This is the case in respect of member *m* in Figure 4.2: (*vz*) is less than (*vx* + *em*). However, for member *n* (*vz*) is greater than (*vx* + *en*). This household would therefore only grow *On* of its requirement (using member *n* to do so), while the balance of requirements (*OR* – *On*) would be purchased with part of the income earned by member *m* in wage employment.

Alternatively, we can say that the net cost per unit of time saved by purchasing rather than growing subsistence requirements (*the opportunity cost of purchase*) is given by (*vz* – *vx*). A comparison of this cost with an individual's opportunity wage rate will determine whether a member can earn more in alternative employment than it costs to save a unit of his/her time in subsistence production. We can state this household's labour allocation criteria as follows. Member *n* will be the first to be considered for subsistence production, because he/she is the cheaper producer, and will be employed in subsistence production rather than wage employment, because his/her wage rate (*en*) is less than the opportunity cost of purchase (*vz* – *vx*). Since some of the subsistence requirements remain outstanding ($OR-On$), member m will then be considered for subsistence production. But, as his/her wage rate (em) is above the opportunity cost of purchase, he/she will be allocated to wage employment rather than to subsistence production, and the balance of requirements will be purchased.

Other Z goods

The analysis outlined above can be extended to the consideration of other Z goods which are produced by the application of time and market inputs on the family farm and are directly consumed by the household. In most of southern Africa a very important category of Z goods, which are obtained and retained by working the land, relates to the benefits of acquiring arable land under traditional land-tenure arrangements. According to these arrangements members of a chiefdom are allocated land rights, which they maintain as long as they continue to cultivate the land. Together with the allocation of arable land for the exclusive use of the household goes the right to clear a homestead site and build housing units, as well as a number of communal rights within the chiefdom. These latter include access to and the use of water for washing and drinking, grazing for livestock, grass for thatching, and wood for building or fuel (see Chapter 9 below for a fuller discussion of traditional land tenure in southern Africa).

All the household has to do to maintain these rights is to continue to cultivate its allocated area to some extent. In terms of Figure 4.2 the PX line for these goods would have a very small slope, since the market input costs involved are negligible. The time costs would also generally be small:

    1) because the minimum cultivation needed can be done as part of the time input for, say, production of the staple food requirement and can be quite adequately performed by the lowest wage earners or by non-wage earners; and

    2) because related labour inputs in, say, collecting firewood or cutting thatching grass can often be done in the slack winter period or by low-potential wage earners, e.g. cattle herding is done largely by boys of school age.

Thus the cost of procuring these goods through traditional tenure arrangements ($Px.Xi + Wi.Ti$) will generally be much lower than the market cost of purchasing them directly (Pz).

In this connection it is interesting to note that in utilizing government-established ranches for breeding and fattening, farmers in Swaziland are reluctant to pay any charge for 'grazing', but are prepared to pay a 'management' fee. Under traditional tenure the right to utilize grass comes automatically with membership of a chiefdom and is virtually costless in terms of both market inputs and time. The actual use of this right does entail herding time and therefore has a cost. Thus while a charge levied on the mere rent of pasture is unacceptable, a charge for managing livestock on it is not.

Another Z good acquired by continued cultivation of the household's allocated area is the social security afforded by continued membership of the chiefdom. By retaining land use rights, an indigenous farm-household ensures a means of livelihood in periods of unemployment or old age. According to Hughes (1979, p. 277), there is 'ample evidence that many regard its [land's] role as the basis of a social security system as one of the most important of all the economic roles that it has.' As in most of Africa, formal state social security does not exist and most wage earners do not accumulate much, if anything, in the way of retirement pensions. Direct application of labour to the land is therefore often the only (and the cheapest) way of providing some security against sickness, unemployment or old age. It ensures that a means of subsistence, through land rights, will continue to be available if needed. It should be noted that the decision to obtain such goods by applying labour on the farm has nothing to do with the current productivity of this labour in terms of crop or livestock output. This helps explain why it is not infrequent that land will continue to be cultivated at very low levels of productivity.

In so far as cattle provide non-marketable consumption goods (milk, meat, hides, bridewealth, security, prestige) that are obtained by the application of time and market inputs on the farm, they too are equivalent to Z goods. However, cattle are also saleable and, like maize, become a means of generating income when they are exchanged for cash. However, unlike maize whose marginal value in consumption falls rapidly once basic needs are met, some of cattle's Z-good properties (i.e. prestige and security) will continue to have a high value as incomes rise above subsistence levels. Thus, even when basic needs have been met and income levels are high, cattle may continue to be retained as consumption goods rather than marketed. The costs of keeping extra cattle are small. Virtually no market input costs are involved, given the communal grazing system, and, as we have already noted, herding time costs are kept low by using schoolboys. Furthermore, for some of the Z goods conferred by cattle, such as security or prestige, there are few if any realistic alternatives to be purchased in the market place.

When a need for cash arises, the sale of cattle will be one of the possible means of meeting these needs. In this case, cattle sale will be chosen if it is the least costly alternative. For example, selling a cow would mean giving up the security, prestige etc. conferred by the marginal beast and would save on the cost of keeping it (which we have indicated is small). Alternatively, the needed cash could be obtained from selling leisure and working for an extra t hours in income-earning activities. The decision whether to work more or to sell a cow would depend on the subjective evaluation of t hours' lesiure against the benefits conferred by the marginal cow, less the costs of keeping it. Of course, the sale of a cow may have the added advantage that the cash can be obtained more quickly than by having to work for it. This may often be the deciding factor and one which is related to a further attribute of cattle: their use as an accessible savings account.

Cash cropping and multi-person households

Thus far we have looked at a two-person household situation and suggested that the time of each member could be used in either the production of non-marketable Z goods on the farm or in income-earning wage employment off the farm. Most indigenous farm-households in southern Africa have more than two producing members, and it is of course also possible to apply labour to income-earning activities on the farm by growing a crop, not for own consumption, but for sale. In so far as these activities generate income, they resemble wage employment. However, in terms of their returns to the labour input of household members, they will be more akin to crop production for own consumption. Indeed the same activity, e.g. growing maize, can supply both Z goods (food for own consumption) and income (through the sale of the crop). The decision to allocate the time of a household member to crop production or wage employment, then, will depend on the comparison of that member's wage rate with the opportunity cost of purchasing subsistence requirements, until such time as these requirements are met. Thereafter the decision will rest on a comparison of the member's wage rate with the net commercial return to crop production, i.e. the sale price less input costs. Since the sale price of, say, a bag of maize, will be less than the cost of purchasing the equivalent quantity of maize in the retail market, the net commercial return will be less than the opportunity cost of purchase. Thus, after subsistence needs have been met, the minimum wage rate above which members will be allocated to wage employment will be reduced.

This is not to suggest that there is a large difference in the subjective evaluation placed on producing one more or one less bag of grain. Rather it recognizes that the decision to produce for own consumption depends on: 1) the cost (or possibility) of purchasing the balance of subsistence requirements that are not grown and; 2) on the value of the labour time needed to produce the balance. This is different from the decision to grow grain for sale, which is based on: 1) the market value of grain produced in excess of own consumption requirements and; 2) the value of labour time used to produce the excess. A special case is where purchased food supplies are not reliably available and it is therefore necessary to grow the whole of one's subsistence requirement. Such a decision is quite independent of the market price of the subsistence crop, and represents the well-accepted 'own production of food first' criterion. This criterion represents a special case of our more general concept, where the opportunity cost of purchase is so heavily compounded by the risk of not being able to purchase requirements, that labour will be used to produce all own food requirements, however high its opportunity cost in alternative employment may be. But once these requirements have been met, labour will only continue to be used in producing the subsistence crop for sale if the market returns from doing so are greater than those that can be earned in alternative employment.

The question of risk is clearly an important factor in these decisions. There are risks in procuring the necessary household food requirements through crop production or wage employment and purchase. Where reliable food retail markets are available and retail prices are fixed, as in much of southern Africa, the risk element with wage employment relates to the chance that one's actual earnings turn out to be less than expected. This risk applies whether cash is being sought for food purchases or to obtain other essential market goods. To rely on farm production to obtain food needs also involves the risk that the harvest will be less than expected. Relying on farm production to generate cash to purchase essential market goods involves the additional risks associated with marketing the crop.

It is of course possible to discount wage earnings to take account of inherent risks (à la Todaro) and explicitly to recognize variability in crop production. However there are good grounds for thinking that these refinements would add a degree of complexity to the analysis without significantly changing the nature of the conclusions reached. We are primarily concerned with the allocation of farm-household labour between farming and wage employment. In this respect our decision criterion, which depends on the relative returns to members' time in wage employment compared with crop production, is quite compatible with risk aversion behaviour, since it is those household members with relatively good job prospects, i.e. contract mine workers, the educated and the skilled, who have the lowest risks of not finding employment. These will be preferentially allocated to wage employment both on account of their higher wage-earning potentials and the relatively low probability of them not generating the expected levels of cash income.

The question of risk is of course important in considering different crop production strategies, because of the implication that risk minimization involves a cost in terms of income maximization (see, e.g., Low, 1974). Such a conflict does not so clearly exist when we are considering the allocation of labour between crop production and wage employment. Indeed it is becoming increasingly common to see wage employment per se as a risk averting strategy (Guillet, 1981, p. 12; Sumner, 1982, p. 501). Stark and Levhari (1982, p. 192), for example, suggest that:

> an optimising, risk averse small-farmer family confronted with a subjectively risk increasing situation, manages to control the risk through diversification of its incomes portfolio via the placing of its best-suited member in the urban sector, in which income variance is distributed independently from agricultural production.

In leaving the risk factor out of our analysis it may be that we are underestimating rather than overestimating the value of wage employment vis-à-vis crop production.

In going on to consider multi-producer households, it will simplify the analysis considerably if we standardize farm-household labour units in terms of their efficiency in crop production. While one standard labour unit will be deemed to be equally as efficient as all other units in crop production, we would not expect the wage-earning potentials of each unit also to be the same. If they were the same there would be no comparative advantage among the household labour units. Given the size of the wage-rate differentials that face farm-households in southern Africa, it is reasonable to assume that some comparative advantage in crop production versus wage employment does exist.

Standard labour units are measured on the horizontal axes of Figure 4.3. The OA axis represents labour units used in crop production and the WH axis is again the corollary of this: labour units allocated to wage employment. The labour units are arranged in increasing order of comparative advantage in wage employment from left to right.

Money is measured along the vertical axes. For a crop, say maize, that may be grown for own consumption or to generate income through sale, the market input costs per standard labour unit, commercial returns and opportunity purchase costs are represented by the OC, OM and OP^7 lines respectively. The linear relationships reflect constant efficiency in the use of time and market inputs for all standard labour units. Returns to scale are also assumed to be constant since flexible land availability implies that as more standard labour units are applied to crop production, efficiency does not fall due to increasing labour to land ratios. The wage line WW' is curved and, in comparison with the constant returns to cropping, represents increasing comparative advantage in wage employment from left to right.[8]

Since we have assumed constant returns to crop production, a household's

A model of the indigenous farm-household in southern Africa 43

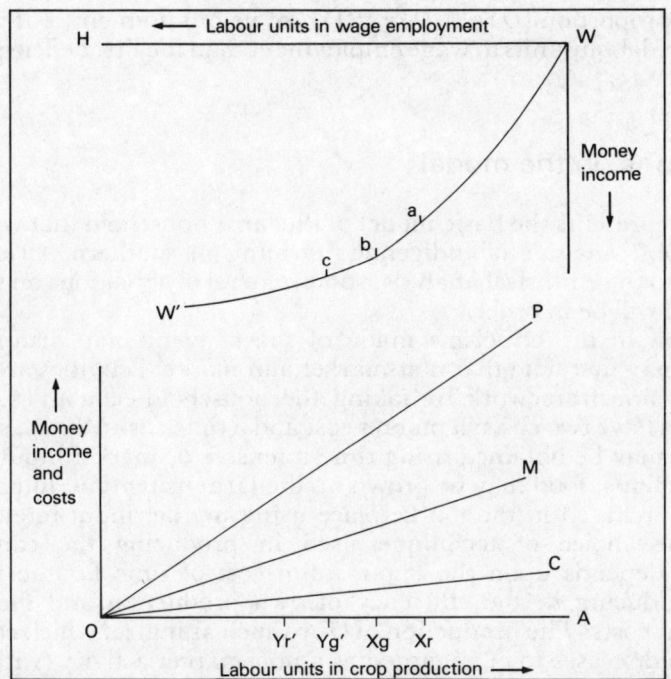

FIGURE 4.3: *Household-economics farm-household model: the multi-person household subsistence and cash cropping versus wage employment*

subsistence requirement can be measured directly in terms of the standard labour units needed to grow it. Say, for the farm-household (X), maize requirement can be met by allocating OXr standard labour units to its production on the farm. The wage rate for the standard labour unit at Xr is given by the slope of the WW' line at the point vertically above it (point a). Since the slope of the opportunity cost of purchase line is less than that of the wage line for the standard labour unit at Xr, that labour unit will be allocated to wage employment rather than to the production of the subsistence requirement on the farm. Only labour units to the left of Xg will be allocated to the production of the subsistence crop requirements on the farm, since to the right of point b the slope of the WW' line is greater than that of the OP line. This household would be a deficit maize producer, purchasing the proportion $(OXr-OXg)/OXr$ of its requirement.

A second household (Y) with similar levels of efficiency in maize production and wage-employment opportunities, but with fewer consumers per producer, may be able to meet its consumption requirements with only OYr' standard labour units. This household would allocate OYr' labour units to maize production. since at Yr' the OP line has a greater slope than the WW' line. It would even go further and allocate OYg' labour units to maize production, since the slope of the WW curve to the left of point c and Yg is less than that of the OM line. To the right of Yg' and point c, labour units earn a better return in wage employment than growing maize for sale to generate income. This household would, in contrast to the first, be a surplus producer, selling the surplus proportion $(OYg' - OYr')/OYr'$ of its requirement, but would still allocate more labour units to wage employment than the first deficit-producing household.

Observations on the model

Figure 4.3 represents the basic model of the farm-household that will be used for subsequent analysis of indigenous farming in southern Africa. Before proceeding to the empirical analysis, some general observations on the nature of the model will be in order.

In relation to the criticisms made of the conventional farm-household model, we may first note that non-market and market activities are included within the same framework by taking the household-economics view that commodities have two costs: a market cost and a time cost. Wants, such as the staple food, may be obtained using time-intensive or market input-intensive techniques. Thus, food may be grown on the farm using time-intensive technology or purchased in the marketplace using market input-intensive technology. The choice of technique used in producing the consumption commodity depends upon the opportunity cost of time for the household member producing it, the efficiency of own production and the different market input costs. The production of crops such as maize, which can be consumed or sold, ceases to be regarded as a non-market activity (with the crop valued at the retail price) when basic needs are met and surpluses are exchanged for cash in the market. Their production is then regarded as a market activity (with the crop valued at the farm-gate price), directly comparable with other market activities, such as wage employment.

Second, the point at which such a changeover between non-market and market activity takes place, in relation to subsistence crop production, depends on household members' wage rates in relation to the purchase price of food as well as on the structure of the household (consumer/worker ratio). In contrast to the implication of the Nakajima model, it does not necessarily follow that larger households will produce smaller surpluses or larger deficits than smaller ones. Indeed, if larger households have smaller consumer/worker ratios (as is the case for household Y compared with X in figure 4.3 above), and benefit from complex cooperation, as is often the case, then the opposite is implied, and this is consistent with empirical observations (see Table 4.1).

Third, neither constant returns to household members in wage employment nor diminishing returns to labour on the family farm are necessary assumptions of the model.

While these factors make this model more relevant than current subjective equilibrium ones, for analyzing the allocation of time between market and non-market activities and farm and non-farm employment, the allocation of time between productive activity and leisure is not given explicit treatment. There are two reasons for this. First it is felt that the allocation of time between work and leisure is less significant in relation to agricultural development in southern Africa than the allocation of labour between farm and non-farm activities. Second, as Nakajima (1970) has demonstrated, so long as some family labour is marketable, the allocation between farm and non-farm work can be ascertained without needing to know anything about the utility function and this clearly has advantages in terms of analytical simplicity.

It is possible, however, to give some recognition to the increasing subjective valuation of leisure as incomes increase by regarding leisure as a highly time-intensive non-market commodity. As such, leisure may be purchased at the cost of forgoing income that could have been earned with the time taken as leisure. Evidence that leisure is shared between household members is provided by Evenson, Popkin and Quizon (1980, p. 329). If this is so, the result of taking away productive time in equal proportions can be regarded as reducing the slopes of the WW', OP, OM and OC lines in Figure 4.3, since each work unit now produces less income or crop than when it took less leisure. However, the *relative* slopes would remain the same, so that the allocation of work units between activities would remain unaltered.

We may note that an implication of this is that if farm-household incomes rise as a result of an increase in wage rates, more work units will be allocated to wage employment than before, but each work unit would also take more leisure so that, not only would proportionately fewer work units be allocated to farm production, but these units, in common with all the farm-household work units, would apply less effort (work fewer hours) in production.

Although the adoption of a geometric approach to the analysis means that only relatively few aspects of behaviour can be considered at any one time, the limitations of simplicity are balanced by the advantages of gaining a broad understanding of the relationships involved. Many factors that affect farm-household behaviour are left out of the analysis. No account is taken of seasonal variations in labour requirements in farming, or of the lumpiness of different types of household labour, for example. Factors such as intercropping maize with pumpkins, the value of certain weeds as a relish, the preference for certain maize varieties for fresh consumption, the extent of storage losses and variations in soil quality have all been ignored. Sociological factors, such as the problems that wives with migrant husbands have in receiving extension advice or in obtaining credit or tractor hire, have not been considered.

Thus, in common with all models, reality is grossly simplified. Nevertheless it is considered that the model does incorporate elements which give rise to some of the most significant relationships that bear on the question of indigenous agricultural development in southern Africa: the relationship between farm production and off-farm wage employment opportunities; the relationship between farm production for own-consumption and for sale; the relationships between the prices of crop inputs and outputs, retail food supplies and labour in wage employment; and the inter-relationship of all of these with farm-household composition.

Quantification of the geometric model would enable more variables to be considered but would also pose difficulties. The problems involved with estimating comparative advantages and standard labour units could be overcome by entering individual member's efficiencies in different tasks through the season into a programming framework. However, the data specification problems would be formidable (e.g. are women more efficient than men at weeding and if so by how much?) and the exercise would need to be done on an individual household basis, since as Chayanov (1966, p. 60) observed:

> every family, depending on its age is in its different phases of development a completely distinct labor machine as regards labor force, intensity of demand, consumer/worker ratio and the possibility of applying the principles of complex cooperation.

In addition, of course, the relative efficiencies of the components of this machine as well as its intensity of operation change over time.

In view of the controversy on the validity of assumptions and integrity of purpose in the specification and quantification of programming models in the study of indigenous farming situations (Farrington, 1976; Low, 1978; Palmer-Jones, 1977, 1979; Upton and Casey, 1974; Upton, 1979), there are perhaps some methodological advantages to be had by keeping the model and analysis at a more general level. Furthermore, as Evenson, Popkin and Quizon (1980, p. 356) point out, 'the modern version of household economics is itself still quite primitive. It has not reached a point where the commonsense analysis of data with simple statistical tools can be ignored'. The analysis in Part II is therefore confined to examining the assumptions upon which the model is based and to formulating and testing certain hypotheses and implications of the model in relation to the development of indigenous agriculture in southern Africa. Before examining the model in relation to contemporary farm-household behaviour patterns and development issues, we will use the general arguments upon which it is based to reinterpret the historical development of agriculture in two countries in the region: Botswana and Lesotho.

Notes

1 Hunt (1979) found Chayanov's theory of the family farm to be well suited to indigenous farming in eastern Kenya, where the prevailing socio-economic conditions resembled those of much of southern Africa today.
2 Similar quantifications of the Nakajima model have been reported by Strauss et al. (1981); Lau, Lin and Yotopoulos (1976); and Ahn, Sing and Squire (1980). While the estimation procedures used vary between applications, they are all based on the same theoretical framework, and thus suffer from the same basic theoretical shortcomings.
3 The data in Table 7.19 suggest that the direction of causation in Africa is as Chayanov found, since the oldest and youngest households both have the smallest households and cultivated areas. In Mbere, eastern Kenya, where traditional land tenure prevailed at the time, Hunt (1979, p. 258) obtained a correlation coefficient of 0.6 (significant at .001 level) between household size and cultivated area.
4 While constraints other than land (e.g. capital) may cause returns to labour to fall, even where no land constraint exists, it is commonly recognized that land and labour are the major resources in small-scale African farming. Also, as we show in Tables 7.11 and 7.19, capital assets tend to increase together with increasing availability of labour and land.
5 The independence of household characteristics and the production side of the Nakajima model is brought out in empirical applications. Strauss et al. (1981, p. 39) state, for example, that in their analysis the effects of changes in household characteristic variables on consumption were examined in relation to the consumption side of the model and, 'since these variables do not enter into the production side, these are the total effects'.
6 The opportunity cost of taking a particular action is measured in terms of the benefits forgone by not taking an alternative action.
7 In regions other than southern Africa, where the opportunity to purchase does not exist

because of poor market developments, the opportunity-cost-of-purchase line in effect has a very steep slope because of risk compounding. In this special case all the labour required to produce subsistence food needs will be so allocated and the balance will be allocated to wage employment or commercial crop production, according to the relative returns in each.
8 The shape of the WW' curve is determined by the comparative advantage of different household members in wage employment compared with farming. It does not imply that, as a farm-household sells more labour, wage rates decrease because the household faces a (monopolistic) downward-sloping demand curve.

5 Historical developments re-examined

The household-economics model developed in Chapter 4 brings out the importance of the linkages between market and non-market production processes at the household level. At a macro-level the equivalent linkages between the development of the modern market sector and that of the indigenous subsistence sectors have not been adequately treated by orthodox neo-classical development theory (see Low, 1982b, pp. 49–64), which does not take us beyond the simple notion that the introduction of a market structure enabling the supply of new technology represents the basic change needed to stimulate the transition from subsistence to commercial farming (see Norman, Simmons and Hays, 1982). Such changes over the last fifty years in southern Africa have, on the contrary, been associated with the transition of formerly self-sufficient farming communities to sub-subsistence deficit food producers today.

Although they have markedly different agro-climatic characteristics, Botswana and Lesotho are two of the countries in the region that have followed this same development path. In this chapter we interpret the historical development of these countries in the light of the farm-household model developed in Chapter 4 and the household-economics thinking upon which it is based. The analysis suggests that household-economics thinking, which caters for the effect of non-market factors within a neo-classical framework, has a contribution to make to development theory. In subsequent chapters we will show that it can also provide practical guidance to policy-makers and development planners seeking to encourage the transition from subsistence to commercial farming in Africa.

A household-economics interpretation of agricultural development in Botswana and Lesotho

The processes of historical development of the agricultural economies of Botswana and Lesotho exhibit remarkable similarities. Murray (1980) and Spray (1975) have documented how Lesotho changed from being the granary of the Orange Free State before 1900 to a labour reserve for the Witwatersrand today. Kerven (1979) notes that the Tati reserve in Botswana was referred to as the granary of Matabeleland in the late nineteenth century by European travellers. Yet by 1943 the area was being described as 'wickedly grazed out'. In 1971, with half the male population in wage employment elsewhere, the area was said to be not so much farmed as used as a bank for Batswana absentees' savings, which are kept in the form of starving cattle (Kerven, 1979, pp. 3–4).

These are extreme cases, perhaps, but are by no means unique in the history of the region (see, e.g. Bundy, 1979 and Robertson, 1935, p. 5).[1] An examination of how these changes have come about reveals the influence of modern-sector development and indigenous institutions on the present day problems of migration and low levels of production in indigenous agriculture.

In both Lesotho (Spray, 1975) and Botswana (Schapera, 1947, p. 6), the indigenous populations were self-sufficient before the coming of the Europeans. Although barter trade existed, its scale was minimal (Schapera, 1947). The Europeans opened up a whole new consumer-goods market. As Schapera (1947, p. 123) commented in the 1940s, 'the Tswana can now obtain the products of factories all over the world'. Thus a new demand for market goods was created which required households to allocate more of their labour time to market production than they previously had done.[2]

The labour time needed to earn money to meet the new consumer demands could be obtained by sacrificing leisure or by reallocation of labour from subsistence to market production. The labour thus released could be employed in cash cropping, trekking cattle to market or wage employment. Evidence from Lesotho indicates that around 1875 many Basotho followed the typical 'vent for surplus' path and increased their efforts in traditional farming to produce surplus grain for sale to mining camps in South Africa. The rationality of this option is brought out by the observation of missionaries living in the area at the time:

> The valleys of Basutoland, composed as they are of a deep layer of vegetable mould, watered by numerous streams and favoured with regular rains in the good season, *require little more than a modicum of work to cover themselves with the richest crops* (cited in Murray, 1980, p. 5).

Such low labour-input options were not available to the Batswana on their less fertile and more distant lands. They therefore sought wage employment in the diamond and gold mines of South Africa, being reluctant to sell their cattle for reasons which we will consider in more detail in Chapter 9. Initially they were reluctant to be away for the normal six-month mine contract. Thus in 1903 the Rand gold mines made a special concession in respect of Bechuanaland recruits and reduced the contract period for them to four months (Schapera, 1947, p. 57). The Batswana timed their absences to fit in with the farming calendar, leaving around February and returning in October or November (Schapera, 1947, p. 54). At this early stage the Batswana seem to have behaved very much in accordance with Barber's 'periodic disguised unemployment' hypothesis (Barber, 1961).

The orthodox 'vent for surplus' behaviour did not apply to all Basotho, since many also sought wage employment outside Lesotho, and not all Batswana migrants were only absent in the slack season. However it can be argued that, by and large, the early response to an induced demand for market goods was met in ways that did not disrupt traditional subsistence farming.

Neither did the desired goods substitute for subsistence farm production to any great extent. Initially, manufactured articles replaced locally crafted ones and new luxuries were acquired. Purchase items included tea, sugar, door and window frames, clothes, guns, utensils, cattle and ploughs (Schapera, 1947, p. 122; Spray, 1975). The benefit of ploughs to cash-cropping Basotho

50 *Historical developments re-examined*

farmers can be appreciated in terms of the extra crop revenue they could expect to obtain in return for their investment. To the subsistence-farming Matswana migrant, it meant that he could complete his farm work sooner and sign on for a longer mine contract.

From about 1930, the picture of market participation superimposed on subsistence farming changed. Both the Basotho and Batswana increasingly became deficit producers of their basic food requirements and purchasers of the balance, a situation that has persisted to this day.

Murray (1980) has provided a succinct and vivid account of how Lesotho moved from being a substantial net maize exporter before 1920, to a substantial net importer from 1930 on. This change is reflected by the data presented in Table 5.1.

Murray (1980, pp. 12–15) stresses the role of the modern sector (urban bias) in causing the change. The imposition of grain marketing restrictions, the importation of cheap American and Australian grain, and market slumps are said to have 'inhibited mercantile exchange in Basutoland'. No doubt this was the case, but the limitation on mercantile exchange does not explain why the Basotho became net maize purchasers – indeed such restrictions would tend to limit this possibility. Clearly other non-market factors were also at play. Murray draws attention to population increase forcing a larger proportion of the population to settle in the less fertile mountain regions, and to disease and drought.

The movement of an increasing proportion of the population to the mountain regions was probably the most significant factor.[3] This resulted in the ratio of the area planted with maize to that planted with wheat falling from 2:1 in 1931 to 1.4:1 in 1938 (Colonial Annual Reports). Wheat is better suited to the mountain regions than maize, but the bulk of it is exported and maize is the preferred food. Thus, although the total acreages of both maize and wheat were said to have increased between 1931 and 1938, wheat exports expanded (barring the drought-affected years of 1933 and 1934) while net maize exports did not (see Table 5.1).

While wheat did often substitute directly for maize as a subsistence food, the fact that the bulk of it continued to be exported indicates that it was being sold in order to buy the preferred food (maize meal). Whether wheat was consumed directly or sold to purchase maize meal, the movement to the mountains, and the shift from maize to more labour intensive wheat, as well as reductions in fertility due to massive overgrazing, made it more expensive in terms of time to obtain a household's food requirement through traditional farming. This, together with an increased demand for mine workers following a gold price increase in the mid-1930s, resulted in 'a vast flow of emigration from Basutoland' (see Table 5.1) over the next decade (Murray, 1980, p. 9).

In Botswana a similar process was operating. As the data in Table 5.2 indicate, there is a close relationship between the imports of maize meal and the estimated number of absent workers. The imports of sorghum (the other major subsistence crop) fluctuated with the climate. Heavy sorghum imports in 1933 reflect the drought in that year and it is significant that in 1938, when there were two-and-a-half times as many migrants, the less dry conditions compared with 1933 precipitated an even greater volume of sorghum imports.

TABLE 5.1 *Net maize and wheat exports and gold mining employment: Lesotho, 1928–37*

Year	Net maize Amount thousands of bags	Exports Value thousands of dollars	Wheat Amount thousands of bags	Exports Value thousands of dollars	No. of Basotho employed on gold mines[a]	Percentage of male adults[b]
1928	+ 86	+ 48	118	131	14 448	8.4
1929	+ 62	+ 36	72	64	15 939	9.2
1930	– 55	– 28	132	105	20 917	11.9
1931	– 140	– 63	104	91	28 292	15.9
1932	– 94	– 41	197	168	28 653	15.8
1933	– 356	– 217	56	45	31 217	17.0
1934	– 137	– 96	90	89	35 000	18.8
1935	– 93	– 49	181	152	41 000	21.8
1936	– 207	– 145	96	66	45 399	23.8
1937	– 51	– 35	171	132	39 452	20.4

Sources and notes:

Colonial Annual Reports, 1928–37

a) 1929–33 average numbers employed, Pim (1935)
   1934–7 year-end estimates, Colonial Annual Reports
b) Male adults taken as 60 per cent of de jure male population

52 Historical developments re-examined

TABLE 5.2 *Grain imports and labour migration in Botswana, 1928–38*

Year	Grain imports, thousands of bags[a]			Average number of migrants officially employed in South Africa (thousands)[b]	Percentage of male adults[c]
	Sorghum	Maize	Maize meal		
1928	7	19	13	3.9	7.2
1929	14	11	12	4.7	8.4
1930	2	2	11	5.7	10.0
1931	1	8	14	4.9	8.2
1932	2	5	12	5.7	9.4
1933	17	5	19	6.7	10.8
1934	2	2	16	7.9	12.4
1935	3	3	30	10.2	15.6
1936	5	8	25	10.8	16.1
1937	7	2	24	12.4	18.0
1938	20	8	34	16.5	23.3

Sources:
    a) Colonial Annual Reports, 1928–38
    b) Schapera (1947, Appendix A)
    c) Male adults taken as 30 per cent of total enumerated population

As in Lesotho, population pressure and overgrazing caused reductions in the productivity of labour in traditional subsistence farming for the Batswana, and it became cheaper for the adult males to enter wage employment and purchase food requirements than for them to grow it on their farms. Thus more men remained on the mines for longer periods. In 1943 Schapera (1947, p. 56) commented that 'most mine labourers are now away twice as long as, say, twenty or thirty years ago'. This caused further reductions in farm production per hectare and per head. In 1937 the resident commissioner in Botswana reported that the acute shortage of labour in South Africa resulted in an undue exodus of labour, to the detriment of tribal welfare. Schapera (1947, pp. 134, 164–7, 198) repeatedly comments on the detrimental effect of substantial male absenteeism on crop and livestock production. He quotes a statement made in respect of labour reserves in South Africa, which he argues is equally applicable to Botswana and reflects the views of other writers on the subject (e.g. Houghton, 1964, p. 318):

> The mere absence of the men for the greater part of the year is invariably reflected in the cultural operations of the land and the resultant low yields. Even while the responsible male times his visit home to coincide with the ploughing and seeding season, agriculture suffers. It allows of no preparatory cultivation nor does it enable him to take advantage of favourable rainfalls. It necessitates leaving to the women and to juniors the major part of the work. There can be no organized system of working. The standard of agriculture, therefore, is low and there can be no development (cited in Schapera, 1947, p. 166).

The foregoing historical interpretation of developments in Lesotho and Botswana can be summarized as follows. Initially, surplus labour with a low opportunity cost in subsistence farming was used to generate the cash income necessary to meet the new demand for market goods. High-opportunity-cost labour needed to produce the subsistence food, which was either unavailable or relatively expensive in the market in terms of the time needed to earn enough money to purchase a unit of it, was retained in traditional farming. As the population expanded, the time needed to produce a unit of food in traditional farming *increased*, due to decreasing fertility of the cultivated land. As the market sector expanded, purchased food became more accessible and less expensive, due to transport improvements and food imports. Thus, the time needed to earn the money to purchase a unit of food in the market sector *decreased*.[4] The decrease in the cost of purchasing food relative to growing it encouraged more people to leave for wage employment even when it conflicted with subsistence farm production, and the increasing availability of jobs enabled more people to do so. The pure 'vent for surplus' effect ceased to prevail, since migration now tended to be undertaken instead of, rather than in addition to, subsistence food production.

The exodus of migrants, although great, did not reverse the process of declining productivity in traditional agriculture as conventional marginal-productivity theory would lead us to expect.[5] On the contrary, increasing migration contributed to declining levels of production per worker and per hectare. Because of traditional tenure arrangements and the nature of the modern-sector job opportunities, most families remained on the land and the migrants oscillated between their urban workplace and their rural home. The retention of a rural home base, which required no monetary payment but only the presence of some household members, enabled the household to maintain access to a wide range of household necessities, such as food, shelter, water, fuel, grazing and security, which could be procured cheaply with low-opportunity-cost family labour. Thus wives continued to cultivate (albeit less effectively than before) and migrants' land holdings were not reduced in favour of non-migrants. The pressure of the land therefore remained, even though the effort put into cultivating it was reduced.

Radical writers like Meillassoux (1981) and Simson (1979), who liken the pattern of oscillating migration in twentieth-century Africa to the more permanent rural exodus of nineteenth-century England, fail to appreciate a fundamental difference in the socio-economic environment from which these migrants originated. As Elkan (1960, p. 138) has pointed out, the towns in England drew their populations from agricultural labourers rather than small peasant farmers. These farm labourers had no rights to land and were already entirely dependent on wages before they entered the industrial labour force. They therefore stayed in the towns because the wage employment prospects were better there (though not very good) and, for them, the countryside offered no compensating non-monetary benefits, such as those related to indigenous land use rights in Africa.

Contributions to development theory

At the aggregate level the increasing food gap in Africa has been explained by a combination of rising urbanization and growth in non-agricultural incomes with attendant large shifts on the levels and composition of food demand. This has been accompanied by a disproportionately slow shift of an inelastic supply schedule, particularly where the resulting pressures for food price increases are dampened by policies designed to mollify urban consumers (Aboyade, 1983).

The household-economics interpretation of this process in southern Africa differs from those based on previous applications of neo-classical development theory in that it emphasizes the relationship between market and non-market production at the household level. This leads us to view development in terms of the effect that expansion of the modern sector has on the market versus non-market and farm versus non-farm production activities of indigenous households. Thus, at the macro-level, the analysis focuses on the relationship between the market-orientated modern sector and the non-market orientated indigenous sector. Unlike conventional theories, which account for duality between sectors in terms of institutional constraints either at the indigenous farm level (e.g. Lewis, 1954) or the urban industrial level (e.g. Todaro, 1969; Lipton, 1977), it is recognized that institutional constraints on perfect factor mobility at market prices exist in both the modern/industrial and indigenous/farm sectors. In the modern industrial sector, real wages are kept relatively high by pressure from influential groups. In the indigenous sector, relatively low productivity is a consequence of and, to some extent, is compensated for by non-market household production, which is facilitated by indigenous institutions.

The incorporation, within a neo-classical framework, of non-market factors in the analysis of economic development, mirrors the approach adopted by micro-Marxists, such as Meillassoux (1981), and political economists, such as Hyden (1980), who also emphasize the role of non-monetary elements in 'precapitalist' modes of production. These writers argue that indigenous structures and modes of production can have as strong an influence on the pattern of development and response to market expansion as the way in which the market itself is introduced and controlled. This school suggests that neo-classical analysis, which seeks to explain behaviour in purely economic terms, is confused by the fact that the system of circulation of goods in indigenous African societies is conditioned by non-market factors (Meillassoux, 1981). However, while Meillassoux and his followers attribute the roots of underdevelopment to failures of capitalism to produce a dynamic transformation of indigenous economies, Hyden stresses the strengths of indigenous peasant societies in the face of expansion of the market and the barriers that these societies pose to the progress of capitalism.[6] Hyden (1980, pp. 19–20) argues that Marxist and marginalist economists alike have overemphasized the market as the determinant of African development and that the indigenous peasant economy 'has the ability to survive and also affect the mode of operation of the market economy'.

While the micro-Marxist approach has made important contributions to the study of the role of the indigenous modes of production in influencing agricultural development and commercialization in Africa (Eicher and Baker, 1982, p. 40), the abstract nature of the models that have been developed has limited their capacity to provide guidance to policy-makers and development planners. The household-economics approach has the potential to overcome some of these shortcomings by analyzing the influence of non-market factors on farm-household behaviour within a neo-classical framework.

In Part II we will apply the farm-household model developed in Chapter 4 to an empirical analysis of indigenous farming in southern Africa. We will focus on a number of contemporary development issues and show how household-economics thinking can provide policy-makers and development planners with a clearer understanding of the likely impact of development initiatives on farm-household production.

Notes

1 Nor have such cases been confined to southern Africa. Gerhart (1975, p. 35) refers to Hay's (1972) study of the economic history of the Luo in Kowe, Kisumu District in Kenya:

> After 1930, Hay found, famines in 1931 and 1943–44, the collapse of cotton prices during the depression, the discovery of gold nearby, and eventually the labour demands of World War II drew men off the land. Labour migration and local trade became important as sources of cash income. These plus increasing population pressure, shorter fallow periods and soil erosion led to a gradual de-emphasis of the agricultural sphere within the economy as a whole. By 1945 labour migration was the accepted pattern.

2 Much has been made of the influence of the hut tax in forcing men into wage employment, and it is probably correct to say that some administrators did see the tax in this light. But Schapera (1947, p. 142) cautions against placing too much emphasis on its influence, since a considerable amount of migration was already occurring before its imposition at the turn of the century.
3 Movement from high-potential to medium- or low-potential agricultural areas in the face of increasing population pressure has been a common occurrence elsewhere in Africa (see Johnston, 1978, pp. 79–81, 85; Heyer, 1981, p. 116).
4 In some respects this process is analogous to a reversal of the development of cash-crop production described by Fisk (1964), in which increasing utility of money through the development of the modern sector stimulates cash-crop production which becomes more profitable as the scale of cash cropping increases. Here the relative utility of subsistence production compared with wage employment is reduced through the expansion of the modern sector which lowers the real market price of food, while subsistence production becomes less profitable due to decreasing land fertility.
5 Nor did the terms of trade move in favour of food production, since deficits were either imported or supplied by large-scale modern sector farmers.
6 Heyer, Roberts and Williams (1981, p. 5) also suggest that peasants are well placed to resist rural development initiatives aimed at increasing their production and commercialization if these initiatives conflict with their best interests.

Part II
Field study:
regional evidence and analysis

6 Focus on Swaziland

The empirical analyses presented in Part II are based mainly, though not exclusively, on material relating to Swaziland. The reason for this is that many of the ideas contained in this book were formulated while working in that country between May 1974 and February 1981, during which time the author had the opportunity to obtain relevant farm-household data. However, there happen to be other advantages in focusing on Swaziland. Apart from the obvious analytical advantages of concentrating on one rather than a group of countries, particularly for micro-level study, the choice of Swaziland has a number of points to recommend it.

First, while Swaziland is typical of countries in the southern African region in terms of land tenure, culture, climate and history, it does not suffer from some of the extremes experienced elsewhere in the region. As de Vletter et al. (1981, p. 45) point out, the indigenous rural sector is not so obviously underdeveloped as in Botswana, Lesotho or Transkei. Swazi farmers do not in general suffer from lack of rainfall as in Botswana or from such disadvantages as Lesotho's mountainous and eroded terrain. The country has enjoyed a stable political environment since independence in 1968, and has been free from a minority white government and the disruptions of war experienced, for example, by Zimbabwe.

Second, unlike Botswana but in common with Zimbabwe, Zambia and Malawi, the agro-climatic environment is varied so that a range of cropping possibilities (subsistence as well as cash) exists. Third, as in the whole region, there has been long-standing contact with the monetary economy and this has taken the form of modern-sector development in agriculture and industry within the country (as in Zambia, Zimbabwe, Malawi and Botswana) as well as participation in the industrial development of South Africa through international migration. In short, Swaziland exhibits socio-economic characteristics that are typical of the region as a whole, has good agricultural potential and, over the period of analysis, has been free of political instability and drought.

Geography and climate

The Kingdom of Swaziland, the second smallest country in Africa (17 368 sq km), is surrounded by South Africa and Mozambique. The country is divided into four well-defined topographic regions running from north to south in roughly parallel belts as shown in Figure 6.1.

The highveld has an average elevation of 1300 m (ranging from 900–1900 m). Annual rainfall is between 1000 and 2000 mm, with an average of 1270 mm, of which 75 per cent falls in the summer season from October to March. Average mean temperatures range from 22.6°C to 10.8°C. The

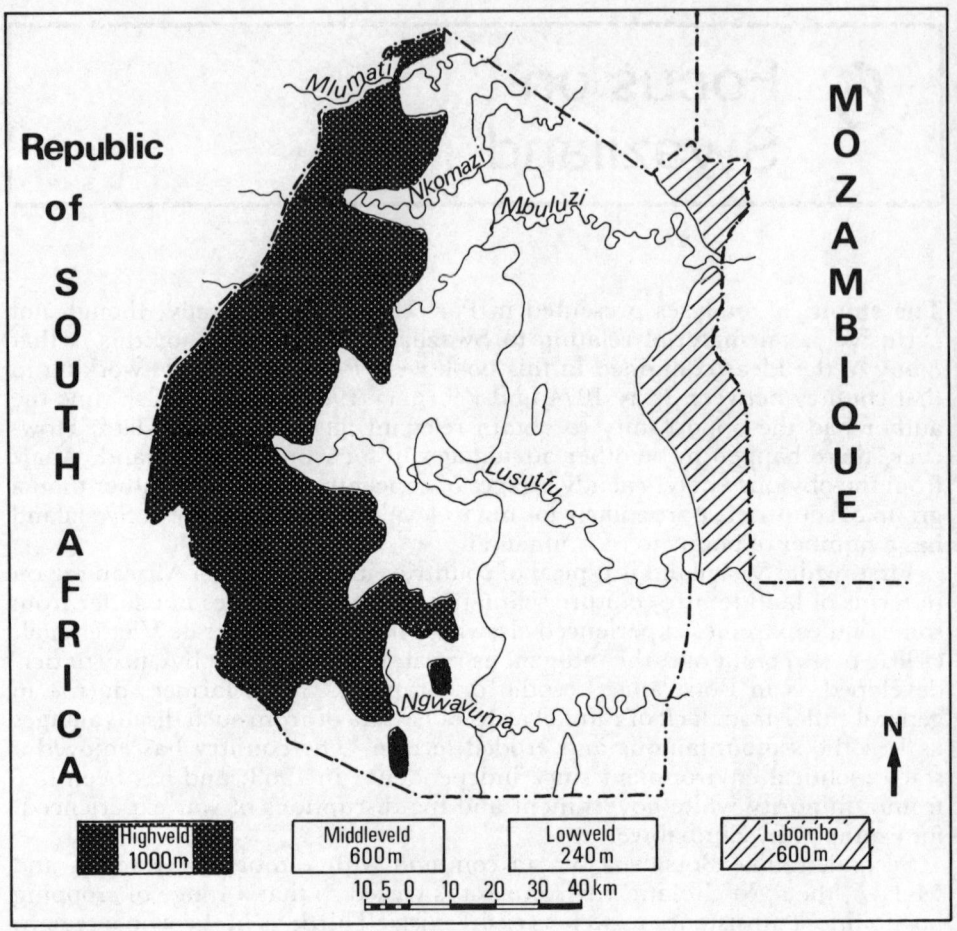

FIGURE 6.1: *Ecological regions in Swaziland*

natural vegetation is short 'sour' grasses and woodland. Livestock graze all year round and the main crops grown are maize, tobacco and potatoes.

The middleveld is characterized by rolling terrain averaging 700 m in elevation (ranging from 1000 m in the west to 350 m in the east). Annual rainfall is between 750 and 1150 mm with an average of 940 mm. Average mean temperatures range from 26.2°C to 11.7°C. Long grasses cover most of the area and the main crop is maize, with tobacco, cotton, beans, vegetables and sorghum also being grown by indigenous farmers. Cotton, citrus and pineapple are the main crops grown on large farms or estates.

The lowveld is flat or gently undulating, with an average elevation of 200 m. Rainfall is variable, averaging 660 mm, with a marked drought hazard. Average mean temperatures range from 29.8°C to 15.4°C. The original sub-tropical savanna climax has given way to sparse woodland, thorn scrub and tall 'sweet' grass. Maize is the major crop grown by indigenous farmers but sorghum is also widely grown. Cotton and cattle are the main cash crops. Estates grow sugar and citrus under irrigation (about 25 000 ha are irrigated) and there are also a number of large ranches.

The Lubombo is a plateau rising from the lowveld, in the extreme east of the country, with a similar agro-climatic environment to that of the middleveld.

History

The Swazi people are descendants of the southern Bantu, who migrated southwards from the lakes of central Africa many centuries ago. In the sixteenth century, the Swazi people lived near Maputo, the capital of present-day Mozambique. Led by Chief Ngwane II, they later moved into what is now south-eastern Swaziland. Here they absorbed the existing Nguni and Sotho clans and brought them under the Dlamini hegemony. The Swazi Nation came into existence when Mswati II was proclaimed King in 1840.

British traders and Afrikaner settlers first came to the area in the 1840s. In the 1880s gold was discovered and prospectors persuaded the then King Mbandzeni to grant concessions, the extent of which is said to have exceeded the territory of the Nation. In 1894 Swaziland's independence was guaranteed by the British government, and its present borders were specified. The British administration of the territory commenced in 1902 after the end of the South African War. In 1904 the colonial administration appointed a commission to delineate the network of land concessions. Five separate proposals for land partition were drawn up (Crush, 1980). The final proposal, agreed on in 1907, provided the Swazi with reserves covering 37 per cent of the land surface in a patchwork throughout the country. The reserves were arranged so that they included areas under the jurisdiction of all Swazi royals and the locations of royal graves, royal cattle posts and chiefs' kraals. The current (March 1980) state of land apportionment is given in Table 6.1.

TABLE 6.1 *Swazi land apportionment (1980)*

	Hectares	Percentage of total
Total rural areas (excluding urban areas)	1 643 530	100
Swazi Nation Land (including Lifa Land)	874 924	53
Purchased since independence	157 743	10
Total held by Swazi Nation	1 032 667	63
Title-deed farms:		
owned by Swazi citizens	92 520	6
held by expatriates	518 343	31

Source: Baker, C.F., (1980), personal communication

The Swazi nation now holds 63 per cent of the total land area of the country. The bulk of this is Swazi Nation Land (SNL), which is owned communally by the Swazi people and vested in the King, who holds it in trust for the Nation. On this area, arable land is allocated by chiefs to individuals on a usufruct tenure basis. Other non-allocated land within a chiefdom may be used for grazing or other communal purposes by members of that chiefdom. A smaller proportion of the land currently belonging to the Nation (about 10 per cent) is: 1) managed for the Nation on a commercial basis (Lifa or Tibyo land);

2) owned by the government (e.g. government cattle fattening and breeding ranches) or, 3) owned directly by the King. Most of the land purchased by the Nation since independence has been allocated to Lifa/Tibyo or the government. Only about 36 000 ha has reverted to Swazi Nation Land.

Increasingly Swazi nationals are purchasing privately owned land (Title Deed Land – TDL) but the bulk of this is still held by foreign-owned firms running large estates (sugar, citrus, forestry), in which the government often has a controlling share.

Since independence in 1968 a modern system of government, with cabinet ministers at the summit, has governed jointly with a traditional government, the Swazi National Council. Traditional government enjoys substantial power, especially on all matters affecting Swazi Nation Land development, where chiefs maintain customary law and hold power over land allocation. The King is de facto executive head of both the modern and traditional forms of government.

The Swazi rural sector

The Swazi rural sector consists of some 56 000 farm-households with an average resident population of 7.5 persons and 2.5 absentees. The average holding consists of about 2 ha of arable land, and households also have communal access to grazing, thatching grass, water, wood etc. within the area of their chiefdom. Family labour comprises the bulk of the labour force on most farms: hired and community labour together account for only 3–7 per cent of total farm labour. As may be seen from Table 6.2, the major crop in all geographic regions is maize.

TABLE 6.2 *Percentage of households growing and area planted to major crops on SNL*

	Highveld	Middleveld	Lowveld	Lubombo
Maize				
Percentage of households	97.7	98.9	98.7	100.0
Percentage of area	79.7	76.9	65.2	83.2
Sorghum				
Percentage of households	18.3	15.5	23.8	6.4
Percentage of area	3.9	7.0	5.0	9.0
Jugo beans				
Percentage of households	25.5	27.9	23.8	15.9
Percentage of area	3.2	3.0	4.0	0.9
Groundnuts				
Percentage of households	25.6	40.4	35.1	40.3
Percentage of area	3.9	7.0	5.0	9.0
Pumpkins				
Percentage of households	33.7	24.3	33.4	29.9
Percentage of area	3.3	2.4	5.0	1.2
Cotton				
Percentage of households	—	2.2	8.9	1.5
Percentage of area	—	1.5	11.2	2.8
Tobacco				
Percentage of households	2.1	6.1	1.4	1.4
Percentage of area	0.3	0.5	0.5	0.2

Source: Swaziland Government, 1973, p. 50

Fertilizers and other inputs such as hybrid seed are widely used. In 1971/72 one-third of farm-households over the whole country used fertilizer, although in the highveld two-thirds of farmers used fertilizers (Swaziland Government, 1973, Table V). In 1980/81 compound fertilizer for basal dressing was purchased by 65 per cent of farmers in the rural development areas. In the same year 54 per cent of rural development area farmers bought hybrid-maize seed and in some areas up to 90 per cent of farmers were using hybrid varieties (RDA Management Unit, 1981a). However, yields per hectare are well below technical potential and vary considerably from farm to farm and from year to year (see Table 11.5 for aggregate maize yield data). Farm-to-farm variation in maize production was remarked on thus by a UNDP expert:

> All over Swaziland there are kraals which produce excellent maize, and surrounding them are other homesteads which, year after year, produce terrible crops. . . Every year, the poor growers satisfy their needs by buying from their more provident neighbours, and if the year is a very bad one and the neighbourhood does not produce enough, they have to rely upon the local store (Barclay-Smith, 1980, p. 30).

Cattle are held by 60 per cent of households but ownership is probably more widespread than this, as it is common for cattle to be loaned out to relatives to overcome local scarcity of grazing or of herding labour.

A nationwide survey covering 1150 rural households in 1980 recorded 68 per cent of households having absentee workers and 39 per cent with resident wage earners (de Vletter, 1983). Participation of rural Swazi households in the money economy dates from the 1890s, when Swazis were first recruited for work on the newly developed Witwatersrand gold mines. Barker (1965, p. 39) tells us that in 1907 Gwamile, the then Queen Regent, began encouraging young Swazis to go to the mines in greater numbers to earn money to help purchase back some of the concession land. By the census year of 1936 work on the gold mines had become an established and important part of Swazi economic life. In that year the Swazi population was recorded as 153 270. About 10 per cent was reported to be in wage employment and half of these were recruited for work on the South African gold mines. Earnings returned to Swazi households from this latter form of employment amounted to £10 sterling per recruit: enough then to have purchased about half the annual maize requirement of the average rural household. Nowadays every other farm-household purchases as well as grows some of the basic staple.

Average annual cash expenditures are estimated to be about E800[1] per farm-household of which 30–40 per cent is spent on food and 10 per cent each on school fees, clothing, cropping expenditures, household goods, medical and other expenses (de Vletter, 1983; FMS). An estimate by de Vletter (1983) suggests that in 1980 average cash income from crops and livestock was about equal to the average level of remittances received from absentee workers and one-third of the average earnings of resident wage earners. Another national rural household survey (Flaxen, 1972) estimated that 63 per cent of total rural income was attributable to own production in 1972. This represents a slight decrease from the equivalent figure of between 64 and 77 per cent estimated in 1960 (Hughes, 1964, Table 124), and evidence from various recent surveys indicates that, on average, the value of own production now probably does not account for much more than 50 per cent of total income.

The Swazi rural sector is typical of the region:[2] production for own consumption constitutes a significant proportion of total income; cash income is equally important and has been so for a long period of time; wage employment continues to be an opportunity open to most households, and is the most common money-earning activity.

Notes

1 The Swazi currency is the lilangeni (plur. emalangeni – E). One lilangeni equals one South African rand.
2 For example see Hughes, (1974) for Zimbabwe; LASA, (1978) for Lesotho; Alverson, (1979) for Botswana; Marter and Honeybone (1976) for Zambia; Umphawi (1984) for Malawi.

7 Supporting evidence from Swaziland and elsewhere

In this chapter we will draw on evidence from Swaziland and elsewhere to justify using the model developed in Chapter 4 as a framework for analyzing farm-household behaviour and agricultural development in southern Africa. After a brief discussion of the data sources, the case for the model will be made by showing, first, that the evidence does not support the usual assumption of diminishing returns to labour on the Swazi farm; second, that the subsistence orientation of cropping patterns throughout Swaziland as well as regional variations can be understood in terms of the model; and, third, that production variations between Swazi farm-households are significantly influenced by, and can be understood in terms of, the domestic development cycle.

The data base

The data used in this investigation come from a number of sources, the chief of which are the farm management surveys conducted initially by the Economics Section and later by the Monitoring and Evaluation Unit of the Ministry of Agriculture and Cooperatives. These data have been analyzed and presented in a series of Farm Management Survey Reports (hereafter FMS) numbered 3 to 7. The reports consist mainly of mean estimates of a range of farm and household parameters for the random sample of households selected in each of the five rural development areas surveyed. Details of these areas and of the methodology and content of the farm management surveys are given in appendices 1 and 2 below. While some of the tables in the reports will be used directly in support of the arguments, most of the information presented constitutes a further analysis of the primary FMS data.

A number of ad hoc surveys on maize marketing, cattle marketing, farm credit and irrigation farming have also been carried out recently by the Economics Section and Monitoring and Evaluation Unit. These will be drawn on directly and in some instances will also be subjected to further analysis.

The author was involved, in various degrees, with the planning and/or execution of all the ad hoc and FMS studies mentioned above and, for this reason, they form the major part of the data base of this study. However, three other complementary sources of information will also be tapped quite extensively. The first of these is the 1960 nationwide rural survey conducted with the assistance of Natal University in 1959/60, the results of which have been published in Holleman (1964). These data provide a useful time perspective to the rest of the information which is cross-sectional and of recent origin. The second, non-author related, source of information comes from a series of surveys conducted by Fion de Vletter at the University of Swaziland at Kwaluseni. The last of these is a nationwide survey and as such is a useful complement to the FMS and ad hoc surveys, which are area (rural development area) based. The third complementary data source consists of the reports of the Management Unit of the Swaziland Rural Development Areas Programme, including some of the annual reports of managers of individual project areas. In each section the Swaziland data are supplemented with complementary information from elsewhere in Africa, particularly southern Africa.

Where no specific source is given in the following text, the data presented can be taken to come from a further (unpublished) analysis of the FMS or ad hoc surveys. Otherwise the source will be given at the foot of the relevant tables.

Returns to farm labour in crop production

We have already questioned the assumption of diminishing returns to farm-household labour on fixed land areas in southern Africa (see Table 4.1 above). Analysis of farm-household data in Swaziland provides further evidence against the diminishing returns assumption.

Analysis of farm-household labour data

The data in Table 7.1 for example, indicate that Swazi farm-households can and do acquire the right to hold and to cultivate larger areas as their de jure and de facto[1] labour forces expand.[2] Thus, Swazi households with larger labour forces also have larger areas upon which to apply their extra labour. Other things being equal, therefore, we would not necessarily expect to observe that households applying large amounts of labour to cropping experience lower returns than those applying small amounts.

In an attempt to test this hypothesis, correlation analysis was conducted on data from 300 households over 5 rural development areas. The results reported in Low (1982(b), pp. 137–40) indicate that:

    1) maize yields per hour decline as households use more labour in cropping;

    2) maize gross margins per hour remain constant or increase as households use more labour in cropping.

These seemingly conflicting results are explained by further analysis of the data which shows that farm-households applying smaller amounts of labour in cropping and those that apply crop labour less intensively per area of land cropped, complement their labour with purchased power (hire of tractors, oxen or labour) to a greater extent than others. Compared with others these households (applying less labour less intensively) will obtain higher yields for each power complemented hour they apply. But, since they purchase more power per labour hour, their gross margins are reduced and the correlations with labour input become positive.

These results suggest the need to control for the use of power in our analysis. Accordingly, in Table 7.2 only farm-households spending less than E10 on power are included. This reduces the numbers in each cell considerably (to about ten per cell) so that a significant difference is found for Mahlangatsha

TABLE 7.1 *Mean arable areas allocated and cropped per farm by de jure and de facto household workforce (hectares)*

	No. 16–64 year-olds in household			F-sig. level	No. 16–64 year-olds on farm			F-sig. level[a]
	0–3	4–5	6+		0–2	3–4	5+	
Area allocated								
5 RDAs	1.1	1.4	2.0	.001	1.1	1.6	2.0	.001
Northern	0.8	1.1	1.9	.001	1.0	1.3	1.9	.010
Southern	1.2	1.7	2.2	.001	1.2	2.0	2.2	.001
Zombodze	0.9	1.1	1.4	.021	0.8	1.2	1.4	.025
Central	0.8	1.4	1.6	.024	0.7	1.4	1.6	.016
Mahlangatsha	1.6	2.2	2.7	.029	1.6	2.1	3.2	.001
Area cropped								
5 RDAs	0.9	1.2	1.7	.001	0.9	1.3	1.7	.001
Northern	0.8	0.8	1.6	.001	0.8	1.0	1.6	.013
Southern	0.9	1.2	1.7	.001	0.8	1.5	1.8	.001
Zombodze	0.8	1.0	1.4	.013	0.8	1.1	1.4	.031
Central	0.7	1.2	1.4	.032	0.6	1.2	1.4	.020
Mahlangatsha	1.3	2.1	2.4	.013	1.4	2.0	2.9	.001

Note:

a) The significance level of the F statistic, i.e. the confidence with which we can reject the hypothesis that the between and within group variances are derived from the same population. The figure .001 indicates that there is only a .1 per cent probability that we would be mistaken in rejecting the hypothesis. For standard errors see Appendix 3, Table A7.1.

TABLE 7.2 *Farms spending less than E10 on power: maize yield and gross margin/hr by labour hours in cropping*

	Overall mean	Crop Labour Hrs/Farm			F-sig. level
		0–199	200–399	400+	
Maize yield/hr					
5 RDAs	6.7	5.3	7.1	5.6	.001
Northern	3.8	2.8	4.9	3.3	.291
Southern	3.4	4.4	1.8	3.6	.278
Zombodze	8.5	6.8	11.0	8.8	.652
Central	6.4	6.0	7.0	—	.773
Mahlangatsha	7.3	4.8	8.9	7.6	.139
Maize gm/hr					
5 RDAs	34.6	28.7	40.9	34.5	.451
Northern	21.4	20.6	24.3	19.1	.837
Southern	14.0	18.2	4.6	15.5	.472
Zombodze	59.1	48.2	70.6	72.7	.766
Central	27.1	21.0	34.9	—	.617
Mahlangatsha	44.1	24.7	55.8	47.4	.079

RDA only. Nevertheless a consistent pattern emerges. In all areas, apart from the Southern RDA, farms with low amounts of labour in cropping have below average yields and gross margins per labour hour. The data indicate a pattern of labour returns that increases initially and then falls off as greater amounts of labour are applied on the farm.

This household-level analysis was supplemented by field-level regression analysis in respect of local and hybrid maize in two rural development areas (see Low 1982(b), pp. 140–5). Yields obtained from each field per pre-harvest labour hour applied to that field were regressed against two sets of independent variables:

    1) field-level variables that are specific to a particular field; and
    2) farm-household level variables that are common to a group of fields in the same household.

Two labour-input variables relating to each of the above sets were included in the equations:

    (Fl) the pre-harvest labour hours applied per field
    (Hl) total labour applied to cropping on the farm.

The R^2 values for the four equations estimated ranged from .59 to .74. In all four cases highly significant negative coefficients were obtained for the Fl variable (pre-harvest labour applied per field). In all equations, again, positive coefficients were obtained for the Hl variable (total labour applied to cropping on the farm), but in only two of the equations were these coefficients significant at the 10 per cent level.

We can interpret these results as follows. At the field level, increased labour inputs applied to fields of given size and with fixed levels of inputs reduce maize output per hour. But at the household level, those households with greater overall allocations of labour to cropping achieve higher labour returns on fields of similar size and with similar levels of labour and other inputs than do households with a smaller overall input of labour.

Since similar results are obtained by substituting the total labour input variable with other measures of household labour input, such as household size or size of farm work force, it is possible to view these results as evidence in support of Chayanov's 'complex co-operation' factor. Certainly, the analysis of this Swazi labour data provides grounds for questioning the validity of the normal assumption of decreasing farm labour returns and suggests that the assumption of increasing or constant returns has as much validity in the Swaziland context. It is also relevant to note that while the assumption of constant returns on the family farm is not an essential part of the model presented in Chapter 4 above, the assumption of diminishing returns is essential for subjective equilibrium models of the farm-household since they assume constant returns to family labour in wage employment. Until firm evidence of declining labour returns on the farm can be provided, models based on this assumption must be suspect in the southern African context.

For analytical simplicity it is assumed that returns are constant in Figure 4.3. However, this is not an essential assumption of the conceptual model. Increasing returns or decreasing returns, or even a sigmoid-shaped labour returns curve are not necessarily inconsistent with the model. In fact, the data in Table 7.2 suggest that labour returns may take a sigmoid shape. This is not implausible, since one might expect returns to be low for the initial input of workers with little chance of benefiting from 'complex co-operation'. As more workers are added to an expanded area of land and the benefits of 'complex co-operation' begin to apply, labour returns can be expected to increase. Finally there is presumably some ultimate limit to land availability and/or the benefits that 'complex co-operation' provides so that, as even more labour is applied, marginal returns begin to fall. Nevertheless it does simplify the analysis considerably to assume constant returns on the farm, at least over the relevant range.

Other evidence against diminishing returns to labour in farming

Increasing returns to labour have been observed more generally in Africa. In Zimbabwe, Shumba (1985) found that maize yields per adult worker were higher for households with larger adult work forces than for those with smaller ones. And based on a macro-level analysis of the Nigerian experience, Aboyade (1983, p. 11) suggests that 'the marginal productivity of labour in African farming is positive'.

Other students of the African scene have taken constant returns to labour on the farm to be the norm. For example Hunt (1979, p. 258) argues that 'Productive activities are generally characterized by constant returns to scale and therefore for individual households and individual activities average and marginal returns are approximately equal.'

A further general observation on labour productivity in southern Africa is less difficult to understand if the possibility of constant or increasing labour returns on the farm is accepted: the observation that while unskilled off-farm wages are relatively high, farm productivity is very low. This high wage/low labour-productivity paradox has been commented on by the World Bank (among others) in its 1980 Agricultural Sector Reviews of Swaziland and Lesotho.

These observations are difficult to reconcile with Nakajima's model presented in Figure 4.1. If labour stays in farming until $W = VMPa$, and $VMPa$ is declining from the origin, then average labour productivity on the farm would be higher than the average wage rate. To fit the high wage/low labour productivity observations into subjective equilibrium models of the farm-household, we need to replace Nakajima's log-log farm labour returns curve with a sigmoid one (as suggested by the data in Table 7.2), or we need to assume constant farm labour returns with a variable wage rate as depicted in Figures 4.2 and 4.3.

Summary

In this section on returns to farm labour in crop production we have examined farm-household level data which suggest that, once power expenditures have been accounted for, households with lower labour applications obtain below-average returns to labour in maize production. This is supported by field-level analysis, which indicates a positive relationship between total farm labour application in cropping and field-level maize yields per labour hour. While the results cannot be said to be conclusive, they do cast doubt on the almost automatic assumption of decreasing returns to labour on the family farm, which is difficult to reconcile with the general observation of high wage/low labour productivity in Swaziland as well as other southern African countries.

Cropping patterns

The model presented in Chapter 4 above suggests that, up to the point at which subsistence food needs are met, households will cultivate a subsistence crop so long as it is not cheaper to purchase requirements with income obtained from cash cropping or wage employment. After basic food needs have been met, the extent to which labour is allocated to cropping rather than wage employment and the choice of crops grown will depend on the relative returns to labour obtained from various cash-cropping options on the one hand and potential wage earnings on the other. In this section we will first examine the economics of the subsistence-oriented cropping pattern of Swazi farm-households in general, and then consider regional and geographical variations.

The economics of subsistence maize production

Estimated mean farm gross margins (at producer prices) per hour for maize on selected fields are given in Table 7.3.

TABLE 7.3 *Mean maize gross margins per hour per farm on selected fields*

	No. of farms	Mean gm/hr (cents/hr)	S.E. of mean
Area			
Northern RDA	58	5	6.4
Southern RDA	60	14	3.5
Zombodze RDA	51	46	7.4
Central RDA	66	57	12.2
Mahlangatsha RDA	58	42	4.2

The estimates of maize gross margin per hour in Table 7.3 show a wide range and have high standard errors, indicating a large measure of variation from farm to farm. The significantly lower figures for the Northern and Southern RDAs can be explained by the poor rainfall experienced in those areas in the 1978/79 season. These data can be compared with the few corresponding ones available for the major cash crops of cotton and tobacco given in Table 7.4.

TABLE 7.4 *Reported gross margins per hour for cotton and tobacco*

	Cotton	Tobacco
	(cents/hr)	
Source		
FMS Report No. 2 (table (V)A)	24.0	43.3
FMS Report No. 3 (table 7.3A)	—	39.0
FMS Report No. 5 (table 3e)	—	100.0

The cotton and tobacco estimates relate to years experiencing average rainfall and are therefore more comparable with the estimates of maize labour returns from Zombodze, Central and Mahlangatsha RDAs. This comparison would put maize and tobacco on a par so far as labour returns are concerned, with cotton being the least attractive alternative. But in so far as cotton is grown in the lower rainfall areas, it is perhaps more comparable with the Northern and Southern RDA maize data. Looking at it this way, it would seem that cotton and tobacco give returns to labour as good as or better than maize does.

However, cotton and tobacco only compete well with maize in terms of returns to effort when all three crops are grown commercially for sale. As we have seen, when maize is grown as a Z good for food requirements, the returns to labour are not given by the *gross market value* of the product of a unit of labour less the input costs of growing that product (net sale value). They are given by the *gross retail value* of the product of a unit of labour less the input costs of growing that product (opportunity purchase cost).

Formal producer and retail maize prices are gazetted annually by the government and apply throughout the year in question. While a local informal market in maize also exists between relatives and neighbours, there is no information about the prices in this market or their variability through the year. However, according to the RDA Maize Production and Marketing Survey (1980, tables 3e & 3f), up to 60 per cent of sales were made to the formal market in the better maize producing areas, and in most areas over 40 per cent of maize purchased was in the form of maize meal. Thus while farm-households looking to produce maize for sale may be able to sell locally at advantageous prices in some seasons, their fallback price will be the gazetted producer price. Similarly, while deficit-producing households may be able to purchase some of their requirements locally below official retail prices, the latter constitute the maximum they will have to pay for a guaranteed supply. Thus not only do the formal market prices apply to a large proportion of maize sales and purchases, they also act as the guaranteed prices upon which farm-households can base their production plans.

In 1978 the maize meal retail price was 15 cents/kg against a producer price of 9 cents/kg (Fowler, 1980, Tables 11 and 12). Given these prices, the net sale value and net retail value of maize in the two survey areas covered that year are given in Table 7.5. We can see that the net retail value (or opportunity purchase cost) is twice that of the net sale value. This means that labour returns in maize production for own consumption will be given a value twice that of the commercial gross margin per hour.

TABLE 7.5 *Output, costs and net value of maize 1977/78*

	Output	Input costs	Input costs	Net sale value	Net retail value
	kg/ha	E/ha	cents/kg	cents/kg	cents/kg
Central RDA					
Local maize	1264	22.73	1.8	7.2	13.2
Hybrid maize	1604	74.73	4.7	4.3	10.3
Local and hybrid	1402	44.00	3.1	5.9	11.9
Zombodze RDA					
Local maize	1125	30.93	2.7	6.3	12.3
Hybrid maize	1596	59.96	3.8	5.2	11.2
Local and hybrid	1296	46.20	3.6	5.4	11.4

Since the net returns per hour of the cash crops of cotton and tobacco are comparable with, but are less than twice, those of commercial maize, these cash crops will not compete well with maize production for own consumption (with returns based on the net retail value), although they may do so with maize production for sale (with returns based on the net sale value). The implications of this finding can be traced by reference to Figure 4.3, where OM represents net labour returns to commercial maize production and OP represents the returns to growing maize for own consumption (or opportunity cost of purchase). Tobacco or cotton production may give returns higher than OM but, on the evidence available, will not generally give returns equivalent to OP (which has twice the slope of OM). Thus, up to the point where own food requirements are met, farm-households will choose maize production in preference to one of the cash crops. After this point, cash cropping may be preferred to commercial maize production. However a large proportion of households appear not even to produce all their requirements and, like household (X) in Figure 4.3, are deficit producers. In 1960 it was estimated that 55 per cent of rural households were deficit producers (Daniel, 1964). In 1978/9 de Vletter (1983) recorded 53 per cent of farm-households purchasing maize.

Since the evidence has suggested that cash-crop production does not generally provide income-earning opportunities greater than OP (twice commercial maize returns), a majority of deficit households are not likely to grow cotton or tobacco to finance food purchases. Wage employment is the most likely source of finance for this purpose, not only because of its higher net returns, but also because there is less risk that the income required to meet deficit food requirements may not be so realized. Even farm-households growing all their own maize requirements or a surplus for sale (e.g. household (Y) in Figure 4.3) would not necessarily devote all their remaining labour resources to commercial cropping, because the remaining workers will often have a high wage income potential: the lower wage earners having been allocated to subsistence crop production first.

Again the risk factor will tend to make wage employment more attractive than cash cropping for generating income requirements for other than basic food requirements. While there is a clear risk that the money costs and time costs devoted to cash cropping may provide a rather small net benefit if the year is a poor one, or prices are depressed, the income from wage employment is constant and can be relied upon with a reasonable degree of certainty. And the chances are good that the better-qualified household members will find employment without incurring much time or money costs, since employment centres are within easy reach of most rural areas in Swaziland. Even more-distant employment in the South African mines is arranged on a contract basis within the country.

In conclusion, then, empirical application of the time-allocation and Z goods analysis suggests that, even where households have substantial cash incomes and ready access to reliable food retail outlets, it will often be economically rational to be primarily a subsistence cropper. In general, cotton and tobacco are not likely to offer an attractive alternative to maize before subsistence requirements have been met and, after that, will often have to compete with high wage-earning opportunities. This analysis is consistent with the low rates of adoption of these cash crops over the years, despite vigorous promotion efforts and the apparent advantages that cotton and tobacco have over maize in terms of the usual measure of crop profitability: returns per hectare (see Table 7.6).

TABLE 7.6 *Mean gross margins per hectare for maize, cotton and tobacco (E/ha)*

	Maize	Cotton	Tobacco
Source			
FMS Report No. 2 (table 7VA)	44.2	175.7	792.1
FMS Report No. 3 (table 7.3A)	83.9	—	334.0
FMS Report No. 5 (table 3e)	83.7	—	567.5

Regional and geographical variations

While subsistence maize production is the main characteristic of the cropping pattern throughout Swaziland, regional and geographical differences do exist. The data in Table 7.7 indicate that the cropping patterns in the lowveld and Lubombo regions are less subsistence-oriented than in the highveld and middleveld.

TABLE 7.7 *Cropping patterns by ecological region*

	Highveld	Middleveld	Lowveld	Lubombo
1971/72 sample census[a]				
Percentage of cultivated area under				
maize	79.7	76.9	65.2	83.2
cotton or tobacco	.3	2.0	11.4	2.8
Percentage of holdings selling some				
produce	20.5	21.3	38.1	25.6
1959/60 survey[b]				
Percentage of households selling				
maize	6.9	14.1	4.2	15.7
sorghum	1.7	1.4	2.3	8.0
groundnuts	3.6	8.4	8.3	10.0
1980 survey[c]				
Percentage of households selling				
no crops	61.6	65.8	48.5	48.4
crops except cotton				
or tobacco	31.2	26.0	12.8	41.0
cotton or tobacco	7.2	7.5	38.4	10.5

Sources:
   a) Swaziland Government, 1973, Tables II & IV
   b) Holleman, 1964, Table 94, p. 216, and Table 100 p. 230
   c) de Vletter, 1983

Ecological factors affecting cropping potential explain this in the lowveld, where maize production competes less well with cotton. As the data indicate, most of the commercial production in the lowveld is associated with the production of cotton. This is not the case for Lubombo, which has a climate

74 *Supporting evidence from Swaziland and elsewhere*

similar to that of the middleveld where maize does particularly well. Climatic factors do not therefore account for the greater commercialization of cropping in the Lubombo compared with the rest of the middleveld.

TABLE 7.8 *Household production characteristics by region: 1959/60 sample survey*

	Highveld	Middleveld	Lowveld	Lubombo
Percentage of total cash income from:				
wages	88.2	79.8	83.9	58.7
crop sales	.8	4.3	1.2	12.3
cattle sales	1.7	3.8	6.1	16.7
Percentage of households with no wage income	27	42	42	47
Median wage income per household (rands)	61	46	43	15
Average maize surplus or deficit per household (bags)	−2.1	−0.9	−1.3	+4.5
Percentage of households purchasing maize	73	47	54	36

Source: Holleman, 1964, Tables 94, 121, 123 and 132B

The data in Table 7.8 show that, compared with the other regions, the proportion of cash income coming from wage employment in Lubombo was small: more households had no wage income and the median wage income was comparatively low. To compensate for their relative lack of wage income, Lubombo households sold more crops and grew more (or purchased less) maize.

TABLE 7.9 *Household production characteristics by location: 1980 sample survey*

	Rural RDA	Peri-urban RDA
Percentage of households:		
Selling no crops	38.8	59.7
Selling crops except cotton or tobacco	56.7	35.5
Selling cotton or tobacco	4.5	4.8
Receiving regular remittances	35.8	46.8
Having resident wage earners	34.3	51.6
Receiving cash income from crops	55.2	41.9
Purchasing maize	29.8	59.6

Source: de Vletter, 1983

A similar relationship is observed in Table 7.9, where households have been classified as rural or peri-urban.[3] Compared with peri-urban households, the rural ones show similar characteristics to those in Lubombo. Fewer of them have wage earners or remitters. However, on the other hand, more households sell and obtain income from crops and fewer of them purchase some of their maize requirements.

Peri-urban households obviously have better access to jobs and wage employment than their rural counterparts (many of them will have moved to a peri-urban area for this reason). The same is true of other regions in Swaziland compared with Lubombo. Situated as it is, on the eastern border with Mozambique, Lubombo is farthest from job sources both within Swaziland and in South Africa.

In terms of Figure 4.3, the comparatively poor wage employment opportunities facing Lubombo and rural-based households result in a reduction in the slope of the wage employment curve (WW'). According to our theory this is likely to result in deficit maize producers, such as household (X), allocating more labour to maize production and purchasing less. Alternatively it will result in surplus producers, such as household (Y), keeping more labour in cropping and producing more crops for sale. The evidence fits with this reasoning and is consistent with Chayanov's thinking which led him to state that:

> Peasant farms turn to intensive crops *only* when they cannot meet their demands to the necessary extent with an optimal labour payment *and do not have advantageous crafts and trades*. (p. 115, my emphasis).

TABLE 7.10 *Farm incomes and the supply of labour: Uganda 1956*

	Farm income per head (in shillings)	Wage earners as percentage of working population
Toro	61	41
Ankole	49	16
Kigesi	17	35

Elkan (1960, p. 36) makes a similar point about Uganda. He presents data on farm income per head and the proportion of the working population in wage employment (see Table 7.10), and comments on the figures thus:

> Toro has the highest employment ratio. The District's farm income is low (compared with other regions in Uganda such as Lango, Teso, Busoga, Bugisu and Buganda with farm incomes per head over 100/-), but it higher than that of Ankole and Kigesi and although Toro District is not a farmer's paradise, it is certainly capable of a good deal of agricultural development. But its people prefer to raise their incomes by seeking employment and they have indeed exceptional employment opportunities for earning more than minimum wages, and when they leave home in search of work they do not have to travel far. . . It may well be therefore, that their income from the sale of produce is low, not because they do not have the opportunity to grow crops for sale, but because their opportunity to earn money in employment is relatively more favourable or preferred.

The domestic development cycle

Chayanov was perhaps the first economist to recognize the relationship between farm production and the changes in peasant household structure over the course of its development cycle. He argued that:

> Since the labour family's basic stimulus to economic activity is the necessity to satisfy the demands of its consumers, and its work hands are the chief means for this, we ought first of all to expect the family's volume of economic activity to quantitatively correspond more or less to the basic elements in family composition. (Chayanov, 1966, p. 60).

and he went on to show that:

> the demographic processes of growth and family distribution by size also determine to a considerable extent the distribution of farms by size of sown area and numbers of livestock. (Chayanov, 1966, p. 67).

As we see from Table 7.11, cross-sectional data in Swaziland show the same relationships between household size, sown area and cattle ownership.

TABLE 7.11 *Area cropped and cattle held by household size*

	Overall mean	Household size			F-sig. level
		1–5	6–8	9+	
Area cropped (ha)					
5 RDAs (n = 376)	1.3	0.7	1.1	1.7	.001
Northern (n = 78)	1.1	0.5	0.9	1.7	.001
Southern (n = 77)	1.3	0.8	1.2	1.6	.005
Zombodze (n = 76)	1.1	0.8	0.9	1.4	.004
Central (n = 79)	1.1	0.6	1.0	1.5	.005
Mahlangatsha (n = 66)	1.9	1.0	1.5	2.3	.012
No. of cattle held (head)					
5 RDAs	8.3	1.8	6.4	12.3	.001
Northern	10.3	1.5	7.3	17.8	.001
Southern	8.5	0.8	8.6	10.8	.001
Zombodze	5.0	1.1	3.9	9.1	.001
Central	6.5	3.7	5.3	8.3	.186
Mahlangatsha	11.5	2.6	6.8	15.7	.003

The implications of the domestic development cycle have been recognized elsewhere in southern Africa. Murray (1980, pp. 16–17), referring to Basotho rural households, states:

> This means that what anthropologists call the development cycle of the household – the way in which its size and composition changes through time – must be built into any explanation of observed differences in income and wealth between rural households. (pp. 16–17).

In turn this implies the need for our analytical tools to take account of changes in household size and composition, an area where it has been suggested that the model developed in Chapter 4 has advantages over conventional ones.

We will begin our empirical analysis by re-examining 1960 survey data on inter-household production differences in terms of Figure 4.3. This will lead us to consider the effects of the domestic development cycle on Swazi farm-households by categorizing them into groups according to the stages they have reached in the domestic development cycle and analyzing the differences between these groups.

An explanation of 1960 survey results

The findings of the 1960 rural household survey led Hughes (1964) to hypothesize that the rural population could be placed into one of two classes: one primarily dependent on farming but indulging in some money-earning activities; the other consisting mainly of wage earners who attempted to do a little farming. To test this hypothesis, Hughes examined the relationship between wage earning and maize production. Households were divided into four classes according to the wage incomes received, and the median size of the maize surplus or deficit was calculated for each class (see Table 7.12).

TABLE 7.12 *Wage incomes per household and maize deficits per head (lbs) (1959/60)*

	Deficit-reporting households		Surplus-reporting households	
	Number	Median deficit	Number	Median surplus
Wage income (R)				
0	39	200	30	190
1 to 40	16	175	6	150
41 to 80	20	130	7	200
81 to 120	21	66	4	250

Source: Holleman, (1964), Table 128, p. 265

Hughes comments on his results thus:

If the hypothesis, that there was a direct connexion between maize deficit and wage earning, were correct, one would have expected maize surpluses to vary in inverse proportion to wages earned, and maize deficits to vary in direct proportion to these [but] one has the surprising phenomenon of the median deficit *decreasing* with increased wage earnings. In the surplus-reporting section, one also has a tendency for surpluses to increase with increased wage earnings (p. 265).

This observed positive relationship between maize surpluses and wage income is quite consistent with the analysis in Chapter 4, where Figure 4.3 was used to show that household (Y), a surplus food producer, would have a greater wage income than the deficit-producing household (X). This result rests on household (X) having a higher consumer/worker ratio than household (Y). Although no estimates of consumer/worker ratio were made in the 1960 survey, a positive relationship was observed between household size and maize surplus (see Table 7.13).

No similar comparison between household size and wage employment was made in the 1960 report, but more recent data in Table 7.14 indicate that household size is positively correlated with both the area of maize planted (or crop income) and the number of family members in wage employment (or wage income).

78 Supporting evidence from Swaziland and elsewhere

TABLE 7.13 *Maize deficit/surplus by household size (1959/60)*

	Household size			
	1–4	5–8	9–12	13+
Net surplus/deficit (bags)				
Highveld	–2.6	–2.2	–1.4	–2.3
Middleveld	+0.2	0.0	+1.7	+4.4
Lowveld	–2.3	–1.0	+0.6	–1.8
Lubombo	+0.3	+6.1	+3.4	+15.3
Net surplus/deficit (lbs/head)				
Highveld	–165	–67	–28	–29
Middleveld	+11	–0.1	+33	+50
Lowveld	–154	–31	+11	–21
Lubombo	+22	+188	+66	+152

Source: Holleman, (1964), Table 97, p. 226 and Table 98, p. 229

TABLE 7.14 *Correlation coefficient significance levels:[a] household size with crop production and wage income*

		Survey areas				
	Nation-wide[b]	North RDA	South RDA	Zombodze RDA	Central RDA	Mahlangatsha RDA
Household size with:						
maize area cropped	—	.001	.001	.002	.001	.001
crop income	.001	.025	.085	.002	–.295	.268
No. of wage earners	.001	.001	.001	.001	.001	.001
Household wage income	.001	—	—	—	—	—

Sources and notes:
a) The figures presented here are the significance levels of the respective correlation coefficients with the signs attached being those of the correlation coefficients. For example, the figure –.001 indicates a negative correlation which is significant at the .001 level. A one-tailed test is applied since we are interested in whether the observed direction of association is significantly different from zero. The correlation coefficients and related number of observations are given in Appendix 3, Table A.7.14.
b) From de Vletter (1983)

The same positive relationships between household size, maize surpluses and wage income have been observed in Zimbabwe. Survey data from Mangwende (Shumba, 1985) and Chibi South (CIMMYT, 1982) indicate that cattle owners, who have larger households, also generate higher maize surpluses and earn more off-farm income (see Table 7.15).

The fact that crop production and wage income both tend to increase as household size does suggests that variations in wage income and maize sufficiency are connected through household size. Thus, the 'surprising phenomenon' of a direct relationship between maize self-sufficiency and wage income can be explained in terms of household size and composition. This leads us to consider how the domestic development cycle influences the economic behaviour of farm-households.

TABLE 7.15 *Relationship between household size, maize sales and off-farm income in Zimbabwe*

	Household size	Maize sales Z$/year	Off-farm earnings Z$/year
Mangwende			
Cattle owners (n = 40)	8.4	347	159
Non-owners (n = 40)	6.4	168	149
Chibi South			
Cattle owners (n = 46)	9.0	34	124
Non-owners (n = 50)	6.5	5	66

Identifying domestic development groups

Chayanov recognized that households change in size as well as in their consumer/worker ratio as they move through their domestic development cycle. Chayanov was able to concentrate on these two characteristics in his analysis because Russian peasant families were of the nuclear type and exhibited a two-generation development pattern. Fortes's (1970) classification of the domestic development cycle into five stages is also based on a two-generation development pattern:

1) *Establishment*: when a house is built and a farm established. At this stage Fortes recognized that there may still be a continued dependence on the parental group with the transfer of capital resources and the courting and marriage of a spouse.

2) *Expansion*: when the new household becomes more clearly independent and children are born.

3) *Consolidation*: expansion to the fullest point, embodying the highest ideals of family development.

4) *Fission*: the stage where children marry and leave the parental household. This may be associated with the relinquishing of control of domestic resources from the parental to the filial generation.

5) *Decline*: the final stage, which is contemporaneous with and often contributes to the expansion stage in the filial group if the ageing couple are located within one of their children's households.

Although Fortes's paradigm stresses numerical growth and decline of the household, it also recognizes that households of the same size may be at different stages of their development cycle and that size alone is not a good indicator of a household's position in the cycle.

More extended family groupings having three generations will not tend to exhibit such clear-cut numerical changes as they proceed through their development cycle. Often the filial generation will remain in the parental group through marriage and the birth of the first children. A new domestic unit will then be established by parents already with young children. At the other end of the cycle, the fission stage is delayed and, if the delay is for long enough, the decline stage may be avoided altogether. In polygynous households, the stages of expansion, consolidation, fission and decline will be coincidental in sub-sections of the same household. Thus, while it would be possible to identify the life-cycle stage of a nuclear family having a two-generation development pattern with household demographic data alone, more-specific historical information would be required to perform the same task for a three-generation polygynous family.

TABLE 7.16 *Types of Swazi household grouping*

	Highveld	Middleveld	Lowveld	Lubombo	Combined
Family type					
Nuclear family[a]	41.7	40.0	45.0	41.7	42.1
Simple polygynous[b]	6.7	6.7	3.3	10.0	6.7
Extended agnatic[c]	10.0	21.7	20.0	25.0	19.2
Complex groupings[d]	41.6	31.6	31.7	23.3	32.0

Source and notes:
  Holleman, (1964), p. 127
  a) comprises head plus immediate relations in his line (wife, mother and all his children from any wives)
  b) as for a) but with two or more wives
  c) either of a) or b) but with other kin linked in the male line
  d) all groupings not being one of a), b) or c) above.

Accounts of original Swazi household organization (Kuper, 1961; Marwick, 1940) describe the three-generation polygynous family grouping as the norm. While such groupings still exist, they now no longer constitute the norm. According to Hughes's (1964) analysis of 1960 data (see Table 7.16) about half of the family groupings were of a simple nuclear type and less than one-tenth were simple polygynous groupings. In 1980, de Vletter (1983) recorded only 5 per cent of households with more than one wife. However, relatives other than the children of the household head or his wife were commonly present in the household. Married sons or daughters were present in 35 per cent of households, brothers and sisters in 14 per cent and mothers and fathers in 10 per cent. Hughes (1964) describes the modern Swazi household thus:

> The main differences between the majority of homestead groups of today and the larger ones of the past appear to result from the fact that this process of fission now tends to occur far earlier in the life cycle of a homestead. Sons now frequently set up their own homesteads during their father's lifetime, almost immediately after marrying. The same applies to younger brothers of the homestead head . . . Mothers still settle with their sons after their husband's deaths; but whereas in the past this grouping was frequently a 'mother-sons' family, now it is more often a 'mother-son' group; the mother living with one of her sons, the others having separate establishments. (pp. 122–3).

The movement from the three-generation polygynous family grouping towards the nuclear family probably has economic causes, and is not unconnected with the growth of wage employment in particular. Robertson (1976) notes that the existence of wage employment opportunities 'would tend to undermine the three generation household structure in the long run by offering young men the early opportunity of establishing their own homesteads'. Sibisi (1980) points out that, for the Swazi, wage employment has advantages over remaining in the rural environment where there is limited opportunity to acquire the means 'to make eventually the crucial transition to married status' (p. 6).

Whatever the reason for the movement to two-generation nuclear families, it means that there is some justification for the following attempt to identify development cycle stages in terms of household demographic data. The classification adopted is based primarily on household size, and the data used for the analysis are taken from the farm survey files we have been using for most of our previous analyses. Three size groups are isolated: those with populations of one to six, seven to ten, and eleven or more persons (including those working away). All households in the latter category are assumed to be in the consolidation stage (group 3). The smallest households with six persons or less are presumed to be in the establishment stage (group 1) if the household head is less than 50 years of age and if any children under 10 years are present. They are also assumed to be in group 1 even if there are no children but, in this case, the household must have three persons or less and the household head must be less than 40 years of age. All other households with six persons or less are assumed to be in the decline stage (group 5).

Households with seven to ten persons are assumed to be in the expansion stage (group 2) if the household head is less than 50 years of age and 25 per cent or more of the household members are children under 16 years. A household with seven to ten persons may also be in group two if the household head is less than 55 years of age and 50 per cent or more of the household members are children under 16 years. All other households with seven to ten persons are assumed to be in the fission stage (group 4).

Female-headed households are excluded from the above classification and form a separate category (FH). A summary of these classification criteria and the resulting mean values of the basic characteristics for each group are given in Table 7.17.

The basic characteristics of the different domestic development groups are of course determined by the criteria used in selecting the group.[4] The selection has resulted in a fairly even spread of farm-households between groups and has also resulted in farm-households with the same population sizes being split according to age and consumer/worker ratio. The latter is defined here as the number of persons in the household divided by the number between 16 and 64 years of age.

Thus, we have households in the establishment stage (group 1) and decline stage (group 5) with average populations of four to five persons. But households in the establishment stage have much younger household heads and higher consumer/worker ratios than do households of a similar size in the decline stage. Because of the differences in consumer/worker ratio as well as in the values of their time (see page 29, above), we would expect these two groups to have different production characteristics even though they are of the same size. Similarly with households in the expansion stage (group 2) and the fission stage (group 4), although here the difference in household structure is not so marked, and time-value differences would not be so great either.

Since most females who head households are widows or abandoned wives, it is not surprising that the female-headed households category (FH) has characteristics similar to those of households in the fission and decline stages. Households in the consolidation stage have, by definition, the largest average population and, as we would expect, the average consumer/worker ratio and age of household head lie between those of the expanding and contracting groups on either side.

TABLE 7.17 *Domestic development groups: criteria for classification and basic characteristics (5 RDAs)*

	Establishment Group 1	Expansion Group 2	Consolidation Group 3	Fission Group 4	Decline Group 5	FH Group 6
Classification criteria						
Household size	1–6a 1–3b	7–10	11 +	7–10	1–6	any
Age of head	<50a <40b	<50a <55b		other than those in Gp 2	other than those in Gp 1	
Children <10 years	>0a =0b					
Child/population ratio		>.24a >.49b				
Basic characteristics						
Household size	5.0	8.2	14.5	8.6	4.3	9.3
Age of head	37.8	41.7	56.7	63.7	57.0	57.9
Consumer/worker ratio	2.1	2.2	1.9	1.9	1.4	1.8
No. of households	39	72	86	66	62	51
Percentage of households	10	19	23	18	16	14

Resource and production differences between domestic development groups

Resource and production differences between the groups that have been identified are analyzed in Table 7.19. The analysis of variance F statistic is used to test whether the variation between groups is significantly greater than the variation within them. The results are discussed in turn below.

As expected from our previous discussions, the arable area allocated to households (R1) expands and then contracts as households move through the development cycle (i.e. move from group 1 to group 5). A similar situation is evident in respect of farm equipment (R2) and cattle holdings (R3). Female-headed households (FH) seem to fit between the fission and decline categories in all three respects.

These results reflect a typical pattern of accumulation and decumulation, which is emphasized in the literature on the domestic development cycle. Data in Table 7.18, on the rate of net cattle disposals (defined as sales plus own slaughters less purchases, all divided by the number of cattle held), confirm this pattern of accumulation and decumulation. The net voluntary cattle disposal rates for young expanding households (groups 1 and 2) are seen to be lower than those of the other groups. Since these data relate to rates of accu-

TABLE 7.18 *Net voluntary cattle disposals by domestic development group (Cattle Marketing Survey 1980)*

	Establishment Group 1	Expansion Group 2	Consolidation Group 3	Fission Group 4	Decline Group 5	F-sig level
Classification criteria						
Household size	1-6	7-10	11+	7-10	1-6	
Any pre-school children	Yes	—	—	—	No	
More children than adults	—	Yes	—	No	—	
Net voluntary cattle disposal rate (percentage)	−1.2	1.7	7.7	4.1	3.2	.109

Note: A less elaborate classification was possible for this table than for Tables 7.17 or 7.19 because of the more limited data collected on household structure in the Cattle Marketing Survey than the FMS.

TABLE 7.19 Domestic development groups: resource structures and production characteristics

	Establishment Group 1	Expansion Group 2	Consolidation Group 3	Fission Group 4	Decline Group 5	FH Group 6	F-sig level
Resources							
R1 Allocated area (ha)	0.9	1.4	2.3	1.7	1.0	1.2	.001
R2 Equipment value (E)	14.7	19.3	30.3	23.0	7.1	10.2	.001
R3 Cattle held (head)	3.4	7.2	15.0	10.2	3.3	5.9	.001
R4 No. of farm workers	1.8	3.3	5.9	3.7	2.5	3.4	.001
R5 No. of wage earners	.7	1.2	2.2	1.5	.8	1.9	.001
Production							
P1 Cultivated area (ha)	.7	1.1	2.0	1.5	.8	1.0	.001
P2 Maize area	.6	1.0	1.8	1.3	.8	1.0	.001
P3 Percentage of P2 under hybrid varieties	38	36	43	27	28	19	.051
P4 Cash crop area (ha)	.08	.04	.04	.05	.02	.03	.521
P5 Maize income (E)	1.1	11.6	13.2	15.1	5.2	1.4	.033
P6 Other crop income (E)	10.6	15.1	14.4	10.5	4.5	14.3	.510
P7 Crop labour in (hrs)	211	318	531	373	167	276	.001
P8 Crop labour intensity (hrs/farm worker)	143	124	109	119	67	89	.002
P9 Crop labour intensity (hrs/ha)	315	333	306	271	258	294	.316
P10 Percentage of workers in wage employment	29	26	28	27	25	33	.507
P11 Farm expenditure per farm worker (E/head)	19.9	20.2	11.9	13.3	9.5	8.1	.003
P12 Power expenditure per farm worker (E/head)	14.2	7.8	6.1	4.3	8.2	7.4	.002

Note: For standard errors of the means, see Appendix 3, Table A.7.19

mulation and decumulation in a particular year they are independent of historical factors (such as periods of high cattle prices or good employment opportunities) that might affect the measurement of stocks of assets at any time.

Returning to Table 7.19, we see that the resource advantages of farm-households in the consolidation phase (group 3) are quite marked. Compared with the other groups, farm-households in this group have more crop land together with more equipment, cattle and farm workers (R4) to cultivate that land. They also have more wage earners (R5) to provide cash income. These resource advantages result in group 3 households cultivating the largest area (P1), growing the most maize (P2) and being the most extensive adopters of hybrid maize (P3). But the highest area of cash crops and the next most extensive adoption of hybrid maize are accredited to group 1 households, which tend to have fewer resource advantages than any of the other groups.

According to household-economics thinking, group 1 households would have a relatively high propensity to work: 1) because of the relatively high values of time in early years compared with later ones, and 2) because the present value of future returns to productive investment (asset accumulation) is greatest in the early years.[5] Group 2 households are in a similar position and, like group 1 households, also have relatively high consumer/worker ratios. These relatively high demands on workers in groups 1 and 2 are reflected in greater intensity of labour input per worker (P8) and per hectare (P9) in these groups compared with groups having similar workforces and crop areas (groups 5 and 4).[6]

The observed increase in labour intensity per worker as the consumer/worker ratio increases is consistent with Chayanov's hypothesis and has also been observed to hold elsewhere in Africa. Hunt (1979, p. 262) found a significant correlation (at the .01 level) between hours worked per adult per annum and the consumer/worker ratio for twenty-nine households in Mbere, Kenya.

Increased labour intensity per worker is also reflected in increased labour intensity per hectare (P9). As we noted above (p. 68), increased labour input per hectare results in lower labour productivity. However, this consequent reduction in labour productivity per hectare faced by groups 1 and 2 is offset by investing in better yielding (hybrid) varieties (P3) and greater input and power investments per farm worker (P11 and P12). Even though such investments would tend to increase the productivity of farm workers in groups 1 and 2, the proportion of workers in wage employment (P10) is not reduced compared with other groups. This is because these households have a relatively high desire for income. Consequently, the time saved by the adoption of production-increasing technologies (which is encouraged by the relatively high wage value of these workers' time) is spent on income-earning activities, such as wage employment or cash cropping (P4), rather than taken in leisure.

In terms of our formulation in Figure 4.3 above, compared with groups 4 and 5, group 1 and 2 households have relatively steep wage income curves. But the slopes of the younger households' crop returns lines are also relatively steep, because of the adoption of productivity-increasing technology and their propensity to take less leisure. As we noted above (p. 45), if the *relative* slopes of the wage and crop returns do not change, the equilibrium point with respect to the number of work units allocated to wage employment and farming remains unaltered. This reasoning is consistent with the observation that there is little difference in the proportion of workers in wage employment between groups 1 and 2 and groups 4 and 5.

The data in Table 7.19 confirm that there are significant differences between domestic development groups (as we have defined them) both in terms of resource endowments as well as in terms of crop production, adoption of improved varieties and cash crops, expenditure on farm inputs and power and the extent and intensity of work on the farm. Moreover, we have been able to account for these differences in terms of changes in the desire to accumulate, the consumer/worker ratio and wage employment prospects as households move through their domestic development cycles.

While the categorization of groups has been rather crude and the interpretation of the observed differences between them is no doubt simplistic, it is argued that the above analysis has demonstrated that the domestic development cycle has important implications for farm production and the propensity to adopt new and/or more intensive crop technology.

Demographic differentiation

The foregoing analysis of Swaziland data has led us to argue along the same lines as Chayanov: namely that, through the domestic development cycle, demographic factors do have an influence on farm-household production levels, intensity of work, access to resources and the propensity to adopt innovations.

Similar data for Zambia is given in Table 7.20. Household size is positively related to cropped area, propensity to sell maize and level of household income. In general, higher crop sales are also associated with lower consumer/worker ratios. However, since these data have not been categorized in terms of the domestic development cycle, but according to levels of economic advantage,[7] the authors and other commentators ascribe such observed differences to factors other than the domestic development cycle. Marter and Honeybone (1976) lay stress on rural–urban migration as causing the demographic differences and hence the production differences. Likewise Klepper (1980, p. 125) comments on the same data by remarking that the 'very large differences across peasant households and the high proportion of female headed households at the lower end of the range suggest that most of the differences arise from migration and not demographic differentiation of the Chayanov sort'. Again, commenting on his Mpika data, Bwalya (1980, p. 153) says:

> While elements internal to the individual household may have played and may continue to play some role in the growing social and economic differentiation in Mpika on the basis of Chayanov's theory, they have not been the major determinants. Both historical and present exogenous factors have forced the individual household to fail to become full capitalist producers. . . If non-rural family businesses do become capitalist, it should be wondered why the family farm should not become capitalist.

Clearly the political leanings of these writers cause them to play down the role of the domestic development cycle, which suggests a cyclical development

TABLE 7.20 *Farm-household characteristics in Zambia*

	Household size	C:W ratio[c]	Crop area	Percentage selling maize	Crop income (Kwachas)
Favoured areas[ad]					
Group 1	4.6	2.2	1.3	37	14
Group 2	6.4	2.1	3.1	77	74
Group 3	6.7	2.3	4.8	90	220
Group 4	9.7	2.2	10.4	87	902
Unfavoured areas[ae]					
Group 1	3.1	2.8	0.6	8	2
Group 2	5.7	2.4	1.5	24	18
Group 3	6.9	2.4	1.7	29	64
Group 4	12.1	2.5	4.6	42	427
Mpika district[b]					
Group 1	5.5	2.9	1.1	30	5
Group 2	6.6	3.1	2.2	41	23
Group 3	8.4	2.3	5.4	85	277

Sources and notes:
  a) Marter and Honeybone, 1976, Tables 3.2, 3.6, 3.8 & 3.9
  b) Bwalya, 1980, Tables 3, 4, 5, & 9
  c) Mean household population divided by adults (15–55 yrs)
  d) Northern, Luapula, Copperbelt, and Western Provinces
  e) Central, South and Eastern Province

pattern rather than the progressive formation of a dominant capitalist class. However, it is pertinent to note that the influence of the domestic development cycle is not confined to peasant societies. Within any society, peasant or capitalist, household incomes tend to increase as families mature and then decline again as they age. As proponents of household economics have demonstrated (e.g. Becker, 1976; Ghez and Becker, 1975), the productive activities of capitalist households in the United States are influenced by the life cycle, just as the activities of farm-houscholds in Africa are. To be sure, as Chayanov acknowledged (1966, p. 69), other factors also influence relative income. Many of these other factors operating in Zambia and elsewhere in southern Africa (such as extension, market and credit services) tend to exacerbate the difference caused by the domestic development cycle. For example Elling (1981, p. 147) notes that about one-third of farm-households in some provinces of Zambia are headed by women, almost none of whom are registered as farmers. They are 'thereby excluded from any form of credit and few are able to concentrate on agriculture because of domestic and family demands'. In Malawi credit packages for fertilizer have, until recently, been tied to hybrid maize and have therefore only been available to larger farm-households producing surpluses for the market, since local varieties are much preferred over hybrid for own consumption on account of better storing, pounding and cooking qualities.

The nature of the available wage employment opportunities in the region, which favour young adult males, also reinforces the advantages of households in the consolidation phase. As we have seen for Swaziland and Zimbabwe, and as indicated by both Marter and Honeybone and by Bwalya, larger households have resource advantages at the farm level and have greater non-farm income earning potential at the same time.

Migration may accentuate demographic differences between farm-households: apparently when only rural residents are enumerated, or actually when permanent migration causes premature fission of domestic groupings. But to a considerable extent the domestic development cycle will determine which and how many members migrate (Spiegel, 1980), as well as the impact on the remaining members. Even a wife left behind with three young children will be less disadvantaged when her children become working teenagers. This point is brought out by Matlon (1979, pp. 98–9), who observed the effects of the domestic development cycle on poverty levels in northern Nigeria:

> An analysis of data on household size, composition, and age of head, for example, revealed that a life-cycle earnings pattern explained at least part of the poverty incidence. Three groups representing distinct stages in family development were disproportionately represented among the poorest households: (1) households headed by men under 25 years of age, (2) households headed by men 60 years or older, (3) nuclear family units with greater than average size. In each case, households within these poverty subsets were characterized by either extremely unfavourable consumer to worker ratios, or by low land inheritance.
>
> The presence of a life-cycle earnings pattern is important for two reasons. First, it indicates that among traditional small farmers a significant proportion of poverty may be associated with factors internal to the family. As a result only income transfers rather than production orientated policies would be effective in the short run in reducing this type of poverty. Second, since households currently in poverty due to demographic factors represent stages through which most families pass in the course of normal development, if a longer term income concept were applied the degree of income equality would be even higher than that observed.

While ideological imperatives may demand a denial of the effect of the domestic development cycle on farm-household differentiation, this cannot be demonstrated merely by using other factors to explain the differences. Both trends and cycles can be expected to operate over time. If it is to be argued that the trends are more important than the cycles, it is necessary to show that differences between households at one point in time are better explained by development trends than by stages in the family cycle. Our analysis of the Swazi data as well as evidence from elsewhere in the region (e.g. Murray, 1980, pp. 16–17 on Lesotho; Kerven, 1979, pp. 46–7, on Botswana; Shumba, 1983, p. 5 on Zimbabwe) suggest that the domestic development cycle explains a large part of the economic differentiation found in indigenous rural sectors of southern Africa.

Notes

1. De jure labour force refers to all household members from 16–64 years of age, and de facto refers to those in the same age group not engaged in off-farm employment.
2. The statistical test used in Table 7.1, as well as in subsequent tables where group means are compared, is an analysis of variance in which the ratio of the between to within group variance is computed. A high variance ratio (F statistic) will lead us to reject the null hypothesis that the between and within variances are derived from the same population. The level of confidence that we can have in rejecting this null hypothesis is given in the tables as the F-sig. level. The standard errors of the means are given in corresponding tables in Appendix 3, which are numbered as in the text, except for the addition of the prefix A.
3. Peri-urban households include all those situated in the Central and Zombodze RDAs, which border the main urban complexes in the centre and south of Swaziland respectively. All other households are classified as rural.
4. The above classification procedure does not strictly categorize households in terms of their position in the domestic development cycle. Rather it places households into stages of an idealized development cycle on the basis of the size, age and compositional characteristics that best fit the idealized stages.
5. According to Richards (1954, p. 213) 'in peasant economies a man requires his greatest capital outlay in youth . . . the need for large sums of money gradually diminishes.' And Petit (1975) has shown (in a European setting) that old couples on small farms are less prone to invest in farm improvements than younger couples. The former are not active in the search for information concerning new techniques, whereas the latter are the best 'customers' of the extension services. Petit suggests that the goal of the former is to maintain as well as possible the level of their capacity in spite of declining labour force and this may even prompt them to liquidate some of their assets. By contrast the behaviour of the latter group implies that their objective is to expand their productive assets, in order to be ready when a second generation will add to the labour force but also to the consumption needs.
6. The figure of around 100 hours per worker spent on cropping is considerably less than the 1000 hours found by Cleave (1970) to be the norm for adult males in agricultural production in Africa. However, we should note that about 70 per cent of these hours are provided by women and children, who have other tasks (schooling, household maintenance) to occupy them. Also only one dryland crop can be taken per year in southern Africa, whereas in much of tropical Africa there are two growing seasons per year. Moreover, the recorded labour inputs per hectare are not low compared with with estimates for elsewhere in the region. The average number of man days per hectare applied to maize cropping was estimated as 10.3 in Botswana (Botswana Government, 1979) and 32.9 in Lesotho (LASA, 1978). Even assuming eight hours worked per day these would be equivalent to 82 hours/ha in Botswana and 263 hours/ha in Lesotho.
7. Marter and Honeybone use resource endowments and level of agricultural cash income in their group classification. Bwalya's classification is made according to income levels.

8 Adoption of improved crop technology

In Chapter 7, it was argued that the farm-household model developed in Chapter 4 constitutes an appropriate and relevant framework for analyzing the behaviour of rural households in Swaziland as well as elsewhere in southern Africa. In this and subsequent chapters we will examine some of the implications of the model (and the household-economics approach upon which it is based) for the development of indigenous agriculture in the region. In this chapter we will look at the adoption of improved crop technology by focusing on the implications of the model for the uptake and impact of hybrid maize on Swazi farms. It will be argued that, given the prevailing wage employment opportunities, Swazi farmers will adopt hybrid maize in order to minimize the cost of meeting subsistence requirements, rather than to increase surpluses and cash incomes. We will then present empirical evidence to show that this is in fact what has happened.

These arguments and findings will be extended to the adoption of other crop technology in Swaziland as well as elsewhere. In the final section of the chapter we will argue that a general implication of the analysis is that the common advocacy of land-augmenting (labour-intensive) crop technology for indigenous farmers in southern Africa is misplaced.

TABLE 8.1 *Local-maize and hybrid-maize yields (kg/hectare) (1980/81)*

	Local maize	Hybrid maize
Rural Development Areas		
North	693	1137
Central	846	1490
South	973	1400
Mpono-Velezizweni	956	1126
Mayiwane-Herefords	747	994
Lubombo-Mpholonjeni	693	1188
Zombodze	1196	1196
Bhekinkosi-Mliba	889	1052
Hluthi	822	1187
Overall mean	873	1205

Source: RDA Management Unit, (1981b), Chart No. 6

Hybrid-maize adoption in Swaziland

The benefits of hybrid maize

There can be little doubt that the use of hybrid-maize technology on Swazi Nation Land is associated with increased yields. RDA Management Unit records collected by extension workers show this quite clearly.[1] Although the use of hybrid maize is associated with the use of greater amounts of fertilizer, we make the distinction between hybrid and local maize because this is the basis upon which fields were divided for our analysis.

In eight out of the nine RDAs listed in Table 8.1, hybrid maize gave higher yields per hectare than local varieties. In the ninth case the yields were the same. Overall hybrid maize would appear to give a 40 per cent increase in yields per hectare over local varieties. But we noted in Table 7.5 above that input costs per hectare for hybrid maize were considerably higher than for local maize.

TABLE 8.2 *Local-maize and hybrid-maize returns per hectare (1977/78)*

	Central	Zombodze
Yield (kg/ha)		
Local	1125	1264
Hybrid	1596	1604
t-sig level	(.070)	(.073)
Input costs (E/ha)		
Local	30.93	22.73
Hybrid	59.96	74.73
t-sig level	(.011)	(.001)
Net commercial returns (E/ha)		
Local	70.73	91.03
Hybrid	83.68	69.65
t-sig level	(.557)	(.228)

Source: FMS No. 4, Table 3(d); FMS No. 5, Table 3(d)

From Table 8.2 we see that in two RDAs the increased input costs[2] are such that the net commercial return per hectare to hybrid maize is not significantly greater than that for local varieties. Thus although, on average, hybrid varieties give significantly higher yields per hectare than local ones, the extra input costs associated with hybrid varieties result in net commercial returns per hectare that are not significantly different from those given by local varieties. According to this analysis, we would not expect there to be much advantage in adopting hybrid-maize technology.

But we have argued that farm-households will be concerned to allocate the time of their members as efficiently as possible, in which case returns to labour will be a more appropriate measure of the relative benefit of hybrid over local maize than returns per hectare. Reported labour use per hectare data indicate that there is no significant difference between labour input into hybrid maize and into local maize (e.g. see FMS Nos 4 and 5, Table 3(a)). We would therefore expect to observe the same pattern in respect of returns to labour as we did for returns per hectare. The analysis in Table 8.3 shows this to be the case.

92 *Adoption of improved crop technology*

TABLE 8.3 *Local-maize and hybrid-maize returns to labour (1977/78)*

	4 RDAs	North	South	Zombodze	Central
No. of observations					
Local	222	61	69	41	51
Hybrid	179	52	53	26	43
Yield (kg/hr)					
Local	5.1	3.2	3.2	7.9	7.7
Hybrid	7.7	4.3	5.5	15.1	10.4
t-sig level	(.002)	(.051)	(.001)	(.057)	(.118)
Input costs (cents/hr)					
Local	13	11	12	14	16
Hybrid	39	29	37	50	47
t-sig level	(.001)	(.001)	(.001)	(.001)	(.001)
Net commercial return (cents/hr)					
Local	33	17	17	57	53
Hybrid	26	10	13	60	43
t-sig level	(.170)	(.110)	(.414)	(.887)	(.390)

On a per-hour basis hybrid maize gives a 50 per cent yield advantage, but involves three times the cost, so the net commercial returns are not significantly different from those of local maize.

Expected impact of hybrid maize

A GEOMETRIC ANALYSIS
While there seems to be no clear advantage in adopting hybrid maize for commercial reasons, the following theoretical analysis suggests that hybrid maize does have advantages for subsistence producers. To illustrate the argument, we will employ a simple example based on the data in Table 8.3 and apply it to the geometric model developed in Chapter 4. Table 8.4 sets out the

TABLE 8.4 *Derived cost and return parameters for local maize and hybrid maize*

	Local Maize	Hybrid Maize	Wage Employment		
			High	Medium	Low
Prices and Output					
Producer Price (cents/kg)	8	8			
Retail Price (cents/kg)	12	12			
Yield (kg/hr)	6	9			
Costs and Returns (cents/hr)					
Material Input Costs ($P_x \cdot X_s/T_s$)	12	36			
Net Commercial Return	36	36	108	54	18
Opportunity Cost of Purchase $[(P_z/T_s) - (P_x \cdot X_s/T_s)]$	60	72			
Purchase Cost (P_s/T_s)	72	108			

Note: X_s is the amount of input X required by a standard labor unit to produce a unit of subsistence good Z (i.e. maize). T_s is the amount of time required by a standard labor unit to produce a unit of subistence good Z (i.e. maize). The subscript s refers to a standard labour unit as discussed above (pp. 42–3).

basic parameters in respect of local and hybrid maize. The figures are broadly in line with the empirical data and have been chosen in order to simplify the geometric analysis.

We can see from Table 8.4 that the net commercial return is 40–50 per cent less than the opportunity cost of purchase and that while the former is the same for both local and hybrid maize, the latter is greater for hybrid maize. The higher opportunity cost of purchase when hybrid maize is grown implies that the alternative off-farm wage income (Wi) of the marginal worker must be higher before purchases take place ($Wi = [(Pz/Ts) - (Px.Xs/Ts)]$) and more workers will stay on the farm to produce maize for own consumption than would have done so with local maize. But the higher yields provided by hybrid maize mean that fewer workers are needed to supply consumption requirements and, since after consumption needs are met the equilibrium wage rate is reduced to that of the net commercial returns, more workers may leave for off-farm employment. Thus the impact of hybrid maize depends not only on its profitability relative to local maize, but also on the consumption requirements of the household and the alternative wage opportunities of its members.

For a number of reasons the estimates of returns to time spent on maize production cannot be compared directly with wage rates in off-farm employment. A worker who may spend one hundred hours a month in wage employment would not spend all that time directly on maize production if he returned to the farm.[3] On the other hand the twenty to thirty hours he might spend directly on maize production, if he returned to the farm, would constitute only part of the farm-household production time he would contribute if he stayed at home.[4]

To avoid having to make specific assumptions about the equivalence of an hour spent in wage employment with that spent on the farm in maize production, we will refer to the off-farm wage rate in terms of a multiple of the commercial returns to maize. In Table 8.4 we assume three levels of wage that can be earned off the farm: a high wage rate, equivalent to three times the estimated net commercial maize returns; a medium wage rate equivalent to one-and-a-half times the estimated net commercial maize returns; and a low wage rate equivalent to half the estimated net commercial maize returns.

We will use the relationships set out in Table 8.4 in our geometric model to examine the implications for the adoption of hybrid maize, under varying assumptions about the population structures and wage potentials of farm-households.

Consider Figure 8.1 which represents a farm-household comprising twelve population units measured along the OA axis. It is assumed that each work unit can produce twice the maize requirement of a population unit when local maize is grown,[5] or three times this (i.e. +50 per cent) if hybrid maize is grown. Thus six work units are required to grow the household's requirements with local maize, whereas only four are required if hybrid-maize varieties are used.

The OY axis measures maize costs and returns. The OCl vector is the cost associated with the allocation of a given number of work units to local maize production. The vector OMl, OMh, OCh gives the net commercial returns to local maize, the net commercial returns to hybrid maize and the cost of growing hybrid maize respectively. The OBl line gives the opportunity cost of

94 *Adoption of improved crop technology*

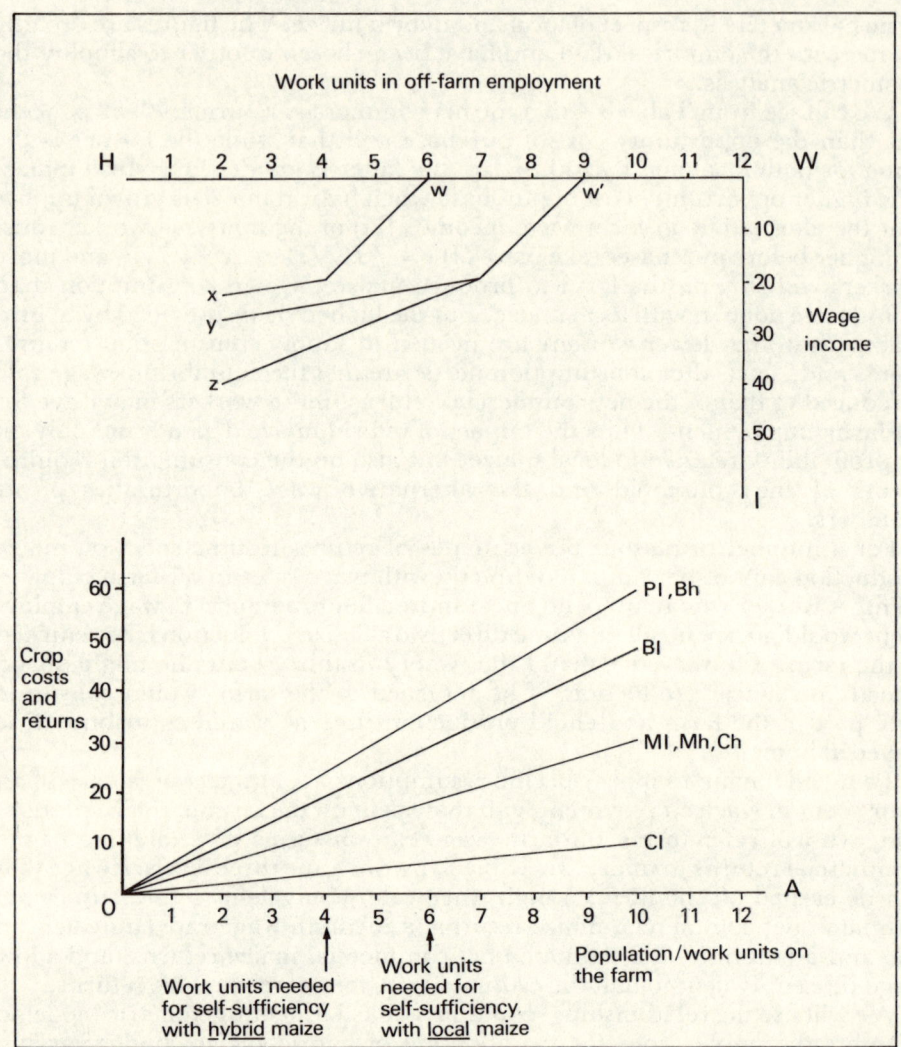

FIGURE 8.1: *Household-economics farm-household model: hybrid-maize technology alternatives*

purchase if local maize is grown. The *OBh*, *OPl* line gives the opportunity cost of purchase if hybrid maize is grown, as well as the cost of buying the amount of local maize that could be produced per work unit. The relative slopes of these lines represent the local and hybrid maize production relationships established in Table 8.4.

The *WI* axis measures wage income and is related to the number of work units in wage employment by the wage lines *wx*, *w'y* and *w'z*. These wage lines represent three households with different population structures and wage employment potentials. Household *x*, having six work units,[6] has a consumer/worker ratio of 2:1 and the wage line *wx*. Two work units command the high wage rate, while two can only expect to obtain wage employment at the low rate. Households y and z have much lower consumer/worker ratios with nine of the twelve population units being work units. However, household y has a lower wage potential than household x. Both households have two work units that can command the high wage rate, but the remaining wage earners in household y can only expect the low wage rate, while those in household z can expect the medium rate. In all households the first two work units have not been included as wage earners, because it is assumed that these workers will remain on the farm to maintain usufruct rights whatever their wage rates may be. Let us now examine the effect of the hybrid-maize technology on households x, y and z in turn.

Household x

With local maize, household x could just meet its maize requirement by allocating all six available work units on the farm. But over the last two work units the slope of the wage line, wx, is greater than that of the opportunity cost of purchase line, OBl, so it will be advantageous to allocate these units to wage employment, and purchase the last one-third of requirements. The cost of producing maize on the farm would be $(4 \times 12 = 48)$ and this added to the cost of purchasing what the last two work units could have produced $(2 \times 72 = 144)$ amounts to a total of 192. Against this can be set the wage income of the last two units $(2 \times 108 = 216)$, which would leave a net balance of 24. By adopting hybrid maize, household x could do better than this. It would still allocate four work units on the farm, as the slope of wx is less than that of OBh over these work units. The on-farm production costs of growing hybrid maize would be trebled to $4 \times 36 = 144$. But this would be more than compensated for by the fact that no purchases are required, since the higher yields of hybrid maize mean that requirements can be grown with only four work units. So 144 would be the total cost of procuring maize requirements, against which can be set the wage income of 216 to leave a balance of 72. Household x would therefore adopt hybrid maize and, in doing so, would move from being a deficit producer to a sufficient producer. It would not go beyond this, however, and produce a surplus for the market because the hybrid-maize commercial return (OMh) is below the wage rates of the remaining work units.

Household y

Household y would allocate seven of its nine available work units to maize production since the wage potential of these workers is less than either the commercial returns (OMl, OMh) or the opportunity purchase cost with either local or hybrid maize (OBl, OBh). Subsistence production costs with local maize would be $6 \times 12 = 72$. The production of one work unit would be surplus to requirements and would give a net return of $1 \times 36 = 36$ on the market, leaving a net cost of 36 to be set against the wage income of $2 \times 108 = 216$.

The household would do no better by adopting hybrid maize. In this case subsistence production costs would double to $4 \times 36 = 144$, but the production of the last three units would be surplus to requirements and give a net commercial return of $3 \times 36 = 108$, again leaving a net balance of 36 to be set against the same wage income. Household y, being a surplus producer, will be indifferent to the adoption of hybrid maize, since the net commercial return is no better than that achieved with local varieties.

Household z

Household z would be a sufficient producer with local maize, since the slope of the $w'z$ wage line is less steep than that of the OBl line over the first six work units that are needed to grow the household requirements on the farm. The seventh work unit has the same wage potential as the first four wage-earning units, but it would be allocated to wage employment rather than the production of surplus maize for sale because the slope of $w'z$ is greater than that of OMl over the seventh unit. The last two units would be allocated to wage employment for the same reason. Thus the local maize production costs for household z would be $6 \times 12 = 72$ and this would be set against a wage income of $(1 \times 54) + (2 \times 108) = 270$, giving a net balance of 198.

With hybrid maize, household z would only need to allocate four work units to grow the household's maize requirements. The remaining work units will be allocated to wage employment, since the slope of $w'z$ is greater than that of OMh over the remaining five work units. The on-farm subsistence maize production costs would be $4 \times 36 = 144$, and wage income would be $(3 \times 54) + (2 \times 108) = 378$, leaving a net balance of 234. Thus household z would adopt hybrid maize but, as in the case of household x, this would not result in a surplus being produced for the market. It would result in no increase in production at all, since household z was a sufficient producer before and would remain so. It would, however, result in a reduction in the allocation of work units to farming and a movement of labour to wage employment.

A NUMERICAL EXAMPLE

The trade-offs involved in saving purchasing costs or time at the expense of extra market input costs can be further illustrated in terms of a numerical example. This example will also serve to demonstrate the influence of the household wage potential in the hybrid-maize adoption decision, and the increased advantages of adoption as marginal wage rates increase.

We will assume that three labour units are needed to grow the household's maize requirements with local maize, but that only two are needed with hybrid maize. The specified labour units comprise the columns of Table 8.5. For each column, the cost elements that make up each labour unit's full procurement cost are entered: the wage element (Wi), the market input element ($Px.Xs/Ts$) and, where appropriate, the purchase cost element (Pz/Ts). These are summed for all the labour units needed to procure requirements to give the 'full procurement cost' for local and hybrid maize for each of three household situations with different wage potential profiles. Hybrid and local maize cost parameters are again taken from Table 8.4.

In household A the third labour unit's wage potential exceeds the opportunity cost of purchase with local maize(60), so the third of requirements that could have been produced with this labour unit will be purchased instead. The other two-thirds will be grown on the farm at costs of 42 and 62 cents per hour, giving a full procurement cost of 176 cents per hour with local maize.

With hybrid maize the wage element of full procurement costs will be the same, as the same labour units are used. Market input costs are 48 cents per hour more than with local maize but, since this is less than the 72 cents per hour saved on purchasing, the adoption of hybrid maize reduces the overall procurement cost and is therefore worthwhile.

For household B, the hybrid-maize procurement cost is the same as for

TABLE 8.5 *Calculation of full maize subsistence procurement cost for households with different wage potentials (cents per hour)*

	Standard labour units needed to produce household maize needs				
	Local maize			Hybrid maize	
	1	2	3	1	2
Household A					
Labour unit 1 (wage = 30)	30			30	
Labour unit 2 (wage = 50)		50			50
Labout unit 3 (wage = 80)					
Market input costs ($Px.Xs/Ts$)	12	12		36	36
Purchase costs (Pz/Ts)			72		
	42	62	72	66	86
Full procurement cost			176		152
Household B					
Labour unit 1 (wage = 30)	30			30	
Labour unit 2 (wage = 50)		50			50
Labour unit 3 (wage = 50)			50		
Market input costs ($Px.Xs/Ts$)	12	12	12	36	36
	42	62	62	66	86
Full procurement cost			166		152
Household C					
Labour unit 1 (wage = 30)	30			30	
Labour unit 2 (wage = 30)		30			30
Labour unit 3 (wage = 30)			30		
Market input costs ($Px.Xs/Ts$)	12	12	12	36	36
	42	42	42	66	66
Full procurement cost			126		132

household *A* and is again less than the full procurement cost with local maize. But in this case the advantage of hybrid maize lies in the saving made in terms of the opportunity cost of the third labour unit which, at 50 cents per hour, more than compensates for the extra market input costs of hybrid maize (72 cents against 36 cents for local maize).

For household *C*, hybrid-maize adoption is not worthwhile because the saving made on the opportunity wage cost of the last labour unit is only 30 cents per hour, and this is not sufficient to compensate for the extra 36 cents per hour market input costs of hybrid compared with local maize.

Standard gross margin analysis tells us that, since the average commercial returns from hybrid maize are no better than those obtainable with local maize, hybrid varieties are not likely to be widely adopted by the average producer to increase marketed surpluses. However Table 8.6 indicates that this standard analysis is not very relevant in Swaziland where the average

TABLE 8.6 *Percentage of households selling maize and reporting regular selling (1977/78)*

	Number of observations	Percentage of Households	
		Selling in 1977/78	Selling most or every year
Rural Development Area			
North	76	18	11
South	76	38	18
Central	76	9	2
Mahlangatsha	32	25	19
Zombodze	71	7	5
Lubombo	64	17	9
Mpolonjeni	76	8	4
Bekinkhosi	48	10	8
Mliba	40	5	0

Source: RDA Maize Production and Marketing Survey, 1980, Tables 3a and 3b.

producer does not grow maize for sale. The analysis based on our farm-household model suggests that for these subsistence producers hybrid maize may have advantages:

1) because it may be cheaper to provide food requirements by using hybrid seed and purchasing less maize (e.g. households x and A) or;

2) because labour released from the production of household food needs may be able to earn more in wage employment than the extra costs of meeting requirements with hybrid rather than local maize (e.g. households z and B).

In addition the household-economics 'full cost of procurement' analysis given in Table 8.5 demonstrates that, as the wage rate of the marginal labour unit increases, hybrid-maize technology, which reduces the time required per unit of output, becomes more advantageous in subsistence production (e.g. compare the reductions in full procurement cost with hybrid against local maize of 24, 14 and −6, as the marginal wage rate decreases from 80 to 50 to 30).

In summary, then, the foregoing analysis leads us to conclude that subsistence producers may adopt hybrid maize for reasons 1) and 2) above. However, we would not expect hybrid-maize adoption to encourage more farmers to become commercial maize producers, or to result in more maize being marketed, since commercial returns are not improved thereby.

Observed impact of hybrid maize

Hybrid maize has been widely adopted on Swazi Nation Land in general and in Rural Development Areas in particular. Table 8.7 gives an indication of the extent of hybrid-maize uptake in the four original RDAs. While there have been some difficulties in recording all crop input sales and there has been a lack of continuity of records in some RDAs, the general picture is unmistakable.

There have been area by area variations in the rates of uptake, as is demonstrated by the data in table 8.8 on the proportion of farm-households adopting hybrid varieties.

TABLE 8.7 *Hybrid-seed uptake in four RDAs (tonnes)*

	4 RDAs	North	South	Mahlangatsha	Central
Years					
1973[a]	7.2	3.2	.7	3.3	n.a
1974[a]	12.2	4.6	1.8	5.3	.5
1975[a]	21.6	3.7	5.1	9.7	3.1
1976[a]	27.6	1.2	4.1	13.9	8.3
1977[a]	n.a	n.a	5.0	13.5	20.0
1978[a]	41.3	4.3	5.0	15.3	16.7
1979[a]	68.6	12.7	4.0	12.6	39.3
1980[b]	104.0	15.2	18.6	16.6	53.6

Sources:
a) Project Managers' Annual Reports (1973-9)
b) RDA Management Unit Inputs Report (1980/81), Table 5

TABLE 8.8 *Hybrid-maize adoption compared with surplus production and off-farm employment*

Maize Production Category	Area No.	Percentage of Households		
		Adopting hybrid maize	Producing a surplus	Having more than 50% of adults in employment
A - Good Production Areas	1	97	88	47
	2	70	68	31
B - Intermediate Production Areas	3	67	53	46
	4	41	49	32
	5	53	40	29
	6	87	39	43
	7	96	31	57
	8	93	28	45
C - Poor Production Areas	9	4	16	22

Source: RDA Monitoring and Evaluation Unit, 1980, Tables 2a and 2c

These area differences in adoption rates cannot be explained by the length of time that an area has been receiving project inputs, since the newest development areas (7 and 8) have two of the highest adoption rates. Neither was there found to be any significant correlation between the population densities of the nine areas and their uptake rates (RDA Monitoring and Evaluation Unit, 1980, p. 10). However, there does appear to be a relationship between the rate of hybrid-maize adoption in an area and its suitability for maize production. Such a relationship has been observed elsewhere. In the United States, Griliches (1957) showed that the inter-state variation in the rate of hybrid-maize adoption could largely be explained by the relative suitability of each state for maize production. Similarly in Africa, Gerhart (1975, pp. 25-6) has shown that differences in adoption rates between Kenyan farmers, some of whom adopted hybrid maize at a rate faster than Iowa farmers in the 1920s and 1930s, were largely due to agro-climatic factors. Within Western Kenya adoption rates in the higher altitude, high rainfall zones were around 90 per cent by 1973, whereas they were less than 20 per cent in the medium altitude, low rainfall zone. From these and other data, Gerhart (1975, p. 34) concludes:

> In sum, there are good reasons to believe that differential profitabilities play an important part in explaining the substantial differences in adoption between the high and moderate rainfall zones and, consequently, in the overwhelming importance of agroclimatic zones as an explanatory variable in the sample taken as a whole'.

On the basis of our knowledge of the nine RDAs surveyed and the data collected on the proportion of households producing surpluses of maize, we can divide the nine areas into three categories according to their maize-producing potential. This categorization is given in Table 8.8. Areas 1 and 2 are placed in category A, since these are traditionally good maize-growing areas and over two-thirds of households surveyed produced a surplus. Area 9 is placed in category C, since this area is situated in the lowveld which is 'considered marginal for maize production' (Agricultural Research Division, 1974, p. 14). Only one-sixth of the households surveyed in this area produced more than their household requirements. The remaining six areas are placed in the intermediate category, B, with between one-third and half of the surveyed households producing a surplus.

The areas in categories A and C conform to the hybrid-maize adoption pattern experienced in the United States and western Kenya, with the higher potential areas having a higher adoption rate of hybrid maize and a higher proportion of households producing a surplus. But a positive relationship between surplus production and hybrid-maize uptake is not evident in respect of the areas in category B. In fact the correlation is negative ($r = -.74$) and is significant at the .1 level. This indicates that areas which have a relatively high proportion of surplus-producing households have a relatively low adoption rate.

While high adoption rates in category B areas are not associated with high rates of surplus production, they are associated with high rates of off-farm employment. There is a positive correlation ($r = .84$ significant at the .05 level) between the proportion of households adopting hybrid maize and the proportion having more than half their adult workforce engaged in off-farm employment.

These observed relationships, between hybrid-maize adoption on the one hand and surplus production and off-farm employment on the other, are consistent with the expectations formed on the basis of our theoretical analysis. Namely that, given a marginal commercial return to hybrid maize, there will be a greater tendency to adopt, 1) in areas with relatively high aggregate returns to wage labour curves (e.g. $w'z$ compared with $w'y$) and, 2) by deficit as opposed to surplus producing households (e.g. household x compared with household y).

Household-level analysis is complicated by the tendency we have already noted for the larger households at the consolidation stage in particular to have considerable resource advantages, to be more commercially orientated and to obtain better returns to labour in maize production. This is reflected in the household-size analysis given in the Maize Production and Marketing Survey Report (RDA Monitoring and Evaluation Unit, 1980) and reproduced in Table 8.9.

TABLE 8.9 *Household size related to cash cropping, maize selling, and hybrid-maize adoption*

	No. of observations	Mean household size	t-sig. level
Cash cropping			
Some cash crops	48	9.06	
No cash crops	511	7.33	.001
Maize selling			
Planning to sell	238	7.59	
Not planning to sell	150	6.21	.004
Sell regularly	179	8.12	
Never sell	377	7.21	.002
Hybrid-maize adoption			
Use more hybrid than local seed	147	8.53	
Use less hybrid than local seed	114	7.86	.150

Source: RDA Maize Production and Marketing Survey, 1980, Table 4(a)

While cash-crop growers and maize sellers have significantly larger households than non-cash-crop growers or non-maize sellers,[7] the size of households growing more hybrid maize than local maize is not significantly different from others. Table 8.10 presents a further analysis of this survey data for Group B households having some wage earners.

TABLE 8.10 *Mean household sizes and adoption rates for deficit and surlus producers (Group B households with wage earners*

	Percentage adopting	Mean household size
Type of Producer		
Deficit producers (n = 143)	75	10.3
Surplus producers (n = 138)	63	11.1
Significant Levels		
Chi squared	.045	
Student's t (one-way)		.076

These data show clearly that the lack of size difference in association with hybrid-maize adoption (as opposed to cash crops or maize selling) is related to the higher adoption rate of smaller deficit households than larger surplus households.

The lack of relationship between the adoption of hybrid maize and the production of surpluses for sale is also demonstrated by the analysis of FMS data presented in Table 8.11. In two out of the four areas a greater proportion of adopters sold maize compared with non-adopters. But in the remaining two areas it was the other way about, and in no case was the difference statistically significant.

TABLE 8.11 *Proportion of households selling maize: hybrid-maize adopters compared with Non-Adopters*

	Percentage selling			
	All households	Adopters	Non-adopters	t-sig. level
RDA				
North (n = 75)	23	29	18	.409
South (n = 75)	20	19	21	.953
Zombodze (n = 76)	8	13	4	.362
Central (n = 78)	17	11	24	.261
4 RDAs (n = 304)	17	17	16	.837

A more consistent pattern emerges when the analysis is conducted according to domestic development-cycle groupings (Table 8.12). In all areas the lowest rates of adoption occur in groups 4 to 6. These households have relatively low consumer/worker ratios and, being the older households, can be expected to have poorer wage opportunities than households in groups 1 to 3. These households may therefore be represented by household y in Figure 8.1. Households in the consolidation stage (group 3) have lower consumer/worker ratios than groups 1 and 2, but have considerable resource advantages and reasonable wage prospects. They may be represented by household z in Figure 8.1. Groups 1 and 2, having relatively high consumer/worker ratios and good wage earning prospects may be represented by household x in Figure 8.1. The evidence presented in Table 8.12 supports the theoretical analysis, which predicts lower adoption rates in households of type y compared with those of types x and z.[8]

TABLE 8.12 *Proportion of households adopting hybrid maize: domestic development cycle groupings compared*

	Percentage Adopting			
	Establishment and Expansion Groups 1,2	Consolidation Group 3	Fission, Decline and FH Groups 4,5,6,	Chi^2 Sig. Level
RDA				
North (n = 75)	44	42	39	.906
South (n = 75)	71	68	28	.002
Zambodze (n = 76)	50	50	35	.410
Central (n = 78)	61	77	42	.027
4 RDAs (n = 304)	57	64	37	.001

The project manager of Mahlangatsha RDA (the best maize-producing area) noted in his annual report for 1977 that the continuing increase in the uptake of hybrid maize (among other crop inputs) was not reflected in a similar increase in the sale of crop surpluses and commented that 'presumably some farmers prefer to grow good (hybrid) maize for subsistence as well as a cash surplus' (Adams, 1978).

The forgoing analysis helps to explain why continued increases in the use of higher-yielding hybrid maize have not been reflected in similar increases in the production of maize for sale. Indeed, at average production levels, it *only* makes sense to grow hybrid maize for subsistence purposes, and the evidence seems to indicate that this is the purpose for which not only some, but most producers have adopted hybrid maize.

Fertilizer and tractors in Swaziland

The hybrid-maize example, which we have dealt with at some length, applies equally to other yield-increasing and labour-saving innovations, such as the use of fertilizer or the hire of tractors. There are two other inputs which have been rapidly adopted by Swazi Farmers, as the data in Table 8.13 show.

TABLE 8.13 *Fertilizer and tractor uptake in four RDAs*

	4 RDAs	North	South	Mahlangatsha	Central
Compound Fertilizer (tonnes)					
1974[a]	409	162	85	98	64
1975[a]	n.a	99	n.a	126	112
1976[a]	n.a	n.a	75	139	264
1977[a]	n.a	n.a	110	251	375
1978[a]	737	74	52	254	357
1979[a]	955	292	94	264	305
1980[b]	1288	258	378	258	394
Tractor Hire (hours)[c]					
1975	1352	811	141	399	—
1976	3426	2108	628	690	—
1977	4531	1340	917	776	1498
1978	6148	1750	1367	993	2038
1979	4958	1299	1308	816	1535

Sources:
  a) Project Managers' Annual Reports, Mbabane, Swaziland
  b) RDA Management Unit Inputs Report, (1980/81), Table 3
  c) Tractor Pool Annual Reports, Mbabane, Swaziland

As with hybrid seed, the adoption of these other technological improvements, which increase yields per labour hour have not been associated with much increase in marketed-crop output. This is because, as with hybrid seed, the innovations have been adopted by most farm-households because they save time in the production of subsistence food Z goods and allow more time to be spent on income-earning activities or the provision of other non-market Z goods or leisure.

In extending the traditional income-leisure model to incorporate the Z goods approach to consumer behaviour, Sharir (1975) likens the household to a consumer receiving his income in kind. The household's available time is divided between home production (e.g. housekeeping, travelling to work) and leisure. Leisure time may be enjoyed as such or used in work. The household can buy time-saving goods (e.g. the services of a maid or pre-cooked foods), and the more such goods are purchased, the more home production time is saved and the amount of time that can be spent on either leisure or work activities is increased. Thus the household can buy leisure indirectly in this way. Leisure time can also be sold in return for more consumption by working. The effect of the introduction of an improved good (e.g. a more powerful vacuum cleaner), that increases the productivity of home time, is that it increases the total amount of time that can be spent at work or in leisure. Sharir (1975) notes that if 'leisure is a normal good its desired amount is increased. But since the total amount of time to be spent at leisure or work activities increases, one usually expects hours of work to increase as well'.

Following Sharir we can think of innovations that increase the productivity of subsistence cropping as being analogous to household labour-saving devices (washing machines, carpet sweepers, microwave cookers etc.), which involve a substantial increase in material input costs ($Px.Xi/Ti$), but save on time and therefore reduce the full labour costs of completing household tasks. As for hybrid seed in Swaziland, a Western household may invest in an automatic washing machine because: 1) it may get the household's washing done more cheaply than before, when some of it was being sent to a laundry service or, 2) because the time saved on washing may be spent on activities that give greater benefits than the extra costs of doing the household washing by machine rather than by hand. Only rarely will the purchase of a washing machine result in a housewife deciding to undertake washing as a commercial enterprise. More often the time saved will be used to seek employment away from the home, to undertake other household tasks, or in leisure activities. So too with the maize production technology in the Swazi farm-household environment. In our simplified analysis we have considered wage employment as the only alternative activity but, in reality, there are a whole array of alternative market and non-market activities that may be taken up with the time saved, ranging from beer-brewing and handicrafts to child care and adult literacy classes.

Appropriateness of labour-intensive versus labour-saving technology in southern Africa

The question of the appropriateness of labour-intensive or labour-saving technology for indigenous farm-households in southern Africa takes on a new complexion when it is viewed from a household-economics perspective. Eicher and Baker (1982, p. 234) have observed that for Africa as a whole although 'the relative percentage of population in agriculture will decline in most countries, the absolute number of people in agriculture will likely increase in most countries over the next 10–20 years'. It is generally accepted that this applies equally in southern Africa. Brand (1974, p. 258) concludes that 'increasing employment opportunities will have to be found in the various countries of southern Africa for some considerable time to come'. Lipton (1978) argues that a 6 per cent per annum growth rate in agriculture is needed if full employment is to be achieved in Botswana, since agriculture is the key sector as far as productive employment is concerned.

These arguments, together with evidence of increasing population pressure, at least on good-quality agricultural land, rising overt urban unemployment and projections of relatively slow growth of modern-sector job opportunities compared with work-force expansion, have led academics and planners to advocate development strategies based on the introduction of land-augmenting, labour-using technology (e.g. Brand, 1974; Merle Lipton, 1977; Lipton, 1978).

Lipton argues that, given the need to increase food production and employment in Botswana, extensive forms of crop production and livestock rearing that were once appropriate are no longer so. Accordingly he advocates a development strategy based on:

1) the use of 'appropriate' labour-intensive inputs associated with high-yielding varieties; and

2) a more labour-using mixture of outputs, e.g. a move from cattle to crops (Lipton, 1978, p. 78).

While the above recommendations may appear to be 'appropriate' on the basis of the foregoing macro-level analysis, from a micro, farm-household, viewpoint their appropriateness is less clear.

Lipton (1978, p. 21) observes that the great mass of unemployment in Botswana occurs because the return to labour in crop farming is so unattractive that work is not worth doing. But it is not a question of doing crop work or doing nothing. Time like any other economic resource is allocated so as to obtain equimarginal returns in alternative uses (Linder, 1970). Eicher and Baker (1982, p. 103) put Lipton's point more clearly when they say:

> One of the major constraints on the supply of labor to agricultural activities is the possibility of engaging in non-farm activities which usually yield higher returns to labor. Because the returns to agricultural labor in sub-Saharan Africa are often only $.10 to $.50 an hour, the value of leisure or other non-farm activities does not have to be very high before labor is diverted from agriculture.

Men in Botswana seek urban or mine employment because the rewards are higher and less risky than in farming. While their wives and children remain on the farm to grow crops, they also stay for other purposes; to maintain usufruct rights and a secure home and to bring up children (future productive assets). More labour-intensive cropping methods are not employed on most farms because the returns from the extra effort involved are not expected to compensate for the output lost by switching time spent by resident members from other non-market activities to cropping. Nor is it expected to compensate for the loss of income in wage employment if absentee members return to do more farm work.

Thus labour-intensive technologies in food-crop production are not appropriate unless they result in a reduction in the time required to produce a unit of food, i.e. unless they are in fact labour-saving per unit of output compared with other methods. For the average Botswana farmer, traditional methods of broadcasting unimproved seed over wide areas, which are left unweeded and unmanured, may well continue to be entirely appropriate. To the average farm-household in Botswana, the offer of a high-yielding variety that must be planted on a well-prepared seedbed at high plant densities, and needs to be fertilized and weeded (and also requires a good season's rainfall), is not unlike offering the average Western housewife an expensive new household appliance that is unreliable and is more likely to consume than save household maintenance time.

Another weakness of the aggregate analysis leading to the recommendation for labour-intensive technology is that it takes no account of the effect of increases in market wage rates. For reasons amplified by Lipton (1977), market wage rates in the formal sector are likely to continue to rise relative to the value of food crops. If this is so, the relative amount of time allocated to subsistence production is likely to decrease and labour-intensive technology, which does not reduce the input of time per unit of output, will become even less appropriate.

Notes

1 The management unit yield data in Table 8.1 were estimated by counting the number of cobs in a 5 metre length of a crop row and the number of rows per 5 metre width, together with an estimation of cob size. The FMS data given in the other tables were obtained by weighing the harvested yield from selected fields. Despite the methodological differences, both methods indicate the same order of yield advantage for hybrid over local-maize.
2 These input costs are due to higher costs of hybrid seed and also to the higher rates of fertilizer applied to hybrid seed than to local seed. Thus we are really talking about a 'high-yielding variety plus increased fertilizer' package when we compare hybrid with local maize. The tendency for the adoption of hybrid-maize to be associated with increased fertilizer use has also been observed in Serenje District in Zambia (CIMMYT, 1978, p. 26).
3 FMS labour records (FMS Reports 2–7) indicate that recorded time spent on cropping amounts to about 100 hours per adult per season. In some months, e.g. January (weeding time), the input is three times that of others.
4 An additional complication relates to the discounts placed on wage employment compared with staying at home, i.e. the costs related to finding employment, transport, travelling time, and being away from home and family.
5 A not unreasonable assumption considering that the average consumer/worker ratio is about 2:1 and, under Swazi custom, resources are allocated so that each household can be self-sufficient in maize (as well as other necessities).
6 The number of work units in the household determines the position along the WH axis at which the wage curve originates.
7 The relative advantage of larger farm-households with respect to the adoption of new crop technology has been observed elsewhere, particularly in connection with the 'green revolution' (e.g. see Ballah, 1979; Schutjer and Van Der Veen, 1977; Feder and O'Mara, 1981).
8 In his study of fertilizer adoption in the Ethiopian Minimum Package Programme Areas, Aklilu (1980) also observed a positive relationship between the number of consumption units in a family and the propensity to adopt as shown below:

	Group A	Group B	t-sig. level
Mean farmer characteristic			
Index of fertilizer use	45.3	95.9	.05
Consumption units in family	3.2	10.6	.01

This is the only other known study in Africa where technology adoption has been related to this type of 'demographic pressure' effect.

9 Non-market benefits of land-use rights and cattle ownership

The development of indigenous agriculture in southern Africa, through the introduction of improved technologies or extension and education, is often thought to be seriously hindered by prevailing attitudes to land-use rights and cattle ownership. For example:

> The communal character of land ownership and the obligations that go with it tend to be a drawback to the emergence of progressive farmers (Yudelman, 1964a, p. 575).

> The oft-expressed expectation has generally been disappointed that agricultural extension work and instruction would reconcile communal tenure and agricultural improvement (Bauer, 1974, p. 227).

> Another difficulty arises from the role of cattle in tribal life... The result is continuous overgrazing of the pastures by poor quality animals whose half starved condition makes them an economic liability rather than an asset (Houghton, 1964, p. 319).

At the same time, attempts to change the land-tenure system or limit stock numbers are met with fierce resistance:

> However, although the need for the introduction of individual tenure may be both evident and urgent, it is often strongly resisted. Indeed the more urgent the need for the change because of population growth or the emergence of new opportunities, the more emphatically tribal authorities or particular groups of individuals may resist it. (Bauer, 1974, p. 227).

> Stock limitation has been persistently urged by the authorities, but in no other aspect of economic adjustment has resistance and conservatism been so tenacious. (Houghton, 1964, p. 319).

Clearly development initiatives in southern Africa need to be based on an understanding of the attitudes to land and cattle, and an appreciation of how these attitudes may affect the outcome of such initiatives. In Chapter 4 it was suggested that the non-market benefits of maintaining traditional land use rights, and of keeping cattle beyond the point of satisfying basic subsistence needs, could be analyzed within the framework of the household-economics approach. In this chapter we will argue that such an analysis can help us understand traditional attitudes to land and cattle. In the succeeding two chapters we will follow through some of the implications of the analysis for migration and rural development.

Land attributes

Land tenure in southern Africa

The extent of the non-market benefits of retaining a rural base are determined, in large measure, by customary land-tenure arrangements and the rights that these give to members of the community. Hughes bases his very thorough analyses of land tenure in Swaziland (1972) and Zimbabwe (1974) on a classification of 'rights', beginning with the 'Right of Avail' which is:

> 'held by the community as a whole but in which every member of that community automatically participates. From this participation (one might say from this share of the "Right of Avail") flows the rights to make use of what the group considers to be reasonable use of the natural resources available to the community, including land.' (Hughes, 1972, p. 62).

From this Right of Avail each group member derives other rights: the right of accommodation, right of tillage, right of pasture. right of water, right of stover, right to hunt, right of way, right to delve, right to collect. None of these in themselves establishes a firm legal relationship between an individual or family group and a particular parcel or parcels of land. Actual occupation (of a residential site) or cultivation (of arable lands) is necessary to change these 'preferential rights' into the complex of rights that Holleman (1949, p. 37) has called 'Bantu ownership'.

Hughes describes the concept of Bantu ownership as being analogous to the 'ownership' of Western law in that, once acquired, it gives the 'owning' group the right to demand that anyone seeking to dispossess them of it should show very good reason indeed for doing so. Moreover, it includes the right to exclude other members of the community from making use, without permission, of any land over which Bantu ownership has been acquired. It differs from Western ownership in that it does not include the right to alienate the land to those who are not members of that land-holding community; in that it can be lost through prolonged failure to use the land; and in that continued exercise of this Bantu ownership is entirely dependent on continued acceptance as a full member of the community. The 'group' holding Bantu ownership is normally the homestead group, the group of people living in a single homestead, i.e. the farm-household according to the terminology that we have been using.

The various roles of land

The implication of this land-tenure system, which is typical of southern Africa, is that the function of land as a producer of crops is not the only economic role that it has. Hughes argues that it is not even the most important of land's roles. The six principal economic roles of land identified by Hughes (1974, p. 25) are:

    1) as a dwelling place;
    2) as a source of raw materials: for building, domestic needs and handicrafts;
    3) as a grower of crops;
    4) as a provider of grazing for one's stock;
    5) as a potential source of money income; and

6) as the basis of a 'social security' system for oneself and one's dependants.

Hughes argues that the first two roles and the last, which are closely related, are the most important ones from a household's point of view. He also notes that the producing roles of land are often not fully exploited. He points out that there are no technical or customary reasons why crop and stock production should not be increased greatly on either communal areas in Zimbabwe or on Swazi Nation Land. Apart from large areas left fallow, yields per acre are 'distressingly low' and could be easily increased, since there are few households who have not seen examples of how these increased yields could be brought about. In particular land's potential as a provider of income has hardly been tapped and this is not for want of technical know-how or desire for money.

Hughes accounts for this behaviour in terms of land's role as a 'pension scheme', which is not provided as a 'nest egg' that can be realized at will, but in terms of the inalienable right to a reasonable share of the natural resources available to the community. Hughes's analysis rests on the word 'available'. He suggests that if individual members of the community were to seek to exploit the available natural resources to their full potential, this would inevitably lead to a shrinkage of the 'Right of Avail'. Lack of commercial cropping on the one hand, and the acceptance of using cattle as a source of cash income on the other, is explained in terms of the different effect of these two activities on the shrinkage of the 'Right of Avail'. Cash cropping, by increasing the value of land, encourages an individual to expand his holding and reduces his willingness to share the land with dependents or relatives. Thus the share of available land for everyone else in the community is reduced. Those who obtain a significant cash income from the sale of cattle, on the other hand, do not advance any claim to any particular patch of grazing.

Hughes's analysis is valuable in that it stresses the non-market aspects of land rights. His analysis is based on detailed field level research in Swaziland and Zimbabwe and provides an accurate reflection of traditional attitudes to land in the region. It is significant that, even under the influence of the considerable political and economic developments that have taken place in the region, the traditional tenure system has undergone little fundamental change. One reason for this, given by Hughes, is that the continuation of the emphasis on the importance of land as a social-security system has been made easier by the expansion of wage employment opportunities in the modern sector. This has reduced the potential conflict between the expansion of cash cropping and the shrinkage of the 'Right of Avail', or the size of the pension fund.

This social explanation for the lack of commercial cropping and low-subsistence crop productivity per hectare can be complemented by our household-economics approach. In Chapter 7 we demonstrated that, on purely economic grounds, cash cropping does not compete well with subsistence maize production and, after subsistence requirements are met, is likely to be rejected in favour of more remunerative wage employment. In Chapter 4 we suggested that the benefits of maintaining a home base rested on the cheapness of providing household goods, including food, as well as the provision of goods such as social security that are not otherwise available. The security aspect of the home base has been mentioned by many writers on indigenous agriculture in Africa (Spengler, 1964, p. 297; Yudelman, 1964a, p. 576; Elkan, 1960, p. 10; Brand, 1974, p. 274; Steyn, 1974, p. 312; Murray, 1980, p. 19). Less often have the relative costs of goods produced in the traditional sector been compared with those in the modern sector. Houghton (1964, p. 317) points out that, even where families have moved into urban areas in South Africa, 'some of them send their children back to the tribal areas to be brought up there by relatives, and because of the insecurity in town many try to retain some rights in the rural economy'. Schapera (1947, p. 167) makes the same point about family migrants from Botswana. Child care, as we have noted, is particularly time-intensive and since time has a higher value in urban than in rural areas, there are obvious advantages in maintaining a rural base, where children can be brought up. The high cost of urban life compared with rural life has also been noted by Elkan (1960, p. 18): food, water, shelter and woodfuel have all to be paid for with hard-earned cash in town. Under customary tenure, on the other hand, these things have zero money cost and require only the time input of relatively low-value household labour.

These activities, child care, fetching water[1] and woodfuel, etc., are household production activities in a household-economics sense and, as such, they are just as valuable to the household as crop-growing activities or the tending of cattle. All these activities are dependent on maintaining the farm-household's 'Right of Avail', and this entails some cultivation. However, maintaining the 'Right of Avail' and the non-market benefits that go with it does not depend on achieving high levels of crop production per hectare. Indeed these other household production activities compete directly with the increased labour inputs needed to achieve high crop yields per hectare. Yudelman (1964a, p. 571) is of no doubt that output could be increased if producers in Africa would increase inputs of labour. But he notes that there exists a level of voluntary unemployment 'in the sense that producers still have high leisure preferences based on traditional value systems whereby they choose to limit their inputs of labour [into cash cropping] rather than to maximise their money returns by forgoing non-economic activities'. Most Western housewives would take exception to an application of Yudelman's view to their circumstances; that by staying away from work to bring up children and maintain the home, they are demonstrating a high leisure preference.

There are therefore sound economic, as well as social, reasons why indigenous farming is not highly commercialized and subsistence crop production per hectare is low in southern Africa. Furthermore these reasons are reinforced by the opportunity to obtain cash income outside farming, which reduces the need for the non-market attributes of land to be compromised by having to produce a cash income therefrom.

Cattle attributes

Cattle, like land, have many economic and social roles. On cattle in Swaziland, Kuper (1961, p. 150) has written:

Their uses are multifarious: they provide food and clothing, they are the most desired reward for loyal service, the medium by which ancestral goodwill is secured for health and prosperity, the closest approximation to currency, the means of ratifying marriage, the modern beast of burden and essential draft animals. They are required on occasions of national and family importance, and a man without cattle is indeed poor and insignificant – he is like an orphan without kinsmen.

The desire for cattle has not diminished with the expansion of the money economy. Indeed the coming of the Europeans and the introduction of the plough enhanced the value of cattle and provided the opportunity to earn money to obtain greater numbers of them. Commenting on the difficulty of recruiting labour before 1900 in South Africa, Robertson (1935, p. 7) notes that 'the farmers had, however, one means of payment available which would induce Natives to sell their labour – payment in stock'.

The propensity to invest wage earnings in cattle has persisted since the period before 1900 (Schapera, 1947, p. 142). In Lesotho the imports of cattle are recognized to be a function of the numbers of men returning from the mines (LASA, 1978, p. VII–8), and the doubling of mine earnings in 1975 and 1976, compared with the previous two years, was associated with a quadrupling of the numbers of cattle imported according to official statistics (see also Eckert and Wykstra, 1980, p. 19).

The attitude to cattle in southern Africa can be understood in terms of the different uses to which they can be put. They may be exchanged for market goods giving superior or more-desired attributes, or they may be used in own consumption. In own consumption they can satisfy both basic needs (meat, milk, draughtpower) as well as provide luxury consumption (prestige, feasts, bridewealth, status). Having such a range of attributes they are, as we noted in Chapter 4, very powerful goods indeed.

Reasons for keeping and selling cattle

The observation that traditional herders in Africa are often reluctant to sell seemingly surplus cattle is commonly explained in terms of the need to maintain large herds in order to supply basic needs and ensure survival of the herd (e.g. Brown, 1977, p. 37; Horowitz, 1979, p. 58; Bembridge, 1980; White, 1981). Few cattle are sold because, it is said, most are required for own consumption. This view implies that, after basic needs have been met, cattle (like maize) will be exchanged for market goods, i.e. sold. If the need to keep cattle for subsistence requirements is the main reason for the low levels of offtake in Swaziland (as suggested by a recent consultancy report – AGROTEC, 1980, p. 77), we would expect the rate of sales of cattle surplus to subsistence requirements to be lower in small herds than in large ones where the margin above subsistence is greater. From the data in Table 9.1 we can see that this is not so. In each ecological region smaller herds have higher sales rates than larger ones (although the difference is only significant for the highveld).

As we might expect, Table 9.1 also shows that cattle subsistence requirements, measured in terms of own slaughter rate, are higher in small than in large herds. For any household the demand for cattle subsistence goods per beast will be greater the fewer the beasts. Thus, the relative need to slaughter

TABLE 9.1 *Cattle sales and slaughter rates by herd size*

	Herd size		t-sig. level
	1–17 head	18 + head	(one tail)
Sales rate (percentage)			
Highvelt	3.9	1.8	.081
Middleveld	3.5	3.3	.450
Lowveld	11.1	6.8	.236
Own slaughter rate (percentage)			
Highvelt	5.5	4.7	.290
Middleveld	5.6	3.7	.070
Lowveld	6.4	2.9	.150

Source: Economics Section, 1980, Tables SA.2 & SA.3

is reduced as herd size increases. That this relaxation of own consumption pressure does not result in greater sales of 'surplus' beasts (as it would for a crop like maize for example) can be explained in terms of the luxury consumption goods provided by cattle.

Let us reject the assumption that stock sales constitute the surplus after providing for own consumption needs, and assume instead that they represent the household's willingness, or need, to exchange cattle for market goods rather than to keep them for 'luxury consumption'. Then, given a fixed short-term demand for market goods, the proportion of cattle that need to be sold to meet the requirement for cash will be greater the fewer the number of beasts held and sales rates, like slaughter rates, will increase as herd size decreases.

This short-term fixed demand for market goods should not be confused with the conventional target-income concept. In terms of the household-economics analysis, the demand for market goods is determined by their relative utility and procurement cost compared to substitute non-market goods produced for own consumption. Thus, as the price of market goods and the attributes they confer change, or as the opportunity costs of time used in non-market compared with market production alters, the derived demand for market goods which confer desired attributes will vary. This analysis is consistent with a short-term target-income concept, but accounts for it in terms of the relative costs of attaining desired consumption commodities through market or non-market production.

Both time-series aggregate herd-offtake data and cross-sectional herd-marketing data provide evidence that Swazi cattle are sold to meet specific cash needs, rather than to maximize income after own-consumption requirements have been met. A time-series analysis was conducted on the assumption that percentage offtake from the Swazi National herd would vary through time and between years, depending on changes in the need for cash relative to the value of the cattle herd. Thus it was postulated that if the growth of the human population or the increase in the need to purchase food requirements are greater than the increase in the value of the cattle herd, the rate of offtake will increase. But an increase in alternative cash incomes relative to the value of the cattle herd was expected to result in a reduced rate of offtake. Annual data for twenty-nine years between 1949 and 1977 gave the following linear regression equation:

$$Y = 6.0 + 7.5 X_a + 0.1 X_b - 0.4 X_c$$
$$(6.1)(4.0)(3.1)(-3.9)$$

Where:
- Y is the estimated offtake from the Swazi herd;
- X_a is the Swazi human population relative to the value of the Swazi cattle herd;
- X_b is the seasonal cash need (reflected in low rainfall and poor harvests in the previous season) relative to the value of the Swazi herd; and
- X_c is the annual earnings from mine employment relative to the value of the Swazi herd.

The adjusted coefficient of determination was .68, the Durbin-Watson statistic 1.19 and the F statistic for the regression 18.4. All the coefficients were significant at the .01 level.

This analysis is reported in more detail in Low, Kemp and Doran (1980a) and represents an extension of a simpler model which related cattle offtake to price and rainfall (Doran, Low and Kemp, 1979). The implication of the 1980 analysis is that the previously observed negative price response is due to price rises increasing the value of the cattle herd relative to cash needs. This interpretation has been challenged by Jarvis (1980), who argues that the negative price response is entirely consistent with profit maximizing behaviour. Jarvis's criticism in this respect is justified, and it brings out the difficulty of using price-response data to argue for or against the commercial motivation of traditional cattleowners (Low, 1980). However the 'sale for cash needs' hypothesis does not rest on the existence of a negative price response (although it implies it), and can be tested without reference to price response, as is demonstrated in the above regression equation.

Cross-sectional cattle marketing information may also be used to test the 'sale for specific cash needs' hypothesis. The analysis of cross-sectional marketing data in Swaziland reveals the existence of a marked regional difference in the patterns of cattle disposal, between the highveld and middleveld on the one hand and the lowveld on the other. The data in Table 9.2 show that sales rates are higher in the lowveld than in the other regions.

TABLE 9.2 *Cattle sales rates by ecological region*

	Ecological Region		t-sig level (one tail)
	Highveld and middleveld	Lowveld	
Sales rate (percentage)			
Herds of 1–17 head	3.7	11.1	.112
Herds of 18+ head	3.0	6.8	.005

Source: Economics Section, 1980, Table SA.1

This regional pattern is also reflected in the proportion of cattle-holders selling and, as can be seen from Table 9.3, was as evident in 1960 as it was in 1979.

Not only are lowveld cattle-holders more inclined to sell cattle than their highveld and middleveld counterparts, they also sell a greater proportion of

TABLE 9.3 *Reasons for cattle sales by ecological region*

	Highveld	Middleveld	Lowveld
Percentage of holders selling			
1959/60 sample survey	24	40	67
1979 marketing survey	25	27	64
Percentage of sellers in 1979 survey selling			
for food	13	13	51
for clothing and farm inputs	17	10	43
for school fees	39	29	23
for medical expenses	9	26	17
for vehicles and building equipment	9	10	26
for bridewealth and stock	17	16	14
because cattle ready for market	13	23	15
Percentage of household population			
in wage employment	16	14	11
households selling some cattle	12	10	9
households selling no cattle	18	16	15

Sources:
  Holleman, 1964, Table 118
  Cattle Marketing Survey, 1980, Tables 1.4 & 1.6

their cattle to meet basic living expenses of food, clothing and farm inputs. The greater need to sell cattle in the lowveld arises from the related low-cropping potential and lower wage incomes, compared with the highveld and middleveld (e.g. see also Table 7.8). Within regions households selling cattle have relatively fewer wage earners than households not selling cattle.

Regional differences are also observed in other aspects of cattle marketing, such as the type of stock sold, the location, outlet and timing of sales and perceived factors limiting sale at various outlets (Economics Section, 1980). Such differences are consistent with the notion that the need to sell cattle in the lowveld is greater than elsewhere, but this does not mean that fewer families keep cattle in the highveld and middleveld. The regional differences observed in cattle-marketing behaviour stem largely from relative differences in the type of attributes provided by cattle in the different regions. In the lowveld, subsistence attributes[2] (or money income to purchase market goods providing these attributes) are relatively important. In the highveld and middleveld these subsistence goods can be obtained more readily from other sources (e.g. cropping and wage employment) and cattle are relatively more important as providers of luxury consumption goods.

The observation by Hughes that some Swazis obtain considerable amounts of cash from selling cattle is consistent with the argument that in some locations cattle will have a greater subsistence function that in others. This should not, however, be confused with the question of commercialization in the sense of selling cattle in excess of those needed to meet basic needs. As we have seen, the greatest cash need is for food and in low-crop-potential areas this need is particularly great and cattle have to be sold to meet it. In the same way cattle keeping in Botswana is said to be much more commercialized than in Swaziland. Sales rates are around 10 per cent compared with an average of

4 per cent in Swaziland. Much of this difference, though, has to do with the difficulty of growing food crops in Botswana (as well as poorer wage opportunities), and hence the greater emphasis on cattle for providing basic needs.[3]

Overgrazing

This view of cattle keeping, based on the various attributes conferred by cattle, puts a different interpretation on the cause of overgrazing, which is usually attributed to 'the tragedy of the commons' (Gordon, 1954). Clearly there is a relationship between communal tenure and the attitudes to cattle keeping, and we would agree with critics like Jarvis (1980) who argue that the effect of communal grazing is that it considerably cheapens the cost of maintaining cattle. However, cheapening the cost of maintaining cattle not only encourages investors to hold on to them longer before selling to maximize income, but also reduces the cost of the various attributes obtained through cattle.

We saw in Chapter 2 how tobacco farmers in Malawi substituted modern goods with superior attributes for traditional ones. In much of southern Africa there has been a similar substitution: the plough for the hoe, the gun for the spear, enamel vessels for clay pots, brick buildings for mud houses. Among the lists of goods purchased with cash earnings, cattle have continued to feature strongly (Schapera, 1947, p. 142; van der Wiel, 1977, Table 40; de Vletter et al., 1981, Table 16). This suggests that, for at least some of the attributes that cattle provide, superior and cheaper substitutes have not been available in the marketplace. Under customary tenure it is cheap to maintain cattle (fodder is free and herding is done by low-cost family labour) and this reduces the cost of obtaining attributes through cattle compared with other means. A change to private tenure, which increases the cost of keeping cattle and therefore of the attributes attached to them, will only reduce the derived demand for cattle if their related attributes are thereby made more expensive than similar or substitute attributes that can be obtained from other market goods. The recent experience of tenure reform under Botswana's Tribal Grazing Lands Programme (TGLP) suggests that the derived demand for cattle is not much reduced by a change to private tenure.

Under the TGLP a number of large-herd owners were provided with private grazing rights on ranches, for the development and upkeep of which they were given government loans. The scheme was successful in its immediate aim of removing stock from the commons but, as Lipton observes (1978, Vol. II, p. 56), the TGLP looks like making the overgrazing problem worse in the medium term. The ranchers seek above all to increase their herd sizes and, according to Lipton, almost every allottee said that his main reason for taking a ranch was 'to multiply my herd'. Help with doing this is their main request at meetings with government officers. Fencing, controlled breeding and improved water and pasture are seen as the methods of achieving the improved productivity which is aimed at increasing herd size, not cash income. Lipton states that the TGLP farmers propose to bring back on to the commons excess beasts that cannot be accommodated on the ranches. Odell and Odell (1980, p. 8) confirm Lipton's observations and our analysis:

a premise that exclusive rights would provide an incentive to reduce stock numbers to sustainable levels has been invalidated by strong traditional pressures that call for increasing cattle numbers as much and as quickly as possible. Already most ranches are overstocked and some are already seriously overgrazed.

Increasing the cost of keeping cattle through a move to private tenure will only reduce the derived demand for cattle when other goods are available that readily and more cheaply provide the luxury attributes for which cattle above subsistence needs are presently kept. This may be brought about through a change in land tenure as Doran, Low and Kemp (1979, p. 45) have suggested:

> de Wilde (1967, Vol. 1, p. 56) probably has misunderstood evidence for factors that he assumes will change attitudes of stockholders towards cattle holding in East Africa. In his discussion of the Kikuyu, Baringo, the Central Nyanzan tribes of Kenya, and the Sukuma of Tanzania, he argues that increased cash-earning opportunities (through cash cropping) have induced a change in attitude to cattle holding as far as the Kikuyu are concerned. Under similar circumstances, however, the Baringo, Central Nyanzan, and Sukumu people showed no tendency to reduce herd size. At the time that this observation was made, the Kikuyu had obtained individual ownership rights to agricultural land, whereas the other groups had no such rights. . . For the Kikuyu, it would therefore seem that land had replaced cattle as the desired symbol and store of wealth (luxury consumption) whereas, for the other tribes, this shift had not been possible.

However, the emphasis here is on the effect of a change in land tenure in providing a substitute luxury consumption good for cattle rather than reducing the cost of keeping cattle on the commons. As Lele (1981, p. 55) has observed for Africa as a whole, the stress placed on destocking and pasture improvement by technicians has had little impact 'because of the complex socio-cultural and environmental factors . . . and the absence of more profitable and less risky ways of investing the surplus resources of cattle owners.'

In Swaziland it was expected that stock numbers could be reduced by the introduction of production-increasing technology, which would enable herders to obtain higher incomes with fewer improved stock than they could with more unimproved stock. However, production improvement initiatives, such as controlled grazing, bush clearing, pasture reseeding, stock breeding and fattening ranches have not resulted in herders keeping fewer cattle under better conditions. Indeed there is some evidence that marginal improvements in productivity (increased calving rates, weaning percentages, cow to bull ratios) have resulted in a reduction in sales (Low and Fowler, 1979, pp. 52-61; Doran, Low and Kemp, 1979). The logic of such production-increasing strategies suffers from the failure to recognize that cattle are kept for consumption as well as production purposes. Solutions to the cattle production and overgrazing problems in southern Africa that do not recognize this dual role of cattle are likely to be counter-productive, as they have been in Botswana and Swaziland.

In this chapter we have provided some empirical evidence to support the view that land and cattle provide substantial non-market benefits to Swazi farm-households. That customary land tenure and attitudes to cattle keeping have considerable negative effects on agricultural development, as it is normally conceived, has not been in dispute. The nature of these negative effects will be discussed in the next two chapters on migration and rural development. However in these discussions we will recognize, even emphasize, the influence on farm-household production behaviour of the non-market benefits to be had from maintaining cattle and land-use rights.

Notes

1 Shapiro (1978) found that in north-western Tanzania on average each woman in his sample of 70 farm-households spent 90 minutes per day (556 hours per year) fetching water.
2 For example, 68 per cent of the meat from own slaughtered cattle is used for consumption in the lowveld, against 55 per cent in the highveld and middleveld. Most of the balance is used for ceremonial occasions (Economics Section, 1980, p. 18).
3 In relation to the 'sale for specific cash needs' argument, it is interesting to note the contrasting findings in two successive papers in the Overseas Development Institute's Pastoral Network Series. Cole (1979), commenting on the Bedouin of Saudi Arabia, says that they do not need to sell their animals because they are receiving money from a government subsidy scheme and are therefore not greatly in need of extra cash. Meadows and White (1979), on the other hand, observe that the Maasai in Kenya have recently forgone their reluctance to sell female cattle as a result of their increasing desire for cash.

10 Labour migration: a comparative-advantage approach

In this chapter we will present an interpretation of the causes and effects of labour migration in southern Africa based on the household-economics argument, which has been developed in previous chapters. We will challenge the radical view that emphasizes coercion and asset confiscation as the prime causes of migration and will uphold, and expand on, the more orthodox view of migration as a function of economic opportunity. The existence of early discriminatory measures aimed at, and having the effect of, extracting labour from the land cannot and will not be denied. However, it will be argued that the deleterious effects of migration on agricultural production has its roots in the nature of the indigenous social structure as much as in the domination and exploitation of modern capital. Hence solutions that concentrate on the latter and do not recognize the influence of the former have little validity.

In advance of our argument we will present empirical evidence that, 1) is inconsistent with the radical coercion theory of labour-force development and, 2) is at variance with conventional wisdom on the principal cause of low productivity in indigenous agriculture: namely land shortage per se. This will lead us to point out the limitations of existing analytical models of migration in the southern African context and show how the household-economics approach can alleviate some of these shortcomings.

We will first review recent historical research that questions the coercion theory of labour-force development in Swaziland, and point out the empirical paradox of non-utilization or under-utilization of arable land in much of southern Africa, where population pressure is commonly believed to be the major cause of migration. We will then argue that labour-force participation in southern Africa may be better understood in terms of the comparative advantage of household members in market/wage or non-market/farm production, than in terms of conventional theories based on the assumption of declining marginal utility to labour on the land. Finally we will suggest that, in conjunction with indigenous land-tenure arrangements, the comparative-advantage concept of labour-force participation provides an explanation for the observed paradox of under-utilization of arable land, and implies that increasing wage opportunities can lead directly to reduced farm productivity per hectare and per farm worker without involving the land sufficiency question. Empirical support for the argument is provided by the observed effects of recent substantial increases in mine earnings on agricultural production in Lesotho. This wage-income effect on crop production, which has puzzled a number of commentators, can be understood in terms of the household-economics approach.

Conventional theories on the development of labour markets in southern Africa

Although differences of emphasis exist, depending on the ideological standpoint taken, there is general agreement on the nature of the measures used to extract labour in the early years of colonial rule. Knight and Lenta (1980, p. 161), for example, draw attention to 'land appropriation through conquest and legislation, the imposition of compulsory payment, government neglect of indigenous agriculture and overt discrimination in favour of white farmers'. Radical writers (Clarke, 1977; Arrighi, 1970; Crush, 1979; Kowet, 1978; and Palmer and Parsons (eds), 1977) stress the role of colonial administrations in undertaking or backing measures which forced African workers into wage employment. By these means, it is argued, the natural indigenous economy was subordinated to the imperatives of the dominant capitalist sector(s). The transformation of the natural indigenous economy created a surplus of labour, since expropriation of cattle and land assets meant that sufficient subsistence production could not be obtained to reproduce the labour supply. Thus surplus labour found, and continues to find it necessary to migrate to wage employment to obtain part of its subsistence.

Although it is generally not included in the standard argument, some analysts (e.g. Arrighi, 1970) also introduce the element of a rising conventional subsistence level, which increasingly includes non-traditional goods requiring cash for their purchase. Thus Stahl (1981, p. 33) argues that:

> African conventional subsistence levels have risen considerably over the past few decades, above the levels necessary for the basic physiological requirements essential to 'reproduce the labour supply'. Africans have come to expect higher standards of living. But given the manifest inability of the 'homeland' agriculture to develop, this has necessitated a higher level of migration.

The radicals go on to argue that, since part of the migrant's subsistence is drawn from traditional agriculture, the capitalist employer only has to pay a wage equal to the difference between total subsistence requirements and that portion of subsistence requirements derived from traditional agriculture. Through this 'primitive accumulation', the capitalist sector reaps large profits and accumulates capital stocks. In the indigenous sector this process results in disinvestment and a 'restructuring of the asset base'.

The more orthodox view differs in that it de-emphasizes the discriminatory and coercive means used to extract labour. Moreover, the reduction in indigenous productivity is attributed more to the inability of the indigenous sector to respond adequately to increasing population pressures. For instance the social functions of cattle-holding were seen to impede indigenous farming (Knight and Lenta, 1980, p. 164).

Nevertheless, both orthodox and radical writers agree that land shortage was the crucial factor in reducing agricultural production and inducing continued migration:

> Africans had previously enjoyed abundant land, which they had held communally and farmed in a land-extensive way. Land spoilation, through conquest and legislation, destroyed the base on which these economies existed. The curtailment of land available produced overloading by both men and animals, and population

pressure was increased through the introduction of medical and veterinary services. This lowered the quality of the land and reduced farm production (Knight and Lenta, 1980, p. 162).

Contradictory evidence

The development of the Swazi labour market

Compared with some other areas in southern Africa (e.g. Botswana, Lesotho and Transkei), Swaziland enjoys a favourable agro-climatic environment. The average arable land holding under traditional tenure is 2.5 ha (compared with 1.9 ha in Lesotho), and annual rainfall ranges from 700-1500 mm (compared with 500 mm in most arable lands areas in Botswana). Maize yields average 1-1.5 tons per ha compared with 0.25-0.75 tons per ha in Botswana, Lesotho and Transkei. About two-thirds of rural households own cattle. The average herd size is eighteen head and annual slaughter and sale offtake is about 8 per cent compared with 4 per cent in Lesotho and 2 per cent in Transkei. Extension coverage is also relatively intensive with a field worker to farmer ratio of 1:300 in Swaziland compared for example with 1:700 in Botswana and 1:1000 in Malawi. Despite this relatively favourable rural situation, participation in the off-farm labour market is no less prevalent in Swaziland than elsewhere in the region. Around two-thirds of rural households have members in wage employment. This is comparable with Botswana, Lesotho and Transkei and is higher than the 50-60 per cent commonly recorded in Zimbabwe and parts of Zambia.

Recent historical research by Booth (1981) has revealed that the development of the Swazi labour market has followed a rather different course from the commonly accepted one. He writes:

> African labor history is replete with examples of work forces coerced into laboring for wages and under conditions decreed by capital and enforced by the state. . . In Swaziland the case was quite different. The competition for labor between British and South African capital, created a market which the Swazi played with increasing shrewdness for better wages and conditions. (p. 1).

Booth (1981) and de Vletter et al. (1981) point out that competition for labour, between local and South African capital, resulted in the importation of non-local black workers (mainly Mozambican) to make up local shortages. After the war, competition for labour between sugar and forestry industries within Swaziland and the gold and coal mines, and wattle and sugar farms in South Africa resulted in Swazi labour being offered increased wages, free transport, improved quarters (including those for families), recreational facilities and better quality food. While the Swazi response to the new conditions was to become very selective in their choice of employment, they, 'like workforces throughout southern Africa (consistent with the design of mining capital), retained their roles as homesteaders as a source of supplementary income' (Booth, 1981, p. 15).

This historical account of the development of the Swazi labour market contradicts the radical coercion hypothesis. Furthermore, the temporary pattern of migration has not always been 'consistent with the designs of mining capital', since in early colonial times a major concern was the stabilization of work forces (see p. 186, below). De Vletter et al. (1981) point out that, since Swaziland lacks serious population pressure, is not obviously underdeveloped and does not demonstrate extremes of exploitation or conscious political collusion, the 'natural' motives to migrate from the subsistence base may be more clearly discerned there than elsewhere. Certainly the widespread existence of temporary migration and the maintenance of the home base throughout Africa caution against accounting for temporary migration purely in terms of local politico-economic circumstances (see pp. 186–7, below).

Land shortage?

As we have seen, most radical and orthodox neo-classical analysts agree that land shortage and population pressure was and is a major cause of the stagnant absolute and declining per capita agricultural production on traditionally farmed areas. It is this declining per capita production that forces (according to the radicals) or induces (according to orthodox neo-classical economists) labour to seek off-farm wage employment.

However these analyses, based on the hypothesis of land shortage, pose an empirical paradox since researchers commonly find that available arable land is not fully utilized and that with more labour and complementary inputs, agricultural production could be significantly increased (e.g. IBRD, 1980b, Annex 7, p. 22). Knight and Lenta (1980, p. 191) suggest that, since only 73 per cent of dry arable land and 75 per cent of irrigated land was cultivated in KwaZulu in 1972, 'land shortage is not the problem that conventional wisdom would have us believe'.

Certainly in Swaziland the question of land shortage is a moot one. On the one hand discussions of the concessions and land partition tend to stress the aspect of land deprivation (Crush, 1980; Mashasha, 1977; Fransman, 1978). Booth (1981, p. 4), for example, states that: 'Labour was provided for ensuring that the Native areas (numbering 32 in all) would not support their human and animal populations for more than a few years at best, and not at all in a few cases.' On the other hand, Barker (1965, p. 39) has commented that the actual partition of land was carried out with strict reference to their [the Swazis'] interests – they got good land, that is, and were not fobbed off with bad, although it is was necessarily in a patchwork over the country'. And on the basis of the 1959/60 survey data, Holleman (1964, p. 335) concluded that:

> Sufficiency of food production is not at present affected by any regional shortage of arable land. In fact, if the present ratio between arable and permanent grazing is maintained, there appears to be enough fallow land available to ensure adequate food production *at the present level of efficiency* for a normally increasing population for the next two generations. With improved yields per acre, the outlook would be even better.

Even today, referring to the rural development area in Swaziland with the lowest arable area per homestead, Sibisi (1981, p. 2) concludes that there 'is no evidence of a serious shortage of land for farming, especially since land is frequently offered for temporary use in return for ploughing of what remains in the holder's hands'.

No one suggests that land is in short supply in Zambia and most observers recognize that there is enormous potential for increases in production. Yet migration here is as prevalent as elsewhere in the region and has 'left many households without sufficient labour to be able to farm adequately.' (Elling, 1981, p. 95).

In Zimbabwe recent survey data indicate that 50 per cent of households cultivate less than 75 per cent of their allocated arable areas (Bonnerie, 1983). Hughes (1974, p. 29) concludes that communal area land is capable of producing many times what it is producing now and that 'the contention that shortage of land is the main cause of the present problems of tribal areas cannot stand up to any type of critical examination'.

Merle Lipton (1977) has queried whether there is an overall shortage of cultivable land in the South African homelands and has suggested that these areas are in fact undercultivated. Evidence from the Transkei (Westcott, 1977) also indicates under-utilization, with over half of the rural farm-households surveyed failing to cultivate some of their land.

In Malawi, which by most African standards would be considered densely populated, recent surveys suggest that land is not the binding constraint that the World Bank and others have been assuming it is. The 1982 national sample census indicates that for all Malawi 50 per cent of arable land was not cropped. Even in the central and southern regions 40 per cent of arable land was recorded as unused. These findings are supported by micro-surveys. Chipande (1983) notes that in his survey of 158 farmers in the Lilongwe Agricultural Development Division, 15 per cent of farms failed to cultivate all the land allocated to them, and over 35 per cent gave or lent some land away in the last five years.

In Lesotho, even, which is normally used as the prototype for the radical argument, there has been a reduction in cultivated area over recent years from 340 000 ha in 1974–6, to 230 000 ha in 1977 and 1978 (IBRD, 1980b, Annex 7, p. 11). In 1950 there were 80 000 ha (or 25 per cent) more land under cultivation than in 1976–7, despite the addition over this time of 171 000 persons to the resident rural work force, not to mention oxen and tractors (IBRD 1980b, Annex 7, p. 11). Furthermore official statistics indicate better yields per hectare in 1977 and 1978 than in previous years.[1] These yield data suggest that land has not been removed from cultivation in Lesotho because of decreasing absolute profitability of continued cultivation. We will argue later that the reduction in cultivated land area in Lesotho has been due to a *relative* rather than *absolute* decline in profitability of continued cultivation, and has been caused by an increase in returns to off-farm wage employment, rather than decreasing marginal productivity of labour on the land.

Before developing this argument and taking a more detailed look at the Lesotho case, however, it is necessary to consider why it is that conventional migration models mislead us into assuming that high rates of migration from densely populated rural areas are necessarily inconsistent with the under-utilization of farm land.

Migration models and analytical concepts

Conventional wisdom influences and is conditioned by theoretical thinking, which invariably conceives migration decisions as being determined by the point at which falling levels of marginal income from farming equate with a constant wage rate. We have already criticized the Nakajima farm-household model on this account. Bell's (1972) theoretical model of migration in southern Africa, which has more recently been employed by Knight (1978, 1982) is also based on diminishing farm returns and a constant wage rate. Bell's model is an improvement on Nakajima's in that it does take account of non-market factors in deciding how much of a migrant's time is spent in wage employment. However this non-market factor is introduced in terms of subjective indifference curves representing the individual's 'preference for life in the rural village' (Bell, 1972) or 'preference for family life' (Knight, 1978; 1982). The introduction of non-market factors in this way is not very useful analytically, except to show that the time an individual spends in wage employment is less than that which would maximize family money income, on account of his positively sloping preference curve.

Todaro's frequently used migration model is also based on the individual's rural-urban income differential, albeit discounted for uncertainty and other costs of migrating. Thus the available theoretical models condition thinking about migration in terms of diminishing returns to labour on the farm (caused by land shortage), individual rural-urban income differentials and the influence of social-value preference for a rural or family life. Most analyses of agriculture and migration in southern Africa therefore compare the annual or hourly income on the farm (usually average in the absence of marginal estimates) with what a migrant can earn (e.g. USAID, 1980; IBRD, 1975(b), 1980a, 1980b, 1983; ODA, 1981). They come up with conclusions like: 'returns of 6 cents per hour for maize sold on the market or 15 cents per hour for maize used as a replacement for purchased flour can be obtained. By comparison a mineworker is currently earning 56 cents per hour' (IBRD, 1980b, Annex 7, p. 12). Of course a crucial factor missed by such analyses is the question of who in the farm-household earns the 15 cents per hour and who the 56 cents? This is where the household-economics approach can make a contribution by introducing the concept of comparative advantage of household members between market and non-market activities or between farm and non-farm employment. In conjunction with the indigenous tenure system, the concept also helps to resolve the apparent paradox of underutilization of land where there is high population pressure.

The household-economics argument

The comparative-advantage concept

A modern textbook on labour economics points out that any 'economic analysis of female (or male) labour force participation must address itself to the question of comparative advantage in the household sector versus the market sector' (Fearn, 1981, p. 72). Although Fearn has in mind modern households in developed societies, the principle is equally (or more?) applicable to indigenous farm-households in southern Africa.

According to the analysis in Chapter 4 (see Figure 4.3), it is unnecessary to invoke the assumption of diminishing returns to labour on the farm to explain migration to off-farm employment at the farm-household level. Migration to off-farm employment can be explained instead in terms of the comparative advantage in wage employment of certain household members over others. This implies that it will be those members with the highest wage-earning potentials who will leave the farm and those with lower wage-earning potentials, but not so much lower farm-household production potentials, who will remain in the rural areas.

There is a considerable amount of evidence to indicate that this is what happens. Nattrass (1976, p. 69) notes that it 'is a well known and frequently observed fact that migration as a process is selective in respect of age, sex and education level, in that the propensity to migrate is higher among young adult males with above average levels of education'. Evidence on the influence that education has on the ability to obtain regular employment is given by the 1976 Swaziland census data presented in Table 10.1. The chances of obtaining regular employment within Swaziland are better with than without education and much better with secondary education than with only primary certificates.

TABLE 10.1 *Employment rates and educational levels in Swaziland (percentage of 25–64 resident age cohort in employment, 1976)*

	Not in employment	Irregular employment	Regular employment
Males			
no education	34.7	10.1	44.2
primary education	21.9	9.1	58.0
secondary education	12.0	7.0	74.6
Females			
no education	74.7	3.5	7.5
primary education	64.9	4.4	13.9
secondary education	33.0	5.6	54.5

Source: Swaziland Government, 1979, Tables XII.2 & XVI.4

Nattrass (1976, Table 3) provides evidence to show that in South Africa 'the rate of migration amongst the more highly educated is greater than amongst individuals with less schooling'. Billing (1978, pp. 105–6) draws attention to a number of studies in Zimbabwe which provide evidence of a positive correlation between education level and migration. In Botswana and Lesotho the relationship between migration and education is not so clear because of the high proportion of mine migrants, who do not require high levels of educational achievement to be employed. Thus van der Wiel (1977, p. 35) says that the better-educated men are more often able to find suitable employment in Lesotho, and that it tends to be the 'illiterate and poorly educated' who go away to work in South Africa.

However, mine and other employment is sex specific and age specific as is indicated by the data for Lesotho and Swaziland in Table 10.2. These data indicate the decline in absentee and employment rates from the age of thirty onwards. The lower absentee rates for Swaziland reflect the better employment opportunities within the country, but even within Swaziland the employment opportunities are much better for males than for females. There is also a difference in the age at which employment rates decline compared with absentee rates. In Swaziland many regular employees would be classified as temporary migrants but many also have more stable jobs (see de Vletter, 1978). The different characteristics of temporary absentees compared with stabilized workers has been pointed out by Nattrass (1976, p. 73). Her data are reproduced in Table 10.3, to which equivalent Swaziland data has been added. Nattrass concludes from these data that 'migrants (i.e. temporary absentees) on average retire from the modern sector earlier than do the stabilized workers. Of the migrants entering the labour force at 20 years of age, half will retire (from the modern sector) before they reach 40 years of age and three quarters by the age of 50'.

TABLE 10.2 *Age-specific migration and employment rates for Lesotho and Swaziland*

	Age Categories					
	15–19	20–24	25–29	30–34	35–39	40–59
Absentee males[d]						
Lesotho (1966)[a]	15	52	56	50	45	28
Swaziland (1976)[b]	9	20	19	14	13	10
	Age Categories					
	15–19	20–24	25–34	35–44	45–49	55–64
Regular employees within Swaziland[c]						
Resident males	15	40	60	58	46	34
Resident females	10	17	18	14	10	5

Sources and note:
   a) Knight & Lenta, 1980, p. 185
   b) Swaziland Government, 1979, Tables XVII.2 & XIII.3
   c) Swaziland Government, 1979, Table XVI.1
   d) Absentees refer to those leaving the respective country, mostly for mine employment.

TABLE 10.3 *Comparative age distribution of male workers (1970, except Swaziland = 1976)*

	Percentage of group in each age category				
	Permanently settled workers	All homeland migrants	All foreign migrants	Zululand migrants	Swaziland migrants
Age group					
14–19	13	12	6	13	13
20–24	15	20	25	18	24
25–29	12	21	20	18	19
30–34	10	18	15	16	11
35–39	12	10	11	10	9
40–44	11	7	8	11	6
45–49	10	4	7	5	5
50–54	7	5	5	5	3
55–64	10	3	3	4	2

Sources:
   Nattrass, 1976, Table 4
   Swaziland Government, 1979, Table XVII.2

Steyn (1974, p. 317) also notes the marked decrease in migration after the age of 40, implying that 'a large number of migrants return permanently to the homelands when they reach a more advanced age'. Kerven (1979, p. 46) reiterates this tendency in respect of the Batswana: 'at some point in the life cycle, a seemingly "urban" resident may take up part-time or full-time residence again in the rural areas'. And in Zimbabwe, data from around 1970 indicate that for tribal trust lands in general, as well as for individual reserve areas, the bulk of labour migrants were in the age group 15–45 and that after age 50 most migrants returned to their rural areas (Billing 1978, pp. 93–5).

In terms of our comparative-advantage theory of labour force participation, these data and observations indicate that as male migrants become older their comparative advantage in wage employment is reduced. There are a number of reasons for this:

    1) the wages they can earn, especially in unskilled employment like mining, will decrease with age and some jobs will no longer be available to them;

    2) other members of the household (young, better-educated sons and daughters) will begin to have higher earning potentials; and

    3) the value of the household head's time on the farm increases at the consolidation stage of the development cycle.

Thus, not only does a male's earning potential decrease but the advantages to his time spent in farming increase as he ages – or rather as the farm-household matures.[2] We have seen how the Swazi farm-household at the consolidation stage has considerable resource advantages. The presence of the household head to co-ordinate the use of these resources then becomes more critical. Sibisi (1980) has stressed the importance of the presence of the male head of household in relation to farm decision-taking in Swaziland. Westcott (1977) found in the Transkei that the presence of the male household head increased both the acreage cultivated and the yield per hectare. In Zimbabwe, Shumba (1985) observed that improved crop production performance was associated with fewer household heads being away in off-farm employment. In Lesotho, Guma and Gay (1978) found that the factors responsible for achieving above average crop production performance were: an above average number of sons in the household, an above average cattle herd size and the presence of the male household head. However van der Wiel (1977, p. 38) found that in only 32 per cent of farm-households was the household head permanently at home, and that in these cases able-bodied sons had 'in their turn' migrated to South Africa.

Thus it would appear that the comparative-advantage concept of labour-force participation, which has come to be an accepted part of labour-economics analysis in relation to advanced societies, also has some relevance in relation to migration theory in southern Africa. In modern societies the comparative advantage relates to the question of which household member spends how much time at work (in market production) or at home (in non-market production). In southern Africa the comparative-advantage concept relates to the question of the identity of household members who migrate out of the farm-household for wage employment and the length of time they continue to do so. The implications for land use and agricultural production are discussed in the following sections.

Implications of the household-economics argument for land use and agricultural production

AT THE INDIVIDUAL HOUSEHOLD LEVEL

The first point to make is that, from the point of view of the farm-household, there does not have to be a shortage of land for migration to take place. More specifically, there does not have to be an absolute declining marginal return to farm work for part of a household's labour force to be allocated to off-farm employment. Indeed it is quite plausible that, in the absence of any shortage of land at the farm-household level, absolute marginal returns to labour increase over a certain range due to Chayanov's 'complex co-operation' factor. The implication is that, as labour is withdrawn within this range, marginal labour returns on the farm will fall.[3]

The comparative-advantage concept suggests another reason to believe that marginal returns per farm worker will tend to fall as wage labour is withdrawn from the indigenous farm-household. This relates to the type of members who will tend to leave for wage employment compared with those who remain on the farm. In the prevailing wage employment market in southern Africa, young, educated and adult male members have the best off-farm job prospects. It will thus be the older, less well-educated and female members of the household who are left to do most of the farm work. This is an empirical observation that has also been made for tropical Africa (Okigbo, 1981, p. 15), as well as many other parts of the Third World (Thornton, 1982, p. 8).

Furthermore, because of other household maintenance tasks (household chores, child care, schooling), these remaining members will limit the time they spend on farm production. Just as in Western societies, where it has been found that married women as a group tend to withdraw from the labour force when they have children (Gronau, 1974; Leibowitz, 1972), so African wives with young children will reduce their effort on crop production to attend to the demands of a young family.

Western women withdraw from the labour market when they have children because the value of their time spent in child care is greater that that spent in employment.[4] In the indigenous farm-household the same applies, except that African women have the opportunity to respond to an increase in the value of time in other non-market activities, such as child care, by increasing the returns to time spent on cropping (e.g. combining less labour with the same amount of other inputs) rather than by ceasing crop production altogether. Increasing wage earnings resulting either from general increases in wages and employment opportunities, or from the increasing ability of household individuals to obtain wage employment as they become more mature, experienced, educated etc., also increase household members' time values. In the face of rising time values in wage employment and/or household activities, methods will be sought to raise time values in other activities to the new equimarginal level (Linder, 1970). These other activities include farm production and, as we have seen in Chapter 7, one way of increasing labour returns in cropping is to apply less labour per hectare.

This implies that more land-extensive forms of cultivation[5] that 1) save the time needed for other household activities and, 2) increase returns per labour unit are quite consistent with increased wage opportunities and increased migration. In these ways increasing wage opportunities can lead directly to reduced farm productivity per hectare and per worker. The above argument therefore reverses the normally accepted direction of causation and provides a direct link between migration and low farm productivity, without involving the land-sufficiency question.

AT THE AGGREGATE LEVEL

At the aggregate level the land-scarcity hypothesis is often seen in terms of the capacity of the land in relation to the population it supports. Migration is then seen as a result of population growth outstripping the capacity of the land to produce more intensively.

While it is true that low inherent land fertility reduces returns to farming and encourages migration, it is also necessary to recognize that the existing capacity of land is not only a function of its inherent characteristics. It is also related to the amount of human effort invested in it. It is well known that present land capabilities in Botswana and Lesotho are rather low. However Stahl (1981, p. 43) argues that:

> In Botswana much land is not utilised and virtually all is underutilised. Many workers could be productively employed clearing thornbush and other scrub from potentially productive land. Hills in Lesotho's village areas, which are at present considered unsuitable for growing traditional crops, could be terraced with the many rocks to be found in the fertile soil, and these terraces could undoubtedly support vines, fruit trees, or even olive trees, the oil of which could be produced locally. The many streams and rivers in Lesotho could be dammed to provide reserve water for irrigation of vines and fruit trees in periods of drought. Fish could be planted and harvested in such reservoirs.

While Stahl's vision may appear a little far fetched to some, the point is that currently accepted levels of land capability in Botswana and Lesotho could be substantially increased given sufficient investment of human time and effort.

We have seen that the opportunity for some members to earn relatively high incomes in off-farm employment can result in labour shortages at the farm-household level, which lead to low levels of labour input per hectare. Traditional institutions governing land allocations compound this situation by discouraging households from forgoing their land rights to specialize in non-farm activities, thereby causing the average returns to household labour in farming to fall over time.

While indigenous land tenure systems have considerable flexibility as regards land allocation, this flexibility does not mean that land is necessarily made available to those who are most willing and able to use it productively. Hughes (1972, 1974) notes that, in order to avoid the possibility of their losing their Bantu-ownership of a piece of land, migrant labourers, and others who may be away for some time, often give a 'Temporary Right of Cultivation' to kinsfolk who may not particularly need any additional land. All that is required is that some attempt should be made to cultivate it, so that the migrant's rights may not be impaired. In some areas a considerable amount of land is 'locked up' in this manner under control of people who often cultivate it very indifferently. Of course, for many off-farm workers, the need to give temporary rights of cultivation to kinsfolk outside their respective households does not arise. Those left on the farm will continue to cultivate, even if they may not be able to do so very thoroughly.[6] Because all households have their own land, there is little possibility of supplementing a depleted family labour force with hired labour at a wage rate below the returns that can be expected from the extra labour input. The result is that a proportion of households do not fully utilize their land holdings. Hence the paradox of under-utilization of land even where population pressure is high.[7]

The traditional land-tenure system itself, then, contributes to the reduction in land productivity over time. Not only does it encourage all households to continue cultivating and thus results in less or more marginal land being available per farming household over time. In association with off-farm employment opportunities it also results in a situation where perfectly good arable land lies idle or is indifferently cultivated, and accelerates the process by which households seeking new allocations or additional land are likely to be allocated more marginal and smaller plots. Under this situation, even constant real-wage rates in off-farm employment will induce greater migration over time in the face of declining overall returns to household labour time in crop production.

This process has been evident in southern Malawi where real wage rates have been constant though job opportunities in the estate sector have been expanding. Since few households have been prepared to forgo their land rights, population expansion has resulted in many households now cultivating very small or marginal gardens. The smaller holdings are intensively and continuously cropped with maize/pulse mixes. Maize production per household has fallen below requirements in most cases due to smaller areas, reduced fertility and heavy intercropping pressure. These deficits are increasingly purchased with the income of male migrant workers. Those households without migrant incomes purchase food deficits by working on neighbours' gardens (*ganyu*) or engaging in non-farm income earning activities such as trading or beer brewing. Even in this situation there exist many gardens which are much less intensively cultivated by a significant proportion of households who either have other forms of livelihood or who are critically short of family labour and cannot rely on *ganyu* being available whenever they need it.

Another aspect of the indigenous social structure also has an influence on land productivity over time. This relates to communal grazing rights and the various roles of cattle. The non-market advantages of keeping cattle beyond those needed for subsistence have been elaborated in Chapter 9. These non-market advantages, and the communal grazing system which enhances these advantages, produce the high derived demand for cattle that is reflected in consumption expenditures. The use of migrant wage income to purchase cattle in southern Africa is legendary (see pp. 111, 115 above). Less obvious is the related fact that increased wage earnings reduce the need to sell cattle (Low, Kemp and Doran, 1980a). In whichever way it is expressed, the continued high derived demand for cattle has had disastrous consequences in terms of land fertility in many parts of southern Africa (Robertson, 1935; Pim, 1932, 1935; Morse, 1960; South African Government, 1955).

Thus, while land confiscation by colonial powers has had an important influence on migration and agricultural production in southern Africa, so too have the indigenous social structures which lead to allocation and investment patterns that tend to exacerbate both land availability and land quality

130 Labour migration: a comparative-advantage approach

problems. In addition, off-farm wage employment opportunities have reduced incentives to invest more time in farming, and this has also affected the current productive capacity of the land in many areas.

Micro–macro linkages: an interpretation of aggregate crop production changes in Lesotho

To end this chapter let us take another look at the recent reduction in land use in Lesotho in the light of the forgoing analysis. The cross-sectional data in Table 10.4 indicate that, at the micro-level, farm production assumes less importance as household incomes rise. This tendency is mirrored at the macro-level as indicated by the aggregate time-series data in Table 10.5.

TABLE 10.4 *Percentage rural household income distribution by income source: Lesotho, 1976*

	Income Strata			
	0–199	200–599	600–999	1000 +
Source of Income				
Crops	39	16	3	4
Livestock	30	21	6	12
Sub-total agriculture	70	37	9	16
Off-farm	30	63	91	84

Source: Van der Wiel, 1977, Table 48, p. 88

TABLE 10.5 *Estimates of area planted and percentage composition of rural household income in Lesotho*

	1967–9[a]	1973	1974	1975	1976	1977	1978
Mine wages in maize equivalent (kg/shift)	10	15	22	40	43	39	36
Crop area planted[b] (thousands of hectares)	347	341	303	278	210	239	233
Source of Income[c]							
Crops	n.a	n.a	15	9	6	12	12
Livestock	n.a	n.a	15	12	12	10	10
Sub-total agriculture	41	n.a	30	21	18	22	22
Off-farm	59	n.a	70	79	82	78	78

Sources and notes:
Eckert & Wykstra, 1980, Tables 7 & 8.
a) Mine wages for 1970, crop area for 1969/70
b) Crop area data obtained from Bureau of Statistics official figures.
c) Source of income data estimates based on survey data for 1967–9 (Monyake, 1973) and for 1976 (van der Wiel, 1977).

The substantial rise in wage earnings in the mid-1970s resulted in a decline in the proportion of household income contributed by agriculture from 41 per cent in 1967–79 to 18 per cent in 1976. Not only was labour diverted from farming to wage employment, but labour time spent in farming by those remaining at home was reduced per worker and per hectare for the reasons discussed above. The predicted move to more extensive forms of land use took the ultimate form in Lesotho of the complete removal of some land from cultivation[8] and a substantial increase in the fallow area.

Eckert and Wykstra (1980, p. 15) have argued that 'the most persuasive explanation of the overall area trends is that faced with a sudden rise in money income many households made a choice between additional (low paying) work in the fields and leisure and simply left many fields fallow'. This argument invokes the traditional labour/leisure model, which assumes a decreasing marginal utility of income and implies an increase in leisure and decrease in labour input as money incomes rise. No doubt such a leisure preference applies, especially among wealthier households, and we have indicated how such a leisure preference may be interpreted in terms of Figure 4.3 (see above, p. 45).

However it is also relevant to note that the household-economics approach does not necessarily imply diminishing marginal utilities of income. Rather it implies diminishing marginal utilities of money relative to time. Thus:

> As money income rises, the relative decline in its marginal utility (or marginal product) induces households to behave in ways which conserve time and use money relatively intensively. It has been alleged that wealthy households reveal their low evaluation of money by 'frivolous' expenditures on 'inessential' convenience items, but these expenditures may also be interpreted as an efficient substitution away from their relatively scarce resource, time, and towards time saving, more expensive (in money) convenience items. Such behaviour indicates nothing about the absolute direction of change in the marginal utility of money income'. (Michael and Becker, 1973, p. 141).

For the Basotho, purchased maize meal or ferlitizer represent 'convenience' money-expensive, time-saving items in terms of food procurement. The purchase of maize meal and non-cultivation represents the extreme land-extensive (labour-saving) technology. The alternative of using fertilizer also increases output per unit of time. The use of these time-saving strategies in combination could help to explain the increase in recorded national crop yields (see Table 10.6) that coincided with increased mine earnings. Eckert and Wykstra (1980, p. 19) conclude their analysis of these increased yield estimates by arguing that 'The combination of much higher levels of inputs per hectare being applied to the more fertile and responsive soils is the only rationale that can explain a sudden and sustained jump in the magnitude recorded for yields'. While the extent of the yield increases may be disputed[9] (IBRD, 1980b, Annex 7, p. 6), the household-economics approach provides a theoretical basis for relating a substantial increase in migrant earnings both to the removal of less fertile fields from cultivation, and to the simultaneous increase in input use on the remaining higher potential areas.

Thus a substantial increase in off-farm earnings is consistent with reduced plantings and increased crop yields. However, increased yield per hectare estimates exclude areas where the extreme land-extensive technology has been applied, i.e. those areas left uncultivated, which now have a zero yield. It is significant to note that, on the basis of a breakdown of area data by crop (Eckert, and Wykstra, 1980, Table 8), and the yield data in Table 10.6, total production of maize is only 10 per cent higher in 1976/77 than in 1973/74 and sorghum and wheat production is lower in 1976/77 than in 1973/74. Even

TABLE 10.6 *Crop yields recorded by uniform crop cutting field surveys in Lesotho (kg/ha)*

Crop year	Maize	Sorghum	Wheat	Comments Rain	Evaluation
1960/61	687	783	850	+15%	Normal-good
1969/70	514	688	544	-30%	Drought
1973/74	945	1008	745	+ 3%	Normal
'Normal'[a]	816	896	798		
1974/75	652	684	823	+10%	Normal-good
1975/76	579	555	799	+39%	Excess rain
1976/77	1568	1467	1373	+15%	Normal-good
1977/78	1408	1447	1359	+14%	Normal-good
1978/79	1058	1345	952	-16%	Oct-Nov dry

Source and note:
Eckert and Wykstra, 1980, Table 9
a) Average of the two years 1960/61 and 1973/4

accepting the disputed yield estimates, and assuming a 2.5 per cent per annum growth in the number of farm-households, per household production of maize was no higher in 1976/77 than in 1973/74, and those of sorghum and wheat were lower.

Thus, even though yields per hectare (and presumably per labour unit) have increased substantially, these increases do not represent a significant increase in farm-household production. The World Bank's conclusion that such yield increases cannot have actually taken place, since they imply 'a major breakthrough in Lesotho agriculture' (IBRD, 1980b, annex 7, p. 6), is symptomatic of the simple farm-orientated view of farm-household production, which leads to the assessment of performance in terms of measurements such as crop yields per hectare. We will expand on this theme in Chapter 11.

Notes

1 These official data are the subject of some controversy. However project-level records indicate that while yields may not have increased as indicated by the official statistics, they have not declined over the period (IBRD, 1980b, Annex 7, p. 10).
2 Schultz (1976, p. 8) suggests that the costs of migration are likely to increase with age as familial obligations and ancillary social relationships become less readily ruptured.
3 Note that, according to conventional theory, marginal returns to labour are expected to increase as labour is withdrawn.
4 Some women with relatively high salaries will employ child-care services to enable them to continue to work.
5 Such as less thorough seedbed preparation, broadcasting of seed and fertilizer rather than row planting and fertilizer placement, and reduced weeding.
6 In Malawi some farm-households reach a compromise between keeping some family members on the land full-time and asking others to cultivate it. It is reported that in many of the

villages around Lilongwe young wives join their husbands in town during the dry season and return to the villages to cultivate their lands when the rains start.
7 Rutman (1971) has applied similar reasoning to explain the 'misuse' of land in Transkei. He argues that traditional forms of tenure, absence of leasehold agreements or a monetary price for land use result in inappropriate resource pricing and distorted patterns of use. We would agree with this, but would also point out that the traditional forms of tenure have significant non-market and non-farm benefits and prevailing use patterns seem less distorted when non-market and non-farm production is taken into consideration.
8 Evidence of reductions in crop production as wage incomes rise is provided by Minford and Ohs (1976) for Malawi. They used multiple regression analysis to evaluate determinants of the supply of agricultural labour and found a significant (.05) inverse relationship between the returns to non-farm employment opportunities and the amount of labour used in farming. Elkan (1960, p. 34) noted that in Buganda in 1924 rapid increases in cotton prices resulted in the almost total withdrawal of Ganda workers, who had previously provided a large portion of the local labour supply. Later, when cotton prices were depressed in 1928–9, Ganda began again to provide a large part of the labour supply.
9 In contrast with previous sample surveys, the 1976 sample coverage included crops grown in gardens next to the house and metric measurements were also used for the first time. Re-examination of the primary questionnaire indicates that inclusion of garden plots cannot have resulted in more than a 3–5 per cent change in the national totals. The World Bank (IBRD, 1980b) considers that the yield improvements indicated by the data have not in fact taken place, since project records do not show such dramatic improvements.

11 Rural development: towards a broader perspective

In Chapter 3 we drew attention to the World Bank's concern that per capita food production had fallen in Africa as a whole in the 1970s, despite the fact that this period had witnessed an unprecedented effort by governments and donors to stimulate and expand food production. This effort has been directed in the main through the medium of the rural development project which was conceived of in the following terms:

> Since rural development is intended to reduce poverty, it must be clearly designed to increase production and raise productivity. Rural development recognizes, however, that improved food supplies and nutrition, together with basic services such as health and education, cannot only directly improve the physical well-being and quality of life of the rural poor, but can also indirectly enhance their productivity and their ability to contribute to the national economy. It is concerned with the modernization and monetization of rural society, and with its transition from traditional isolation to integration with the national economy (IBRD, 1975a, p. 3).

In practice, increased production and raised farm productivity have been the primary goals of rural development projects and most projects have been justified and evaluated in these terms. The narrow conception of rural development in terms of farm production alone is a hangover from previous development projects of the 1960s, which concentrated on large-scale agricultural operations (Yudelman, 1981, p. 15). Although project focus changed from the development of a few large commercial enterprises to the development of masses of small subsistence farm-households, project analysis and philosophy remained largely unchanged. The emphasis on farm-specific technical input/output relationships was maintained and rural development projects were seen as vehicles for funding, procuring and supplying technical farm inputs that had proven output potential.[1] The new challenge of rural development was seen in terms of the problems of providing and supplying these inputs to target groups of small farmers in dispersed rural locations. This was where rural development differed from previous project work on large-scale estate development. It was assumed that if the supply problems could be overcome and the inputs successfully delivered, increased market production would automatically follow. Accordingly rural development project planning and implementation efforts, as well as evaluations of project performance, have concentrated on the disbursement of funds, the development of supporting infrastructure and the supply of various inputs to farmers in rural areas.

As anticipated, the input supply problem has not been an easy one to solve. Very few rural development projects in Africa have been implemented according to schedule, and inputs have often not reached the farmer within the time-span or in the quantities anticipated. Herein, it is assumed, lies the reason for the lack of any significant increase in production output despite the considerable efforts that have been mounted. For example, Lele (1979) states that the production impact of rural development projects in eastern and southern Africa has been disappointing compared with achievements elsewhere (e.g. Asia and Latin America) because it has proved difficult to deliver the necessary technical and infrastructural improvements in those sparsely populated and institutionally underdeveloped countries. Such an evaluation is, of course, directly influenced by and follows from the narrow technocratic input/output view of rural development, which assumes that if farm inputs had been successfully delivered, increased farm output would have been forthcoming.

Such a simple input/output approach to the technology of rural development has been challenged by McInerney (1978, p. 9), who argues that it is essential to look for the impact of rural development beyond the listing and valuation of farm input and output changes. Whereas it is possible to view agricultural production of a large estate as the singular activity that determines its existence and by which its performance may be judged, for the farm-household, agricultural production is but one facet of a complex rural system within which it operates. Seen in this light, rural development is, as McInerney (1978, p. 9) puts it:

> not specifically an economic problem, nor a technical one, nor social, nor political. It is a problem of matching (a) the external influences offered by alternative production methods, public investments, or other policy interventions, with (b) the internal characteristics of the rural system as reflected not only by technical parameters but by the nature of the power hierarchy, the distribution of wealth, the land tenure system, farm size structure, the extent of market development, the traditions of interdependence or social obligations, historical and cultural factors, and so on.

While still remaining short of such an all-embracing analysis of rural development, it is possible to go some way to broadening the narrow farm input/output concept of rural development by viewing project implementation and impact in a household-economics framework which includes non-market and non-farm factors in the analysis. These non-market and non-farm aspects of the economy of the farm-household have been given little attention by development planners in southern Africa, even though, as we have shown in the preceding chapters they form an important part of the socio-economic environment in which farm-households operate.

First, we will note that, while African farmers in the region have not been slow to adopt agricultural innovations under certain circumstances, formal attempts to increase production and productivity per hectare have been largely unsuccessful. More recent attempts to increase production have also achieved little success, even though implementation has been good and certain productivity-increasing inputs supplied under the projects have been widely adopted. This leads us to re-evaluate these projects in terms of their non-farm benefits and to suggest that earlier innovations can be interpreted in the same way.

Agricultural innovations and development initiatives

An historical perspective

Indigenous farmers in southern Africa have not been slow to adopt new farming techniques under certain circumstances. The widespread and rapid adoption of the plough in the first half of this century is a prime example of this. In Chapter 4 we noted the early purchase of the plough in Botswana and Lesotho (Murray, 1980; Spray, 1975; Schapera, 1947). Yudelman (1964b, p. 238) reports a similar expansion in plough ownership in Zimbabwe. Between 1900 and 1920 it is estimated that plough ownership in that country increased from 1 per 200 farm families to 1 per 20 farm families. Knight and Lenta (1980, Table 1) provide evidence of similar increases in capital-equipment ownership on African farms in South Africa between 1930 and 1965 (see Table 11.7). Nor has the introduction of the plough been the only change to take place in farming methods. The use of the ox as a draught animal was a necessary complementary innovation. Maize continues to replace other indigenous grain staples (millet and sorghum) and, as Miracle (1968, p. 304) points out, improved maize varieties as well as ploughs have been widely adopted by farmers in Zambia and Zimbabwe. Fertilizer use also expanded considerably in Swaziland, with the use of inorganic fertilizers increasing by 387 per cent during the 1950s (Daniel, 1966, p. 508). In Swaziland these increases in fertilizer use have continued, with the average application of 12 kg/ha in 1960 increasing to 53 kg/ha by 1975/6. Similarly in Malawi and Zambia fertilizer use increased by 12 per cent per annum between 1970 and 1976 (Mudahar, 1980, Table 2).

Despite this early and continuing adoption of improved farming methods, per hectare productivity has remained low and governments and administrators have sought to increase indigenous farm production through a variety of development programmes. However, few of these programmes have succeeded in increasing productivity per hectare or total production to any significant extent. For example Yudelman (1964b, p 144) contrasts the widespread spontaneous adoption of the plough in Zimbabwe with the disappointing impact of a scheme to demonstrate and extend improved production methods in the 1930s. The improved production methods gave yields per hectare up to five times those being achieved with traditional methods but involved labour-using technologies, such as early planting, row planting, manure or fertilizer applications and better weeding.

In Botswana a rural development effort was mounted in the wake of the Pim Commission in 1932. The programme included water development, stationing of agricultural demonstrators in rural areas and the establishment of livestock improvement centres. The production impact was minimal and labour migration out of the territory continued apace. Similarly in Lesotho an agricultural experimental station was established in Maseru as early as 1935 and a crop improvement programme was set up which aimed at increasing production through better cultivation methods, fertilizing and manuring of crops and use of better seed.

In Swaziland the 1948–56 Rural Development Scheme concentrated on improving methods of land utilization. The programme included conservation methods, improved crop husbandry, cash cropping, rural education and consideration of new land-tenure arrangements. Despite the rapid uptake of fertilizers and the introduction of the practice of planting crops on the contour between grass strips (which has been a highly successful conservation measure), the production impact of the scheme was said to be disappointing, failing 'in its efforts to increase food production, introduce cash cropping on an extensive scale and educate the Swazi toward a new way of life on the land' (Daniel, 1966, p. 508). Similar government schemes for soil conservation or education in improved farming methods have been largely unsuccessful in Transkei and Ciskei (Houghton, 1964, p. 308).

In Lesotho a review of seven separate agricultural development programmes between 1953 and 1980 led to the conclusion that 'after 20 years of experimentation with intensive area based projects there is little improvement in production that can be attributed to them' (IBRD, 1980b, Annex 7, p. 32).

Recent experience in Swaziland and Lesotho

The concept of the current Rural Development Areas Programme (RDAP) in Swaziland was first mooted in 1965. Implementation of the first of a series of area-based projects that comprise the existing programme began in 1970. Each development area of around 20–30 000 ha has a project centre where the extension, management, farm-input supply and marketing facilities are situated. Development activities include the establishment, staffing and running of the project centre as well as the construction of basic infrastructure, such as feeder roads, conservation earthworks, stock-watering dams, piped water supplies and health and education facilities. The development strategy of the RDAP was based on the assumption that agricultural production was held up principally because of poor rural infrastructure and shortage of adequately trained extension workers (ODA, 1981). More specifically, on the production side, it was 'hoped that the introduction of hybrid maize would lead to higher yields per unit area which would enable families to meet their consumption requirements from a smaller area of land, thereby releasing land for cash crop production.' (ODA, 1981).

The RDAP has been supported by numerous other internationally funded agricultural development projects such as the UNDP Crop Production and Extension Project, the UNDP Livestock Production and Extension Project, the CIDA Dairy Project, and the USAID Soil Conservation Project. Most donors now agree that the production impact of the RDAP and its complementary projects has been disappointing (ODA, 1981; IBRD, 1980a; USAID, 1980). This is despite fairly good, if lagged, implementation and better than expected uptake of the major production inputs. Figures 11.1 and 11.2 (extracted from Low and Fowler, 1979) give a representative picture of the implementation and crop production performance of the RDAP in general. The area used as an example is situated in a particularly favourable maize and tobacco growing area.

Figure 11.1 shows that, apart from the land development item, physical and financial implementation of the project has been successfully carried out. A number of physical works in addition to those in the original plans have also been completed. These include two drifts, eleven diversions, three artificial waterways, one-hundred hectares of bush clearing and the laying down of sixty hectares of grass strips. Although expenditure was sluggish to start with,

138 *Rural development: towards a broader perspective*

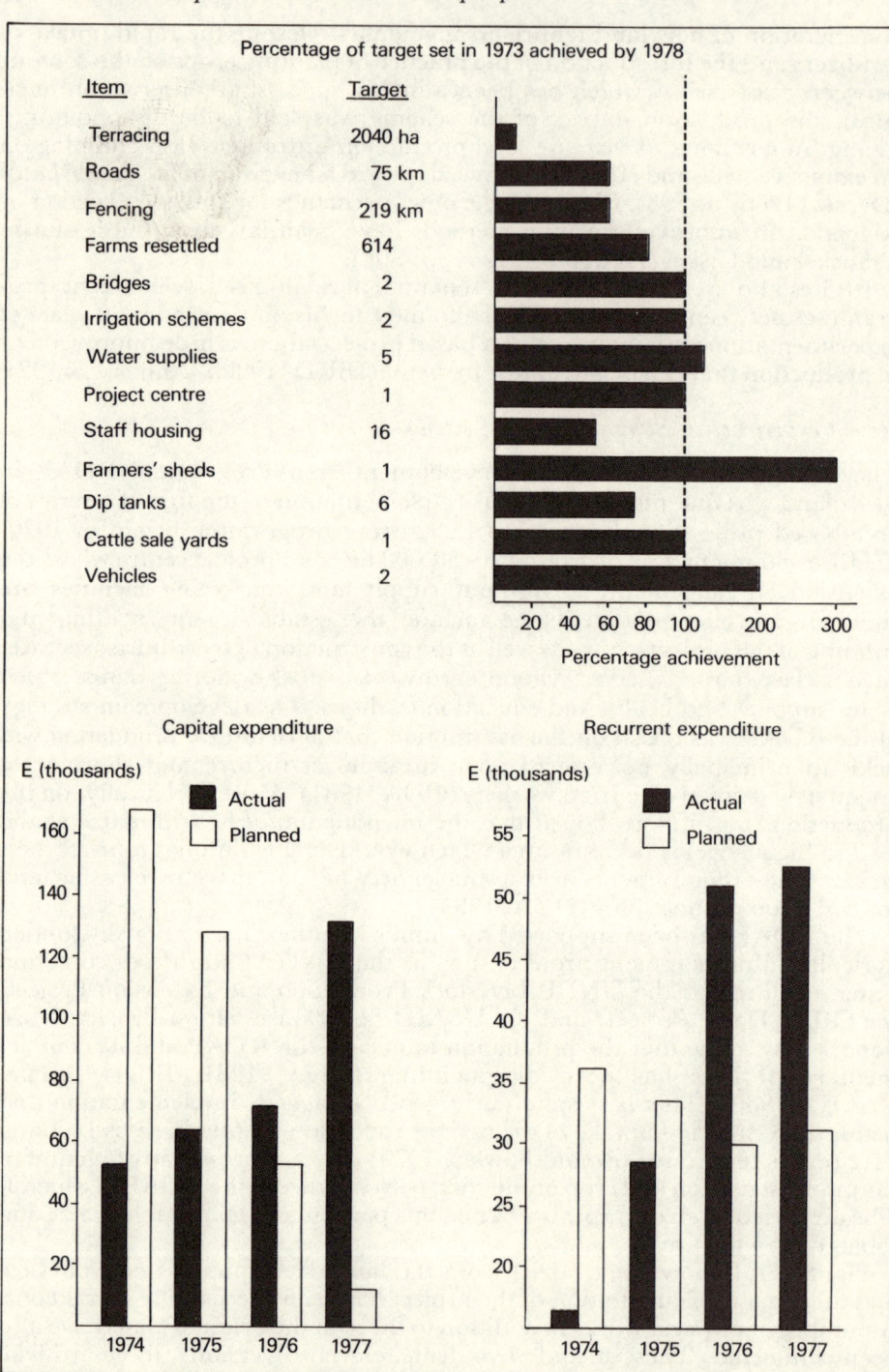

FIGURE 11.1:   *Mahlangatsha RDA: physical and financial performance*

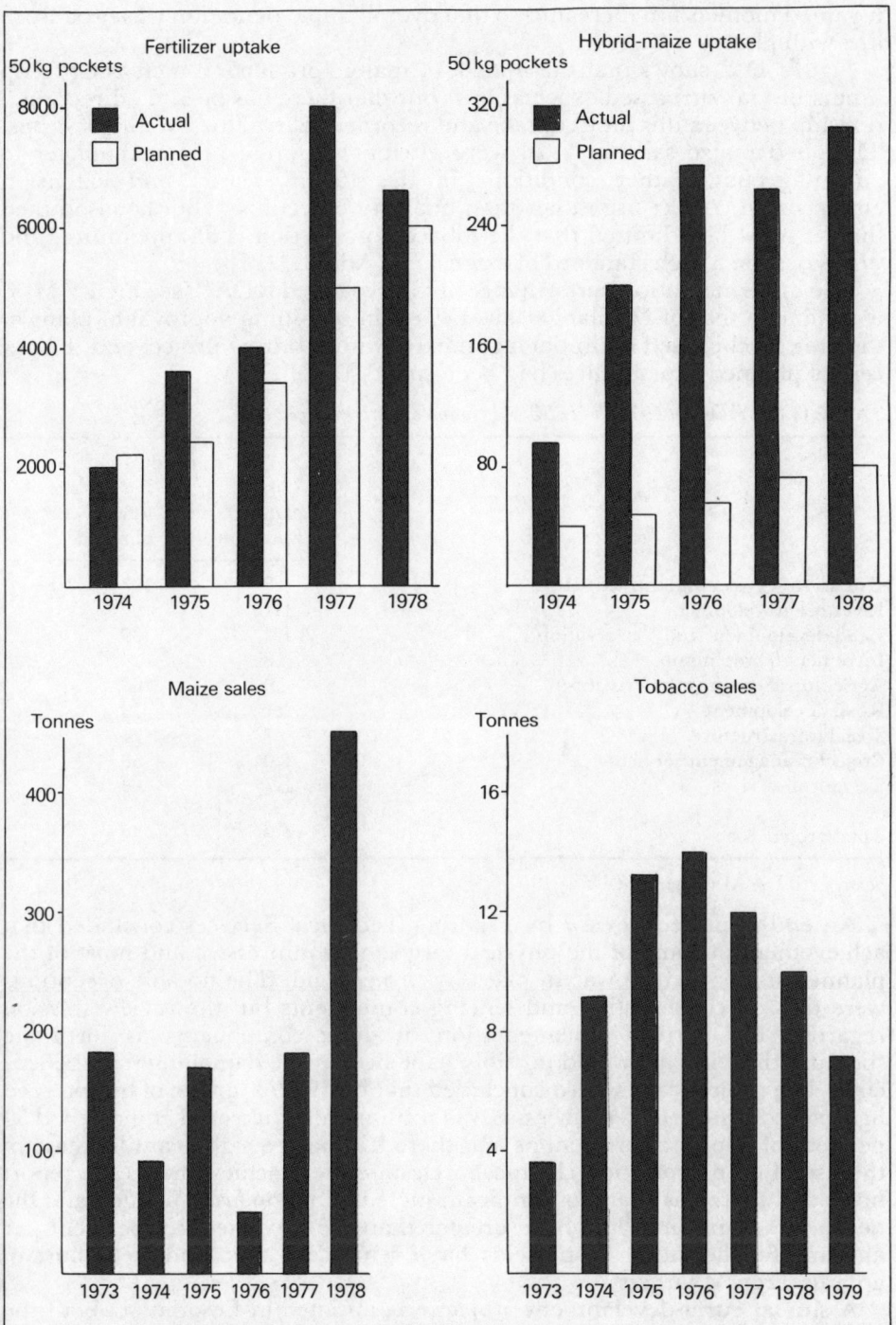

FIGURE 11.2: *Mahlangatsha RDA: input uptake and production performance*

it gained momentum thereafter so that overall implementation was broadly in line with plans.

Figure 11.2 shows that the uptake of major 'production-increasing' crop inputs has far surpassed expectations, but that there has been no direct relationship between this input uptake and recorded sales of the two major crops. The good maize sales in 1978 were attributed by the project manager to advantageous weather conditions in the 1977/8 season and extension emphasis on correct use rather than quantity of fertilizer. But he also noted that 'it must be admitted that the tobacco production is disappointing, and this is despite a high standard of extension' (Adams, 1978).

The implementation performance of the expanded RDAP (see Figure 11.3) is similar to that of Mahlangatsha. Delays in obtaining approval of plans at the area level caused an initial lag in expenditure but by project end, 82 per cent of planned expenditures had been spent (Table 11.1).

TABLE 11.1 *RDAP (1977/8–1982/3): financial performance*

	Expenditure	
	Total planned E million	Percentage of total planned
Extension services and infrastructure	4.8	103
Livestock development	1.7	96
Land development and conservation	1.3	39
Incremental crop inputs	.8	24
Agricultural credit (infrastructure)	.8	103
Road development	2.1	73
Social infrastructure	.7	71
Project management services	1.0	50
Technical services	1.7	98
Total project costs	14.9	82

Source: RDA Management Unit, 1981c

An end-of-project review by Hunting Technical Services concluded that achievement of some of the physical targets was impressive and most of the planned infrastructure was in place by project end. The notable exceptions were the soil conservation and fencing components but the review mission regarded the partial implementation of these components as fortunate 'because their impact would possibly have been more damaging than beneficial'. The project review also concluded that by 1982/3 uptake of hybrid seed had exceeded targets, fertilizer use was substantially increased and reached 50 per cent of appraisal projections and there had been a significant increase in the use of crop-protection chemicals. Despite these achievements the report notes that there has been no significant increase in crop areas planted and the decline in maize area had been greater than the predicted 2.4 per cent per annum. Furthermore, crop yields have remained static and well short of appraisal report targets.

A similar rural-development project was initiated in Lesotho at about the same time as Mahlangatsha RDA. This was the Thaba Bosiu Project, which became effective in 1973 and was intended to assist some 12 000 farmers in the lowlands and foothills south and east of Maseru. Its main objectives were:

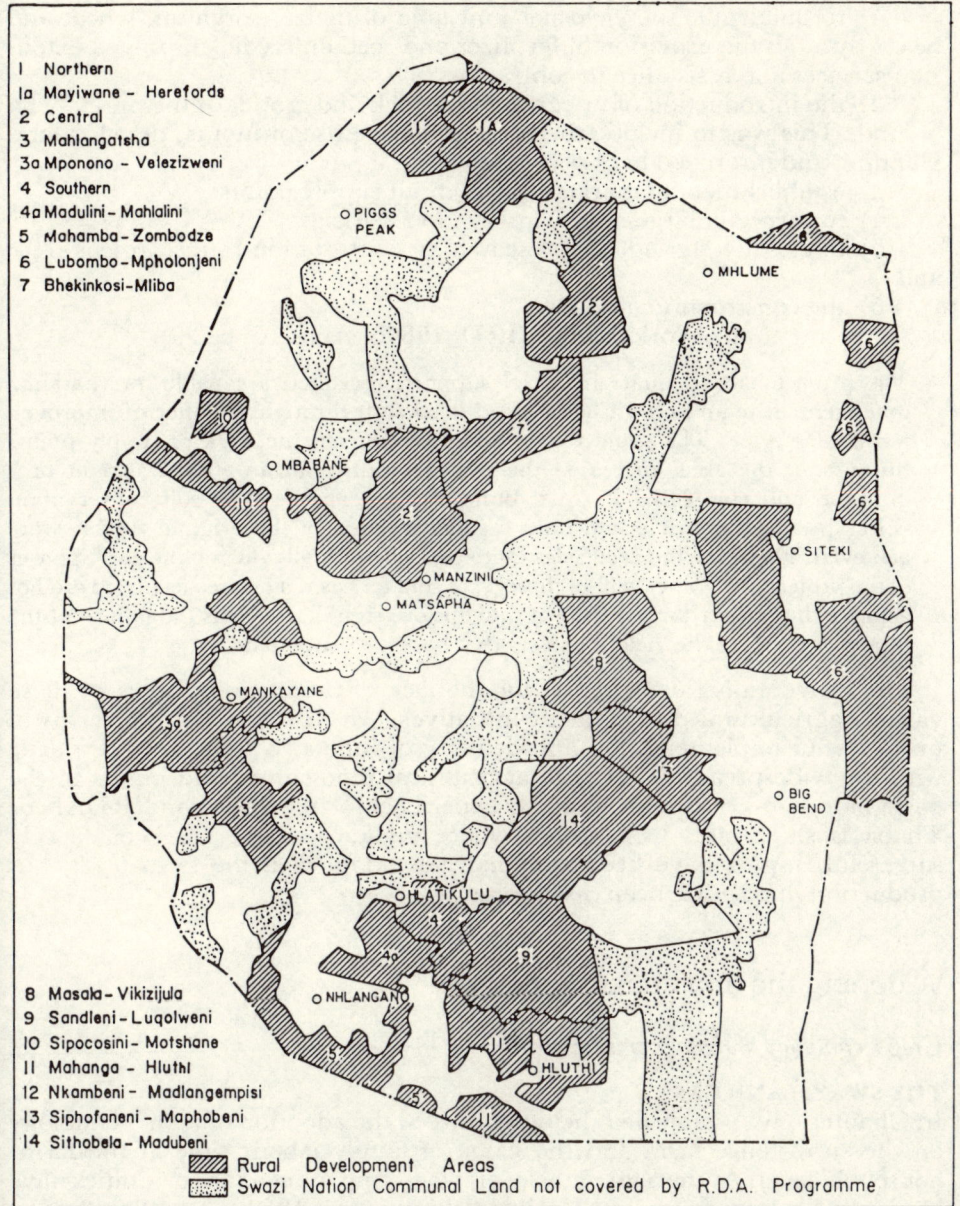

FIGURE 11.3: *Rural development areas programme (1977/8–82/3)*

1) to quadruple the yield per unit area of maize, sorghum, wheat and beans through the provision of fertilizer and seed on credit, improved extension services and assistance to contractors;

2) the introduction of integrated livestock and crop farming on 2000 ha of land. This was to include the more intensive use of inputs, detailed land planning and improved livestock production;

3) establishment of marketing and input supply points;

4) to carry out large-scale conservation works;

5) to conduct agricultural research at a sub-station in the project area; and

6) the construction of roads.

According to the World Bank (IBRD, 1980b, Annex 7, p. 29):

> The project had adequate financial support, recruited a capable international management team and attracted good local staff through the offer of improved terms of service. The project established an efficient network of supply points throughout the area, increased the use of inputs, ran an effective credit programme and completed its road building programme. The soil conservation works proved expensive and only a small fraction of the original targets were achieved. Fertiliser and seed sales increased substantially during the early phases of the project and 75 per cent of these were sold for cash. The area fertilized did not achieve the project targets, but of much more significance was the failure of the inputs to produce the yield increases that had been anticipated.

The conventional explanation for the lack of production impact of these various agricultural development initiatives, which is provided in terms of unsuccessful implementation and delivery of inputs, is difficult to reconcile with the widespread adoption of agricultural innovations and inputs in the past. Nor is it consistent with the experience of the Swaziland RDAP or Thaba Bosiu project in Lesotho, where implementation has been largely successful, inputs have been supplied and adopted at the farm level, but production impact has been disappointing.

Widening the analytical framework

Crop technology and wage employment

THE SWAZILAND CASE

In Chapter 8 we established the link between the adoption of crop technology on the subsistence farm and the value of family labour time at the farm-household level. At the aggregate level, wage employment opportunities have been steadily expanding in Swaziland through the 1960s and 1970s, as the census data in Table 11.2 indicate.

While the inter-census data are not directly comparable because of definitional changes, the data differences are large enough to point to a real sustained increase in wage employment over the last two decades. Of particular significance is the increase in female employment between 1966 and 1976, since it is the females who provide the bulk of the labour hours put into food crop production on the farm.

During the 1970s wage rates also rose quite markedly in both absolute and relative terms. Table 11.3 shows how employment and wages rose rapidly in the first half of the decade, reached a peak in 1976 and have levelled out since then. A similar picture is given in Figure 11.4 produced by Hunting Technical Services in their RDAP project review report.

TABLE 11.2 *Percentage of de facto working-age population[a] in wage employment*

	Total	Males	Females
Census years			
1956	24.6		
1966	30.6	47.9	12.7
1976	36.5	49.1	23.2

Sources and note:
  Swaziland Government (1979b), Tables XIII.2, XVI.3 XVI.5; Colonial Annual Report (1960)
  a) 18 + years for 1956, 15 + years for 1966 and 1976

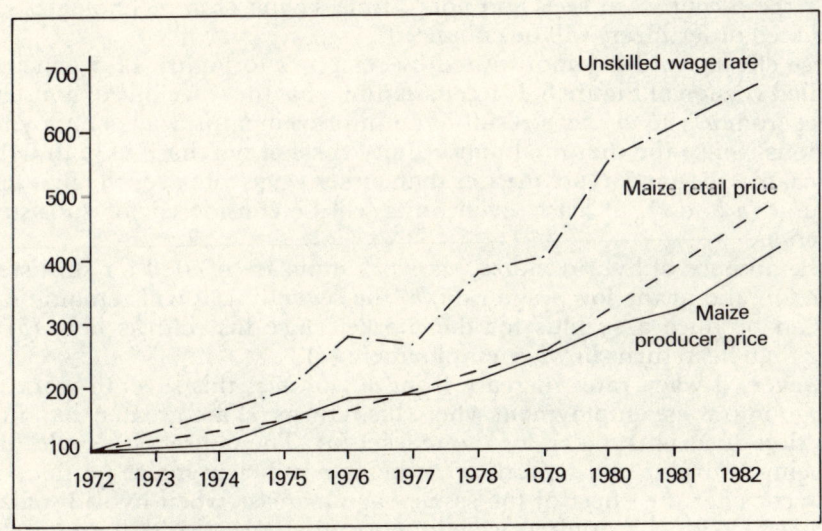

FIGURE 11.4: *Movements in wage rates and maize prices 1972–82*

Source:
  Review of the rural development areas programme final report, annex C, figure C.5, Hunting Technical Services, October 1983

TABLE 11.3 Employment and wage rates (1971–82)

Year	Formal modern sector employment	RSA mine employment	Average monthly unskilled wage in Swaziland (W1)	Average monthly RSA mine earnings (W2)	Index of wages relative to maize price (1971 = 100) for: W1	W2
1971	42 426	6 653	E27	E18	100	100
1972	47 051	6 901	23	21	84	116
1973	57 032	7 859	25	29	91	156
1974	62 061	9 350	28	47	134	249
1975	64 664	16 272	49	79	125	302
1976	66 215	20 462	51	92	105	284
1977	66 225	15 016	53	102	103	298
1978	71 256	14 284	71	112	123	291
1979	73 767	10 397	80	125	117	274
1982	77 357	13 690	125	—	112	—

Sources: Swaziland Annual Statistical Bulletins; *Rand Daily Mail*, 30 July 1977; TEBA Head Office, Siteki

From the point of view of rural production, increasing off-farm job opportunities and wage rates will increase the wage potential of the on-farm worker (Wi) and the full cost of producing Z goods on the farm will increase. In such a situation two types of response can be expected:

1) the equilibrium labour allocation position will shift towards the allocation of more work units to wage employment and less on-farm;

2) the incentive to seek and adopt time-saving crop technologies (e.g. hybrid seed or fertilizer) will be enhanced.

These effects can be demonstrated by reference to Figure 11.5 which is a simplified version of Figure 8.1. Let us assume that the wage line of household y moves from $w'y$ to $w'z$ as a result of an improvement in wage employment conditions. Since the marginal opportunity costs of purchase of both hybrid and local maize (e and d) are greater than either wage rate over the first seven work unit (a and c), at least seven units will be considered for subsistence production.

In the absence of hybrid maize, six work units are needed for subsistence production and at the low wage rate (a) the seventh unit will remain on the farm and produce a surplus for the market since his returns here (b) are greater than his returns in wage employment (a).

However, if wage rates increase from $w'y$ to $w'z$, this seventh work unit would go into wage employment where his returns (c) are greater than in the production of surplus maize for the market (b). The household would move from being a surplus maize producer to being a sufficient maize producer.

Now consider the effect of the same wage increase when hybrid maize is introduced. With the original wage-opportunity curve ($w'y$) the household was indifferent to the adoption of hybrid maize (see Chapter 8, page 95). With the steepened wage-opportunity curve ($w'z$), it now becomes advantageous to adopt hybrid maize and, in doing so, the household will further reduce its on-farm work unit allocation from six to four. This is because only

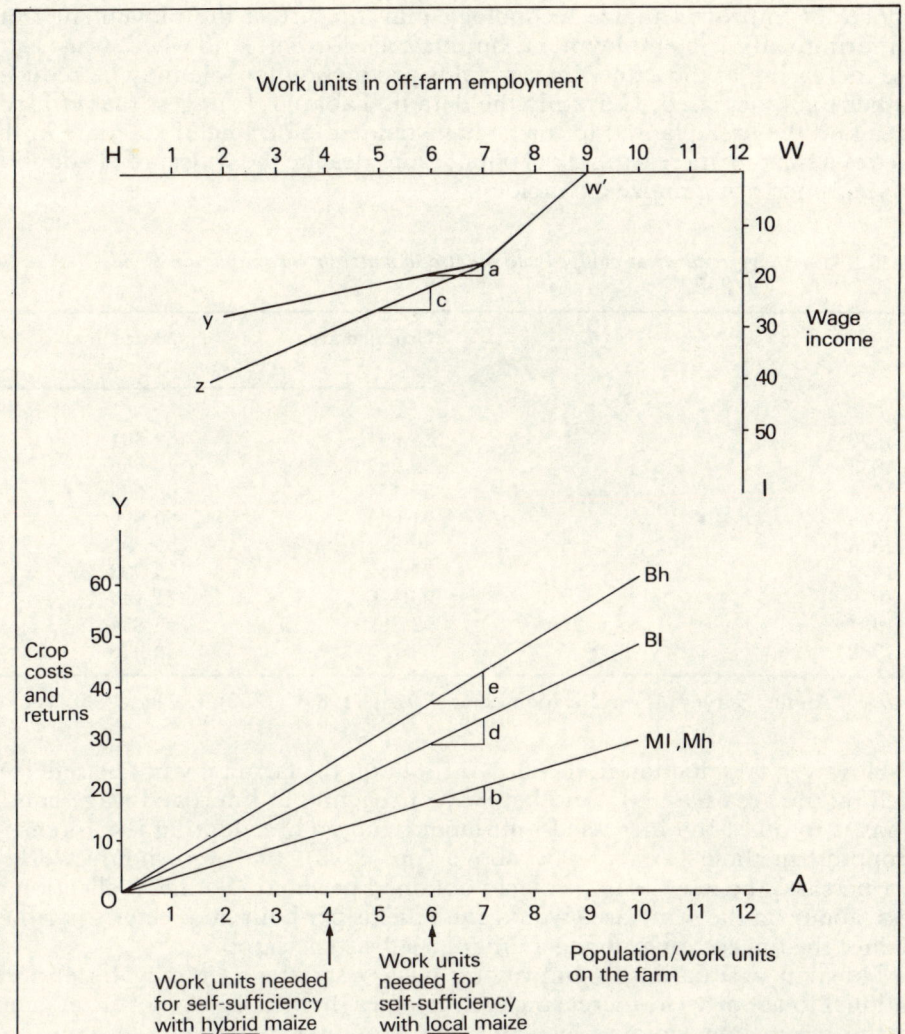

FIGURE 11.5: *Effects of increased wages and hybrid-maize on household labour allocation*

four units are now needed for subsistence production and the next three units all earn more in wage employment (*c*) than the production of surplus maize for the market (*b*).

The net effect of a simultaneous improvement in wage conditions and provision of improved crop technology is to reduce the number of work units allocated to the farm from seven to four.[2] Not only that, a rise in job opportunities and wage rates can lead to substantial increases in total household income. The higher marginal utility of leisure at these higher incomes would have the effect of reducing the work input of each member. We have already noted this effect in relation to the reduction in cropped area in Lesotho in the mid-1970s (see Chapter 10, Table 10.5).

On the basis of this analysis it is possible to argue that the introduction and uptake of improved maize technology may not arrest the movement from on-farm to off-farm employment, but may reinforce it. And where wage rates are increasing at the same time, surplus production for sale may be reduced rather than increased. Certainly the data in Table 11.4 suggest that cropped area and the area planted to maize have tended to decline or stagnate in the face of a steadily increasing rural population, despite the widespread adoption of yield-increasing maize technology.

TABLE 11.4 *Aggregate areas cropped and planted to maize on Swazi Nation Land, 1972–82*

Year	Cropped area	Maize area
	Hectares	
1972	84 691	62 381
1973	89 967	70 555
1974	86 154	68 885
1975	91 634	60 999
1976	89 381	59 799
1977	77 132	53 902
1979	98 416	71 145
1981	92 262	55 654
1982	89 752	58 936

Source: Annual Survey of Swazi Nation Land, (1977), (1980), (1982); Fowler, 1980, Table 4

However, a reduction in the labour input on the farm may not be reflected well by the area planted. Another way of reacting to improved wage conditions is to offset the increased unit-labour charge by adopting less intensive cropping methods. As we saw above (pp. 66–8), the more hours worked per hectare, the less the maize yield obtained per hour. So the application of less labour on the same area would raise yields per hour and, ceteris paribus, reduce the full cost of growing a unit of a subsistence crop.

Thus, in a situation of improving wage conditions, it may be entirely rational to adopt yield-increasing technologies (hybrid maize, fertilizer) and, at the same time, employ less intensive cropping methods. We have suggested that this is what took place in Lesotho in the mid-1970s (see above, p. 131). Of course, from the agronomic point of view, this is the opposite of what should take place and is counter-productive, in that the yield-increasing potential of most of the new technologies is drastically reduced if 'correct' (which invariably means more labour-intensive) husbandry methods are not applied. Nevertheless, we have seen how it may be perfectly rational from the point of view of the Swazi farm-household and it could help to explain why aggregate maize yields on Swazi Nation Land have shown no tendency to increase despite the widespread adoption of yield-increasing technologies such as hybrid seed and fertilizer (see Table 11.5).[3]

Another factor likely to reduce the yield-increasing potential of improved crop technologies is the movement of workers to off-farm employment following wage improvements. This leaves fewer hands on the farm and reduces Chayanov's positive 'complex co-operation' effect.

TABLE 11.5 *Average Swazi Nation Land maize yields (kg/ha)*

		Swaziland	Highveld	Middleveld	Lowveld	Lubombo
Year and Rainfall (mm)[a]						
1972	1091	1762	1602	1658	2226	2132
1973	581	1104	1285	1028	929	1374
1974	698	1577	1717	1640	1175	2055
1975	816	1442	1488	1577	1137	1273
1976	918	1440	1401	1420	1541	674
1977	692	1276	1453	1245	1201	1159
1978	738	1787	1874	1751	1648	2667
1979	541	918	1286	1021	474	426
1980	625	1360	1974	1217	1006	1577
Partial correlation coefficient[b]		.11	.45	.07	−.01	−.13

Source and notes:
   Fowler, 1980, Table 5
   a) Nhlangano-Manzini mean value for October-March
   b) Correlation of yields with time after removing the effect of rainfall. None of the coefficients are significant at the .1 level.

In the Swazi farm-household environment, then, attractive wage employment conditions are likely to encourage the adoption of improved technologies that increase yields per unit of time on the one hand but, at the same time, they are likely to reduce the numbers of workers available for farming and to discourage labour-intensive cropping methods. In terms of yields per area of land, the latter two effects will counteract the positive yield effect of the improved technologies.

It is recognized that the use of improved crop technology is already widespread in Swaziland. One report, for example, noted that 'a majority of farmers are already using improved inputs on their farms. It is no longer a problem of using fertilizer or not' (RDA Management Unit, 1981a, p. 19). Consequently the RDA management is now emphasizing the need to improve husbandry methods. But the forgoing analysis suggests that this may be difficult to achieve while wage employment conditions remain good.

PARALLEL EXAMPLES

In Lesotho maize yield response to fertilizer exhibits a similar pattern to that obtained in Swaziland. According to the results of the regression analysis discussed in Chapter 7, the partial-regression coefficients indicate that fertilizer has a positive and significant effect on maize yields per hour (Low, 1982 (b), Table 7.5). A complementary correlation analysis of the same data, which allows a comparison with similar data available for Lesotho is given in Table 11.6.

These data indicate that in both Lesotho and Swaziland there is a significant positive correlation between fertilizer use and maize *yields* per hectare (and per hour in the case of Swaziland). However there is no such significant positive correlation of fertilizer use with maize *gross margins* per hectare (or gross margin per hour in the case of Swaziland). Nevertheless, in both Lesotho and Swaziland, fertilizer has been widely adopted. In the case of Lesotho the World Bank (IBRD, 1980b, Annex 7, p. 24) concludes that:

TABLE 11.6 *Simple correlation coefficients of fertilizer with maize yields and gross margins in Lesotho and Swaziland*[a]

	Per hectare		Per hour	
	Yield	Gross margin	Yield	Gross margin
Lesotho				
Thaba Bosiu RDP	.334	.058	n.a	n.a
Swaziland				
North RDA (n = 131)	.373	.015	.140	.054
	(.001)	(.433)	(.055)	(.270)
South RDA (n = 130)	.148	−.334	.460	−.167
	(.047)	(.001)	(.001)	(.027)

Source and note:
  IBRD, 1980b, Annex 7, p. 24
  a) Significance of correlation coefficient given in parentheses.

What is clear from existing data is that the use of fertilizer in the absence of a range of complementary husbandry practices does not usually result in large increases in yields. . . This is not atypical of experience elsewhere, *but fertilizer appears to be commonly used in Lesotho as if it were a substitute for good husbandry rather than a complement to it* (emphasis added).

To the Bank Mission, with their narrow farm-production perspective, this behaviour seems quite perplexing. However, it can be understood in terms of a household-economics perspective. As with hybrid maize in Swaziland, fertilizers in Lesotho have obviously not been adopted for commercial purposes (since gross margins are not increased thereby), but to increase the amount of food produced per unit of time. In other words they are a substitute for time-intensive crop production methods (i.e. good husbandry). Fertilizer use represents the substitution of a money-expensive technique for a time-intensive one in the production of a non-market household consumption good. So long as this remains its main function, it is quite illogical to expect fertilizer use to be accompanied by more intensive inputs of time into cropping.

Knight and Lenta (1980) suggest that the same rationale was behind the investment in capital equipment by African farmers in South Africa (see Table 11.7). They note the early growth in the numbers of ploughs and more recently in other forms of capital equipment, including tractors and continue:

> It is interesting that capital equipment increased without there being any significant increase in arable production. Probably the plough (replacing the hoe) and the cultivator, planter and tractor all substituted for labour rather than for land. Family labour thus released could enter or remain longer in migrant wage employment or could avoid arduous hoeing.[4]

In Zimbabwe also, rapid investment in the plough took place during a period when the percentage of able-bodied males engaged in off-farm employment rose from 12 per cent at the turn of the century, to 45 per cent by 1954. Over this same period the acreage cultivated per family rose considerably, with a 140 per cent greater population cultivating 260–270 per cent more land. However, output per family did not increase much: a 140 per cent increase in rural population was accompanied by only a 140–150 per cent increase in output (Yudelman, 1964b, p. 237). In Malawi, Gemmill (1971) found that oxen power was adopted, not because it resulted in any market increase in profitability, but because it reduced the drudgery of hoe cultivation. As Yudelman observes, the plough in Zimbabwe (like capital equipment in South Africa, like hybrid maize in Swaziland and like fertilizer in Lesotho) was adopted as a labour-saving device at a time when off-farm wage employment opportunities, and thus the market value of household members' time, was increasing. Like the other innovations, the adoption of the plough in Zimbabwe did not result in any increase in yield per hectare (the Morris Carter Commission of 1925 suggested that the adoption of the plough reduced per hectare yields) or in any more output per farm-household. Nevertheless it was obviously of considerable benefit to farm-households, where men were released into more remunerative wage employment and women were released from the drudgery of hoe cultivation.

TABLE 11.7 *Cereal production and capital equipment in South African reserves, 1930–69*

	Cereal production (90 kg bags)			Capital equipment (no. in thousands)			
	Total (thousands)	Per capita		Ploughs	Cultivators	Planters	Tractors
Year			*Year*				
1934–6	3120	1.02	1930	185	—	—	—
1946–8	4068	1.25	1950	314	86	47	—
1955–7	3391	0.90	1955	321	106	58	370
1965–9	2341	0.40	1965	341	117	71	2682

Source: cited in Knight and Lenta (1980)

In this context it is interesting to reflect on the rapid acceptance of hybrid maize in Zambia, Zimbabwe and Swaziland compared with the much lower rate of adoption of similar varieties in Malawi, where extension efforts to persuade farmers to grow hybrids have, if anything, been more vigorous but where real wage rates and employment opportunities have remained well below those in neighbouring countries.

Social infrastructure and household production

Although integrated rural development projects of the late 1970s have been justified and evaluated in terms of their impact on farm production, they have typically included a number of social-infrastructural components to which no direct incremental farm production has been attached. The components have included schools, health clinics, water supplies and retail stores. In addition, other infrastructural developments such as rural roads, erosion-control earthworks and fencing on grazing areas were expected to contribute to increased production in a general way.

In Swaziland these components of the development programme were excluded from the plans of eight of the ten areas to be developed under an expansion phase of the RDAP. In the eight areas, designated 'minimum input areas', investments were confined to the directly productive components: input supply sheds and farm inputs, marketing stores, and extension officers, together with their housing and transport. The reasons for limiting the inputs in these areas were 1) that considerable potential was thought to exist for increasing production through the supply of farm inputs and extension alone, and, 2) that the capacity to undertake infrastructural developments was limited, so a wider immediate coverage could be achieved by leaving these components to a subsequent phase of development in most areas.

When it came to discussing the development plans with the chiefs and people of the areas, it became apparent that there was as great or greater demand for the non-productive or indirectly productive infrastructure as for the directly productive 'minimum input' components. In particular water supply and fencing of grazing areas were considered to be the most important parts of the programme, so far as the majority of farm-households were concerned, and communities were dismayed to learn that these were not to be included in the initial development of their areas. Some empirical confirmation of this reaction is given by the results of two related rural household surveys, in which respondents were asked about their perceptions of development needs in their area. The results are given in Table 11.8.

TABLE 11.8 *Percentage of households mentioning particular development needs*

	Rural homestead surveys	
	Initial survey June 1978[a] (n = 457)	Complete survey May 1979[b] (n = 1150)
Water supplies	55.0	51.3
Agricultural assistance	51.2	49.1
Health clinics	29.3	28.6
Transport/roads	24.9	24.7
Education facilities	20.1	22.9
Marketing/shopping facilities	21.0	19.9

Sources:
  a) de Vletter, 1979, p. 77
  b) de Vletter, 1983, section 7

These results were obtained without asking any leading questions or ticking pre-determined items. The categories were made up subsequently from written responses which mentioned an issue(s) related to the specified areas. The perceived need for improved water supplies is quite evident. The agricultural assistance category was composed of a diverse range of activities, which included fencing of grazing areas. Health, education, transport and retail facilities are the other items that featured most prominently. In a pilot survey, conducted in the Northern Rural Development Area, piped water supplies and more schools and classrooms were given as the major desired developments (de Vletter, 1978, p. 29).

The emphasis given to water supplies is not surprising, considering that most households devote considerable time and energy to the procurement of stream water. The demand for fencing is related to the time saved in herding, but it is also associated with the conflicts that exist between the strong desire for children to be able to attend school and attain educational qualifications on the one hand, and short-term opportunity costs in terms of childrens' time on the other. Schuh (1974, p. 21) has suggested that, in Brazil, a major impediment to education is the high opportunity cost of childrens' time. To the extent that fencing reduces the opportunity costs of young Swazi boys, who would normally be expected to herd cattle, it reduces the conflict between the desire for long-term investment through education and short-term need for childrens' time in the farm-household.

In terms of our analysis in Figure 4.3, investment in education has the effect of increasing the slope of the WW' line.[5] To the farm-household this is as legitimate an investment as one in farm improvement, which might be expected to increase the slope of the OM line.[6] Given the benefits of education in terms of job prospects in Swaziland (see Table 10.1), it is hardly surprising that educational investment takes a high priority. Berry (1970) has pointed out that high wages provide both the incentive and the wherewithal for educational investment and that, where institutional pressures exist to keep wages relatively high, the resulting pattern of investment in education rather than farming will lead to increasing rural–urban migration.

The point which emerges from the analysis in the last two sections, is that the distinction between directly productive components such as fertilizers, improved seed and tractors on the one hand, and social infrastructure on the other, is not clear cut from the farm-household's point of view. Water supplies and schooling can be just as productive in terms of increasing the value of a household's labour time and overall welfare as fertilizers, tractors or improved varieties.

Implications for the evaluation of rural development

Early rural development projects were evaluated in terms of the level of funds disbursed and expenditures completed. Evaluation procedures have advanced somewhat since then. The continuing lack of production success has encouraged governments and donors to devote more funds, time and staff to the monitoring and evaluation of all stages of rural development projects (witness the international workshops on this subject, see for example, Imboden, 1980, and Deboeck and Kinsey, 1980).

However, evaluation has been confined to the measurement of farm inputs and outputs and has seldom looked beyond the narrow technical input/output premises upon which projects have been originally justified. Thus the World Bank has now decided against future funding on the Swaziland RDAP, since it is accepted that the internal rate of return, as originally estimated in terms of incremental farm production, will not be realized.

While it is recognized that this is associated with the relatively attractive wage employment situation (ODA, 1981; IBRD, 1980a), which was not considered relevant at appraisal, the project is viewed as a failure since the expected production performance has not been achieved. Like the successor to Thaba Bosiu in Lesotho (BASP), the Swaziland RDAP is now regarded as a service project, assisting with institution-building in the Ministry of

Agriculture and the provision of social infrastructure in the rural areas. On account of similar disillusionment with rural development (as narrowly conceived), United Kingdom aid policy has moved away from 'rural development' towards health and education projects over the last few years.

Most people would surely regard the introduction and use of the ox-plough in southern Africa as constituting a major agricultural development achievement, especially in view of the limited success obtained in promoting oxen cultivation elsewhere in Africa over the last twenty years (Eicher and Baker, 1982, p. 142). Yet this development did not result in increased yields or increased per farm production in Zimbabwe or South Africa.[7] Hybrid maize and fertilizer in Swaziland and Lesotho have provided the same farm-household production benefits as the plough, and have produced similarly negligible results in terms of farm output. The provision of piped water has also increased farm-household productivity, as has fencing of grazing land and the expansion of schools and classrooms. As McInerney (1978, p. 9) rightly says, it is essential to look for the impact of rural development 'beyond the listing and valuation of farm input and output changes'.

A characteristic of rural development projects in southern Africa is not that they have failed to increase farm-household production, but that this production has not been manifested in the narrow farm-output terms in which performance has been judged. Rural development efforts should not necessarily be abandoned on this account. Rather we should take a broader view of rural development and recognize that the basic production unit is not the farm, but the farm-household. Household economics provides an analytical framework which can help us to go beyond the listing and valuation of farm-input and farm-output changes in assessing and evaluating rural development in the southern African environment.

Notes

1 While there have been attempts to change the way in which market outputs and inputs are valued by attaching social weights to them (Squire and van der Tak, 1975), the items included in the analysis were largely confined to those relating specifically to the farm production unit.
2 A similar analysis at the macro-level is given in Low (1981).
3 In Kenya also, the rapid and widespread adoption of higher-yielding maize varieties (Johnston, 1978, p. 83; Gerhart, 1975) does not appear to have resulted in any marked increase in aggregate maize yields. Between 1961 and 1980 average maize yields rose by only 0.1 per cent per annum and total production by 1.1 per cent per annum (CIMMYT, 1981).
4 An interesting observation on the labour-releasing properties of the plough was made by Lewis (1975) about farmers in Mali:

> As the decision makers, but not the labourers, in the family firm, these elders felt that with the labor saving device of the plow they would loose control over the youths who, feeling less needed by the family, would drift away, either to the Ivory Coast or into their own

separate firm. Thus in purchasing the plow, the elder would lose not only its price but also control over labor which he could use to advantage throughout the year (cited in Horowitz, 1979, p. 82).

Lewis gives this as a reason for the early reluctance to adopt the plough by some families. He also notes that in families where youths had already migrated to the Ivory Coast, the remaining elders had tended to adopt the plough.

5 In conventional analyses (e.g. Todaro, 1969; Nakajima, 1970; Bell, 1972) the wage line is fixed (institutionally or by market forces) and the possibility of individual farm-households influencing its slope is not recognized.

6 Westcott (1977, p. 140) has noted the direct substitutability of fertilizer for education in relation to farm-household production in Transkei: 'In the short run,' he writes, 'even the additional supply of fertilizer may be less profitable than other opportunities such as upgrading stock or educating children'.

7 Elsewhere in Africa oxenization has only resulted in marginal production increases. For example, Mettrick (1978) found that in The Gambia, oxenization resulted in a small increase in area cultivated but no increase in yields. Barrett et al. (1982) found that in Upper Volta (now Burkina Faso), area and yield effect were modest but labour inputs per hectare were reduced by 20 to 25 per cent.

Part III
Wider perspectives

12 Policy implications

In laying emphasis on the relationship between market and non-market production on the one hand and farm and off-farm production on the other, the household-economics approach spotlights the need to consider the development of subsistence agriculture in the context of the development of the market economy as a whole and the expansion of the urban/industrial wage sector in particular. We will consider a number of agricultural development policy issues in this light, starting with food-price policy, upon which the World Bank (IBRD, 1981) has placed particular stress in relation to accelerating the rate of agricultural development in sub-Saharan Africa.

Food-price policy

As we have noted, the development of the modern market sector tends to stimulate the demand for market goods and thereby encourages a reallocation of time within the farm-household from non-market to market production. In order for this market production to take the form of growing food crops for sale, producer prices must be such that the returns from the commercial production of food crops are better than those that can be earned from the production of non-food crops or from off-farm employment. Clearly a marketing network must also be available so that the farmer can be sure of disposing of his crop and receiving timely and full payment for it.

Discussion of food-price policy is generally restricted to these production aspects of farm-household behaviour. The argument that low producer prices have brought about disincentives for food production in developing countries is based largely on evidence from studies by Peterson (1979, 1983), Bale and Lutz (1981) and IBRD (1981), none of which has analyzed consumer price policies. From a household-economics perspective the lack of consideration of consumer prices in the food-price policy debate is a serious omission. This is especially so in southern Africa, where the majority of the population are members of farm-households and a significant proportion of these households produce less food than they consume.

To a large extent this situation is a reflection of low retail food prices in relation to good alternative market employment opportunities, notably in wage employment. Raising producer prices will have no influence on subsistence or deficit-producing households whose production does not enter the market, whereas raising retail prices can be expected to induce deficit producers to substitute own production for purchased food. This implies that consumer subsidies which lower retail food prices are inconsistent with a policy of increased food production.

A further implication of this analysis is that an increase in the price of foods based on non-indigenous crops, such as wheat, is also likely to stimulate the

157

158 Policy implications

non-market production of indigenous substitute food crops, such as maize, since purchased food will become more expensive relative to own-grown produce and this can be expected to induce a substitution of own-grown for purchased food. It is now recognized that in many countries food imports have helped to keep retail food prices low, and this has contributed to declining domestic food production.

For example, Caballero (1982, p. 17) argues that in Peru an agrarian policy orientated towards keeping food cheap in urban markets has resulted in consumption patterns based on imports and capitalist coastal production, and that this has contributed to the stagnation of highland peasant agriculture where traditional staples are produced. According to the World Bank (1981, p. 56), a similar policy has been pursued in sub-Saharan Africa and has been accomplished in various ways:

> producer prices are fixed at below market levels; subsidies are provided by selling imported foods at below landed costs; food imports are encouraged when domestic food price levels rise; and imported foods are given an implicit subsidy because of currency overvaluation.

TABLE 12.1 *Wheat and maize imports and utilization: percentage annual growth rates 1971–9[a]*

	Southern Africa[b]	Eastern and Southern Africa	Western Africa
Wheat			
Net imports	3.6 (–0.6)	5.9	10.0
Utilization[c]	2.9 (2.9)	2.5	9.7
Maize			
Net imports	1.0 (–10.7)	44.2	29.5
Utilization	0.7 (– 2.0)	0.3	3.0

Source and notes:
   CIMMYT trade data
   a) All figures exclude South Africa. For southern Africa Zimbabwe is also excluded except in figures in parentheses.
   b) Movements of maize and wheat within the South African common customs area are not included, which means that the recent increases in maize and wheat imports to Botswana, Lesotho and Swaziland are not reflected in the figures.
   c) Utilization is estimated as net imports plus domestic production.

The importation and utilization of wheat in sub-Saharan Africa has been on the increase over the last decade, as the data in Table 12.1 indicate. In eastern and southern Africa and in the southern sub-section of this region, wheat utilization has grown at a faster rate than that of the domestic staple, maize. Moreover, most of the increase in wheat consumption has been met through imports. It is noticeable that maize imports have also increased substantially in eastern and southern Africa, but this reflects reduced production which resulted in the region becoming a significant net importer by the end of the decade, whereas exports almost balanced imports at the beginning. In western Africa growth of maize imports has also been substantial, and this is due in part to increased demand for animal feed. In this region also there has been a marked increase in net importation and utilization of non-indigenous wheat.

Byerlee's study (1983) provides evidence of a widespread and consistent bias in government policy towards providing subsidized bread to urban consumers. While subsidies on wheat consumption may not have been implemented at the expense of producers they are still likely to have reduced local production of indigenous foods through their effect on urbanization. Wheat consumption levels tend to be higher in urban than in rural areas and urbanization is the major factor explaining variations in wheat consumption across tropical countries. To some extent this reflects the higher incomes in urban than in rural areas and the incentive that this gives to consume convenience-type foods which save on the relatively high value of time. Thus, increasing the price of wheat compared to basic staples will not only increase the cost of saving time in this way, but will also make urban living more expensive relative to rural living. In effect it will reduce the real urban wage and this can be expected to result in a reduced rate of urbanization and to an increase in domestic food production and consumption. Evidence for this is provided by a cross-sectional regression analysis of fifty-six tropical countries, in which it was found that high levels of wheat imports are significantly associated with lagging domestic food production (Byerlee, 1983).

Moreover elasticities of demand for wheat range from -0.5 to -0.7 in sub-Saharan Africa, which suggests that increasing bread prices would induce a substantial shift towards the consumption of alternative foods. Given the strong rural–urban linkages that exist in Africa this is likely to result in a substitution by households of non-market procurement (own production) for market procurement of their food needs. This latter effect will be particularly significant in areas, such as southern Africa, where a high proportion of farm-households are deficit food producers.

The above household-economics perspective brings out the importance of food-price policy per se on the promotion of agricultural production. In relation to Africa it has been stated that:

> without better supplies of yield increasing technology, improved tools which allow more efficient use of labor, and money to finance innovation, relative price differences will simply direct resources from one crop to another without quantitatively increasing agricultural output (USDA, 1981, p. 7).

This view is based on the notion that farm-households in Africa are only concerned with farm production for the market, which is far from being the case. African farm-households are also concerned with non-market and non-farm production. Thus, a relative rise in food prices and/or crop prices can induce a substitution of market-crop production for non-farm market production (wage employment), *and* a substitution of non-market food procurement for market food procurement. In either case the absolute quantity of agricultural output would have been increased through price policy alone.

Raising food prices, especially at the retail level, or reducing food aid and commercial imports as a means of stimulating food crop production is a policy that leads to obvious conflicts with other development objectives. First, the political risks are likey to be significant, especially in countries with relatively high urbanization rates, such as Zambia and Zimbabwe. Second, higher food prices will inevitably reduce real incomes of net consuming households and may even have adverse effects on the nutritional status of some of the poorest households. On the other hand, there is little doubt that, as in Peru, the cheap food policies followed by most countries in southern Africa have contributed to the stagnation of indigenous farming in the region and to an increasing reliance on the modern farm sector, food aid and commercial imports for marketed food supplies.

In summary, the implications of the new household theory of consumer choice in Africa are that:

1) retail prices as well as producer prices have an important influence on food production decisions in regions such as southern Africa, where a significant proportion of farm-households are deficit producers of their staple food;

2) policies on the supply and pricing of local as well as non-indigenous foodstuffs in urban areas will influence local food production, since they will affect the real value of time in urban wage employment and influence the migration decision, which in turn has implications for agricultural production at the farm-household level;

3) the above emphasis on retail pricing as opposed to producer pricing and supply highlights the policy conflicts that exist between development in the modern/urban sector and the small-scale indigenous agricultural sector.

Integrated rural development and rural–urban migration

During the last decade, the integrated rural development project has been promoted as a major agricultural development instrument. However, the poor record of these projects in achieving any significant impact on farm production and incomes in Africa has led Eicher (1982, p. 165) to suggest that there is an urgent need to reassess the concept of the integrated rural development project. A major weakness of these projects is that, whereas they have been 'integrated' in the sense that project components have included non-agricultural inputs such as rural roads, schools, health clinics, small-scale industry infrastructure and retail marketing facilities, they have not been integrated in a wider economic sense. In southern Africa integrated rural development projects have been planned, and their goals set, without any reference to urban development or wage employment trends.

This isolated planning horizon reflects the common view that there is a one-way relationship between rural development and agricultural production on the one hand and urban development and wage employment on the other, in which one of the outcomes of successful rural development will be a reduction in rural–urban migration.[1] The potential impact of urban development and wage employment policies on agricultural production and rural development has largely been ignored.

The conventional notion that there is a simple one-way relationship between agricultural development and reduced rural–urban migration has been challenged by empirical research in Latin America and Africa. Data from Peru suggest that the stagnation of small-scale agriculture is a function of the nature and extent of modern-sector development and urban expansion (Caballero, 1982). And Roberts (1982) presents evidence to suggest that, in certain areas of Mexico, agricultural development has resulted in farm-households increasing the proportion of family labour time spent in off-farm wage employment. For Nigeria, Aboyade (1983) shows how the booming petroleum sector 'literally wiped out the domestic production of food', as non-agricultural wages rose and the agricultural sector experienced both out-migration and production decline.

Our household-economics analysis has suggested that similar relationships between urban and rural development occur in southern Africa. On the one hand, expanding wage employment opportunities remove household labour from the farm and reduce its productive capacity. On the other hand, and at the same time, high off-farm wage rates encourage farm-households to seek and adopt time-saving technologies, which enable them to devote more time to wage employment or raise their returns to time spent on farm production.

Both the reduction in labour available on the farm, and the relatively high opportunity cost of household members' time in wage employment, dispose farm-households to think in terms of maximizing returns to time rather than returns to land. This has significant implications for the adoption and impact of yield-increasing agricultural technology, which generally requires relatively high inputs of attention and time in order to realize its full potential in terms of yields per hectare.

For the farm-household with depleted labour resources, on account of rural-urban migration, or with relatively high potential opportunity costs in off-farm employment, it will often not be possible or rational to apply all the complementary increased labour inputs required by a new yield-increasing technology. As with hybrid maize in Swaziland, the technology may be adopted without the complementary husbandry improvements that would substantially improve yields per hectare, because the associated increase in time costs are either unacceptable or not possible for most farm-households.

In this way the potential of yield-increasing crop technologies may be severely limited by rapid expansion in urbanization and wage employment opportunities. The production impact of an agricultural development project, based on the promotion of improved technology, may therefore be influenced as much by urban development and wage policy as by the speed and efficiency with which the project is implemented. This suggests the need to consider modern-sector development, and especially wage policy, in conjunction with rural development. It is not coincidental that the country which has had the greatest success with integrated rural development projects in southern Africa is Malawi, where a strict and deliberate wage policy has kept real wage rates well below those experienced in neighbouring countries.

TABLE 12.2 *Kg of maize per day's wage employment (1982/83)*

Malawi	5.5
Zambia	11.8
Zimbabwe	12.5
Transkei	16.6

The data in Table 12.2 reflect a situation where the producer price of maize in Malawi is below that in Zambia, Zimbabwe or Transkei. However, wages are so much lower in Malawi that a day's wage employment in other countries of the region buys over twice as much maize as in Malawi.

Malawi is recognized to have had the most success in the region so far as the commercialization of the small-farm sector is concerned. The country has been a net exporter of maize in the last eight out of ten years although, compared with Zambia, Zimbabwe and South Africa, a much smaller proportion of the marketed maize crop is produced on large-scale commercial farms. However, even in Malawi the small-farm sector has not been immune to the effects of modern-sector developments. While Swazi and Basotho farm-households have moved out of farming or have purchased inputs in the face of increasing wage rates and opportunities, Malawi farmers have moved out of relatively time-intensive crops such as tobacco and groundnuts into the less labour-demanding maize crop over the last decade. This movement has not been associated with any marked reduction in the price of tobacco or groundnuts relative to maize. But it has occurred over a period when formal employment, mostly in the estate sector, has been growing at a rate of 7 per cent per annum.

Land tenure

Reform of land tenure is typically discussed in terms of the equitable distribution of land resources among the rural population. Hence in Africa, where traditional tenure institutions distribute land fairly evenly among communities, land tenure is often regarded as not constituting a development problem (OECD, 1980, p. 35). The distribution of land is, however, a critical political and economic issue in South Africa, Swaziland and Zimbabwe, where modern farming under private ownership occupies a significant proportion of arable land and there is a trade off between the transfer of land from large commercial to small indigenous farmers, with the potential reduction in marketed surpluses that such a transfer might cause. A central question that arises in this connection relates to the effect that usufruct rights under Bantu ownership have on land productivity and commercialization of land use within the small farm sector.

Whereas, until recently, most studies on land tenure in tropical Africa concluded that indigenous institutions were flexible and not an immediate constraint on increasing production (Eicher and Baker, 1982, p. 98), writers on southern Africa have long since viewed traditional tenure as an obstacle to agricultural development. For example, Yudelman (1964b, p. 223) suggested that the absence of a land market inhibited commercialization, and the distribution of land on the basis of need rather than use prevented good farmers from expanding their operations. He therefore argued for a selective change to individual freehold tenure in southern Africa, but also recognized that any change in the tenure system would have repercussions beyond the subsistence sector, 'for this sector is linked to the wage economy through the migratory labour system'.

The case for individual freehold tenure is supported by Richards, Sturrock and Fortt (1973), who indicate that individual title in the Buganda region of Uganda greatly facilitated the establishment of commercial agriculture there. Kenya is another example where the individualization of land tenure has been associated with a significant expansion in commercial production.

The advantage of individual over communal land ownership is often held to be related to the security of title given by the former type of tenure. This, it is argued, provides the incentive to invest in the land as well as the means to do so through collateral credit. Lack of security and ability to finance land improvements were seen by Maina and Strieker (1971, p. 11) to be two of the main reasons for the low production levels achieved by indigenous farm-households in Swaziland. However, in the development of the Swaziland Rural Development Areas Programme, it was argued that many of the potential improvements in productivity involved the use of short-term inputs, the adoption of which would not be inhibited by lack of long-term security of tenure. Hence the emphasis in that programme on the provision of crop inputs and credit facilities. And, as we have seen, investment in fertilizers and hybrid seed has been substantial.

The security-of-tenure argument is misleading because, as we noted in Chapter 9, Bantu ownership is similar to ownership under Western law in this regard: once acquired, it gives the owning group the right to demand that anyone seeking to dispossess them of it should show very good reason indeed for doing so. From a household-economics perspective, the difference between freehold and Bantu ownership rests not so much on the security of the use right as on the nature of the costs of maintaining the use right. Under freehold tenure there is an opportunity-money cost involved in maintaining use rights, which is related to the productivity and scarcity of the land. Under Bantu ownership there is no money cost involved in maintaining use rights. Instead there are time costs, but these are related less to the productivity or scarcity of the land than to the opportunity costs of using this time in other non-market or market production. These opportunity costs will often be minimal for certain household members and can be covered by labour-extensive subsistence cultivation. Covering opportunity costs of maintaining freehold use rights, on the other hand, requires a minimum value of production per unit area of land.[2]

This does not mean that land held under Bantu ownership will only be used for subsistence production. Where other opportunities for market production are scarce, the land may be used for commercial purposes, as for example with tobacco production in Malawi. Neither does it mean that land held under freehold title will always be used for commercial production. Where other opportunities for earning income are particularly attractive, land may be purchased for non-market purposes. In northern Mexico, for example, Mines and de Janvry (1982, p. 451) report that land is not purchased for profit. Rather, 'migrants buy village land not for profit but for prestige, security and for food for their parents. . . Also land owned in the village means security in case of unemployment in the United States or repatriation'.

What the unit-land value versus the opportunity-time value distinction does imply, however, is that it will often be less costly to maintain use rights and, at the same time, seek off-farm wage employment under Bantu ownership than under freehold title. Moreover, under Bantu ownership there is a greater incentive to maintain use rights on account of the extra non-market benefits that go with it, such as right of grazing, stover, fuel, water etc. The relatively low cost of maintaining use rights, and the additional benefits from doing so, result in most households continuing to retain land-use rights for non-market purposes, even where farming ceases to be the main market-production activity. As we have noted in Chapter 10, this often results in land being held by households that are unable or unwilling to use it productively.

Under freehold tenure, on the other hand, land is more likely to be distributed to those who are willing and able to use it most productively, since those households engaged in off-farm employment will face a relatively high cost in keeping land under-utilized when the opportunities to rent or sell exist.

What this analysis emphasizes is the relationship between the productive use of land under Bantu ownership and freehold tenure on the one hand, and the economic environment, particularly as regards off-farm employment opportunities, on the other. Where off-farm opportunities are scarce or relatively unattractive, Bantu tenure arrangements may not imply less productive use of land vis-à-vis freehold tenure.[3] But where some households find that off-farm wage employment is a more attractive means of market production than farming, there will be less incentive (and opportunity) for them to transfer use rights to others under Bantu ownership than under freehold tenure.

In Chapter 10 we argued that the possibility of undertaking market production off the farm has reinforced the traditional non-market function of land and reduced the pressure for a change in the tenure system. We have seen that in Mexico this non-market function becomes dominant even under freehold tenure when off-farm wage opportunities are particularly attractive in the short term, but involve little long-term security. Long-term security has always been an important function of land under Bantu ownership, and the nature of the off-farm employment opportunities generated by modern-sector development in southern Africa has reinforced the importance of the security role compared with the productive role of land (Hughes, 1972, 1974). At the same time the maintenance of land-use rights for long-term security purposes by most households has reduced the quality and quantity of land available per household over time, so that the short-term attraction of off-farm employment vis-à-vis commercial farming has steadily increased.

In some cases (e.g. Ciskei, Lesotho, Transkei) the point has now been reached where, although the land base is still capable of providing a long-term security for most households, without substantial investments of money and effort it can only provide an acceptable income for a small proportion of households. In these cases, a land-reform policy based on giving households leasehold or freehold title to viable land units (as proposed by the Tomlinson Commission in respect of South African homelands, Houghton, 1961, p. 167) would inevitably lead to the creation of a large landless class, whose living standards would be drastically reduced unless a massive investment in housing, social security and permanent job creation were to be undertaken at the same time. In 1979 a new Land Act was promulgated in Lesotho, which attempts to prevent further fragmentation of holdings by providing for inheritance of land-use rights by a single heir and introduces the possibilities of leaseholding and sub-letting. Spiegel (1981) has suggested that this Act will lead to the creation of a landless class and exacerbate the growing rural differentiation being brought about by more selective labour recruitment in that country.

In other cases, such as Swaziland, where population pressure is less severe and some opportunities exist for the reallocation of land from large to small farmers a gradual change to freehold tenure may well contribute to the more productive use of land without causing unacceptable social disruption. However, it is important to recognize that a change in tenure by itself cannot be expected to have much of an impact. If commodity prices are such that commercial production does not provide returns commensurate with off-farm opportunities, few households will be willing to acquire land for market production and it will continue to be used primarily for non-market purposes.

In arguing for a change to individual security of land tenure in Zimbabwe, Yudelman (1964, p. 225) suggested that the luxury of the form of security given by traditional tenure arrangements could not continue to be enjoyed if economic development was to proceed. The creation of insecurity, he argues, is part of the price paid for fulfilling the evolution of rising expectations. Expectations are rising fast in post-independence Zimbabwe and security through access to land forms part of these expectations. Land under either individual or communal title can provide security, but the experience in Kenya and Uganda that has been referred to, as well as the implications of this study, suggests that, while communal tenure does not preclude commercial production, it is likely to be more readily fostered under individual title than communal tenure, especially where off-farm wage opportunities are likely to continue to expand. Furthermore, individual title to land provides an alternative to cattle as a vehicle for storing wealth and attaining prestige and status (see above, p. 116). Given the severe overstocking problems encountered on communal areas, this is an added potential benefit of freehold tenure that should not be overlooked.

Changes in land ownership and production patterns are already taking place in Zimbabwe. Settlement schemes are being established, small-scale commercial farming on leasehold tenure is expanding and the proportion of marketed output from large-scale commercial farming on freehold tenure is decreasing.[4] Since new forms of tenure for small-scale farming in Zimbabwe are not being developed at the expense of traditional land rights, costs in terms of loss of social security and supplementary benefits attached to traditional rights do not present a substantial barrier to these changes. Zimbabwe may therefore be the first country in southern Africa to provide a test of the extent to which small-scale commercial farming can be better fostered under freehold than under traditional tenure where the modern industrial sector is expanding at the same time.

Notes

1 Gugler (1982, p. 187) reiterates the normal policy prescription that calls for an increase in rural development in order to reduce rural–urban migration. However, he also recognizes that there are some strategies, e.g. mechanization, that 'may displace labour and encourage rural out-migration'.
2 This comparison concentrates on the short-term costs and returns. It may be argued that the freehold title encourages longer-term investments in land with a view to preventing long-term deterioration. However, the extent to which this difference, if it exists, is related to the security aspect is debatable. It probably has more to do with the purposes for which land comes to be used by most owners under the different tenure systems. Since, as we argue

below, there is less incentive and opportunity under Bantu ownership for farm-households to transfer use rights to others who could use the land more productively than themselves, much of the land area held under Bantu ownership is cultivated more for social security than for productive purposes. Investments that may enhance long-term productivity, but have little influence on the social security value of land, are therefore less likely to be undertaken under Bantu ownership than under freehold tenure.

3 The nature and extent of off-farm opportunities in southern Africa compared with other parts of the continent may be one reason why traditional tenure was seen as more of a constraint on production in the former than in the latter.

4 The percentage of maize sold to the grain marketing board by large-scale commercial farms on freehold land fell from 86 per cent in 1981, to 77 per cent in 1982, to 75 per cent in 1983 and to 60 per cent in 1985. At the same time the proportion of communal land maize production entering the formal market had increased from 12 in 1980 to 50 per cent in 1985.

13 Farming-systems research

Farming-systems research has recently been embraced by donor agencies as a promising new approach to developing production-increasing technology that will be widely adopted by small farmers in the developing world. Most national research organisations in independent southern Africa now have a farming-systems research component backed by donor agencies and/or international agricultural research centres. Some countries such as Zambia and Malawi have gone so far as to restructure their research organizations in order to accommodate this class of research. In this chapter we will argue that early applications of the approach in southern Africa point to the need to widen its perspective from the farm to the farm-household. We suggest that household-economics thinking can contribute to this and lead to more realistic expectations being entertained about the likely impact of the approach[1].

Characteristics of the approach

Farming-systems research aims to complement traditional station-based research and overcome some of the weaknesses of the latter in providing extension services with technical packages that are appropriate to the circumstances of small farmers operating in particular rural environments. The characteristics of farming-systems research have been widely documented (Gilbert et al., 1980; Norman et al., 1982; Collinson, 1982; Byerlee et al., 1982). In summary the approach aims to:

1) understand farmers' circumstances;
2) generate hypotheses about how farm productivity can best be improved in the near term given these circumstances and current technical knowledge and;
3) design and test technologies based on these hypotheses on farmers' fields or;
4) direct station research towards more relevant programmes if the technical information base is lacking.

The need for farming-systems research developed as a result of the observation that much of the technology developed from station-research programmes was not adopted by small farmers in developing countries. One of the reasons for this lack of adoption was that the technologies being produced were not consistent with the circumstances of many small farmers. Technologies were seen to be inappropriate for a number of reasons:

1) the natural circumstances (soils, topography, climate) facing small farmers in local specific situations vary from location to location and are generally different from those on research stations;

2) the institutional support services needed to supply inputs were either non-existent or unreliable;

3) the costs and risks of using the new technologies were too high for small farmers relative to the benefits;

4) small farmers had multiple objectives stemming from their need to consume much of what they produced, to minimize risk and to maximize returns to heterogenous resources such as family labour, whose opportunity cost varies through the season as well as for different individuals.

By contrast, the on-station researcher's environment is characterized by particular (often favourable) natural circumstances, availability of inputs, little concern with cost or risk and generally a single objective: to increase output per unit of land.

Farming-systems research methodology is aimed at sensitizing agricultural researchers to the circumstances of their farmer clients. Apart from getting researchers to conduct experiments on farmers' fields, it was recognized that farmers' circumstances are determined by both physical and social factors. This led to the need for inter-disciplinary interaction between social scientists and pure and applied natural scientists. It was also recognized that family farming systems tended to be complex. Within the farm context this complexity was especially evident in tropical areas with long growing seasons where intercropping and multiple cropping were practised.[2] The recognition that family farming systems are complex led to the need to adopt a systems perspective in which interactions between activities could be accounted for. Again this contrasts with the commodity and disciplinary orientation of station-based research.

The characteristics of farming-systems research then are that it is based on first-hand interaction between farmers and researchers, it is interdisciplinary and it encompasses a systems perspective. However this systems perspective is a limited one. Farming-systems methodology tends to concentrate on the interactions among different farming activities and, although some attempt is made to account for the opportunity costs of time and funds used in non-farm market production, little attention is given to the opportunity costs of resources used in non-farm *non-market* production, investment and consumption. Instead research activities and techniques of analysis have focused on how farmers' adoption of new technologies is influenced by natural circumstances, institutional support or cash costs and risks. Farmers' multiple objectives have been less thoroughly treated, partly because there has been little theoretical basis for analyzing multiple market and non-market objectives of households and partly because the other factors can be handled within the context of the farming system. The need to adjust input rates (e.g. fertilizers, plant population) to suit local soil conditions or the management of a new crop to fit into an existing cropping pattern can be established without reference to non-farm activities and intra-household decision-making processes.

Furthermore the relationship between agricultural productivity and household welfare is generally perceived as a one-way process and assumed to be positive, i.e., increased agricultural productivity is perceived as leading to increased household welfare. But, as household economics emphasizes, welfare is a function of the total mix of monetary and non-monetary, tangible and intangible goods. Moreover, perceptions of welfare affect the goals of farm-household members and, in turn, their allocation of resources and management; thus, welfare is not only a function but also a determinant of agricultural productivity (Caldwell, 1983). Where household welfare and the household's commitment to farming are affected by non-farm factors, e.g. the wage employment market, access to consumer goods and household composition, these factors become relevant for farming-systems research aimed at generating appropriate technology for African farm-households.

Farm-household linkages

The need to take a wider (household) perspective is becoming apparent from early FSR studies in eastern and southern Africa, which demonstrate that the linkages between the farm and household are strong and that household factors will often have a significant influence on farm decisions. Some of the results coming out of farming-systems research in southern Africa demonstrate the commonalities that exist in farming-systems research findings and household-economics thinking.

The importance of the time constraint

Diagnostic work in farming-systems research is indicating that farmers very often compromise on crop and livestock management, not because of lack of knowledge or for lack of cash to purchase inputs or because inputs are not available, but because of time constraints. Often seemingly appropriate production-increasing innovations are not adopted because of their implications in terms of time. For example, commenting on the results of experimental work on livestock feeding in the Kenya Dryland Farming Research and Development Project, Tessema (1983, p. 25) concluded that the rate of adoption of innovations was disappointingly poor. He observed that:

1) Kenyan farmers valued their leisure more than the gains they could get from clearing bush to encourage good forage growth;

2) most farmers are grazing their crop residues in situ and realize that they are wasting about 40 per cent of production in so doing. Since they still go ahead with this practice, it seems that, in terms of labour use, farmers choose the least burdensome way of doing a job, even if they are aware that an increased input will give a higher return;

3) the growing of fodder crops creates greater demand for labour and oxen time, which the farmer cannot cope with if he had to carry out operations of ploughing, planting and weeding for food crop production. Thus only a handful of farmers were able to be persuaded to include fodder crops in their cropping system.

Similar examples can be found throughout Africa. In Ghana farmers rejected the labour-using parts of a maize improvement package, such as closer plant spacing and a second weeding, but adopted other parts of the package such as variety and a moderate dose of fertilizer (Bruce et al., 1980). In Malawi farmers saved on labour inputs by spraying cotton less than the recommended twelve times needed to obtain optimum returns per hectare (Farrington, 1977). In Zimbabwe it is reported that 'substantial inducements and price differentials were offered to farmers to follow improved farming practices but only 4 per cent of those in the area responded to money incentives to improve their production methods by adding labour inputs' (Yudelman, 1964a, p. 571). For many of the experimental thrusts that are coming out of farming-systems research work in southern Africa the returns to family labour time or oxen work rates have become primary evaluation criteria (for details, see Low, 1984a, Table 1, and Rockefeller Foundation, 1985).

Influence of the domestic development cycle

Household-economics theory relates differences in behaviour between households to differences in their characteristics and composition and, in particular, to the way these affect the relative time values of members within a household. Farming-systems research methodology recognizes that differences in the economic and natural circumstances facing households will affect their interest in and ability to adopt particular farm technologies. The identification of different recommendation domains in farming-systems research has tended to be based on external factors such as agro-climatic conditions and access to markets or inputs. However as research proceeds the importance of internal household factors in determining appropriate technology is beginning to emerge.

TABLE 13.1 *Characteristics of two recommendation domains in Mangwende, Zimbabwe*

	Cattle ownership	
	Owners	Non-owners
Resources		
Family size (persons)	8.4	6.4
Farm workers	3.4	2.8
Size of holding (ha)	3.9	2.9
Area cultivated (ha)	3.6	2.1
Percentage of farms with head working away	7	13
Percentage of farms with head under 55 years old	17	42
Percentage of farms with woman head	12	30
Crop yields (t/ha)		
Maize	3.2	2.1
Groundnuts	0.7	0.5
Sunflower	0.2	0.04
Income sources (Z$/annum)		
Maize sales	347	168
Vegetable sales	140	84
Groundnut sales	40	26
Off-farm income	159	149
Total income	752	449

In Table 13.1 we see that higher crop yields are achieved by cattle owners than by non-owners. These yield differences are related to management factors. Cattle owners plant and weed earlier and a greater proportion of them winter-plough and apply manure. These management differences are in turn related to internal household factors. As Shumba (1983, p. 5) states:

> While non-owners and owners obtained the same absolute income from off-farm sources, this represents a much higher proportion of total income for non-owners, who have lower productive capacities in farming because of their smaller labour

forces, lack of oxen and greater tendency for the household head to be away. The greater tendency for household heads to be absent in non-owning households is related to the younger age of these households. Job prospects for younger household heads are better than for their older counterparts and wages provide a relatively low risk means for young households to generate the necessary funds to hire cattle and purchase fertilizer. The incentive for members of non-owning households to seek wage employment is therefore quite high and, given their already smaller work forces, this further reduces time available for farm activities and contributes to the lower levels of crop management, lower yields and lower farm incomes of non-owners compared with owners.

From a household-economics perspective the influence of the domestic development cycle on the productive capacity of farm-households is clear. Oxen ownership is a critical factor enabling better crop husbandry, and the distribution of cattle in this society is associated with household development and maturity, which are related to the other factors mentioned by Shumba. They combine to result in poorer crop management by the less-mature non-owning households.[3]

Women farmers

As farming-systems researchers conduct surveys and establish trials in eastern and southern Africa, they increasingly find themselves dealing with women farmers. At farmers' group meetings women invariably outnumber men and it is said that 50–70 per cent of farmers in Africa are women. Given that women the world over are responsible for household production activities (household maintenance, child care etc.), it follows that much of the agricultural work in Africa competes with household production activities for the allocation of women's time.

Farming-systems researchers and farm management economists are accustomed to assessing potential technical innovations in terms of labour demands for competing farm activities. Or alternative market wage activities are accounted for by imputing an opportunity cost of time. Seldom are the demands of household production considered, either directly or indirectly through an imputed opportunity cost.

Rural-household studies are beginning to highlight the large amounts of time allocated to non-farm non-market household activities, especially by women (see below, pp. 181–2). Often the costs of not performing some of these essential or socially necessary tasks (e.g. fetching water or working in another's field) will be quite high and will significantly reduce the real benefits of technologies that compete for the time of household members responsible for such household production activities.

Factors affecting who does what within farm-households and how many hands are available to do farming clearly have significant implications for the appropriateness of new farm technology. In south western Ethiopia, for example, farmers broadcast their maize despite the research station recommendation to row plant. Farmers said they preferred to broadcast because it was a one person operation, while row planting required two people and took longer. Asked why the wives could not assist, farmers replied that they would rather have their wives stay at home to prepare their food and make their coffee.

Expanding the systems perspective

The application of a household-economics perspective can contribute to the effectiveness of on-farm research in three particular areas:
1) understanding farmers' objectives and strategies;
2) defining recommendation domains, and
3) evaluation of new technologies

Understanding farmers' objectives and strategies

Farming-systems research is designed to look at technology development from the farmers' point of view. Understanding farmers' objectives and values is crucial to this:

> The goals and motivations of farmers, which will affect the degree and type of effort they will be willing to devote to improving the productivity of their farming systems, are essential inputs to the process of identifying or designing potentally appropriate improved technologies. (Norman et al., 1982, p. 25).

While farming-systems research recognizes that farmers have multiple objectives, these objectives are generally looked at in terms of the farming system alone. Multiple and intercropping strategies are manifestations of farmers' multiple objectives for cash, preferred staple foods, food security and maximization of returns to farm resources. As Behnke and Kerven state, this concentration on the farming system may have two undesirable results:

> First it may encourage researchers to think of those who farm as primarily or solely farmers, and thereby underestimate the role of non-agricultural activities in the larger household economy. Secondly, an exclusive concentration on farming may ill equip FSR to address one of the major issues in agricultural development in Africa: the withdrawal of labour from agriculture due to rural–urban migration. (Behnke and Kerven, 1983, p. 9).

In southern Africa, as we have seen, farming is seldom the only source of income and in many cases it is not the major one. Wage employment, beer brewing, handicrafts, trading and teaching are common additional sources of income for rural households. While farming-systems researchers are concerned with measuring and increasing farm income, farmers are concerned with stabilizing and increasing their *entire* welfare, much of which may come from non-farm production. Thus in order to understand farmers' goals and objectives, farming-systems researchers need to adopt a household-economics perspective and attempt to see how diverse production activities are combined to maximize household utility. To quote Behnke and Kerven again:

> the acceptability of a farming innovation cannot be adequately judged solely by its technical and economic impact on farming. It must also be assessed in terms of its positive or negative contribution to the household economy as a whole. This will especially be the case when technical innovations require additional labour or capital that could be invested elsewhere, for example, in the search for urban jobs or in the education of children. (ibid, p. 10).

Application of a household-economics perspective will help farming-systems researchers to understand farmer strategies in a household context and thus to search for farm technologies that are appropriate to the overall, farm and non-farm, circumstances facing farmers. Given a household perspective it is possible to see, for example, that one important risk-reducing strategy adopted by many farmers is the search for wage employment by one or more members of the rural household. Over the 1982-4 drought years in southern Africa those households that have had a wage-earning member have suffered much less than those that have not had a reliable non-farm source of income. Clearly where the chances of obtaining off-farm employment are quite good, any farm-based risk-avoidance strategy, such as planting an extra area of cassava, or tied ridging, mulching or insect control must be compared with the returns and reliability of obtaining income from wage employment.

Norman (1983) notes that in the case of Botswana it may be necessary to accept that farmers will be reluctant to invest very much (money or time) in crop production because such investment is risky compared to putting it in to other areas such as livestock and off-farm activities. Such a realization clearly has important implications for the generation of relevant improved agricultural technology for small farmers in Botswana.

Defining recommendation domains

Given the recognition that different farmers face different circumstances, but that resources do not permit research to be geared towards individual farmers, the concept of the recommendation domain has become central to farming-sytems research methodology. The definition of a recommendation domain is a homogenous group of farmers who share the same problems and possess similar resources for solving these problems. This group of farmers is expected to adopt (or not adopt) the same recommendation given equal access to information about it. In much of southern Africa, different recommendation domains occur not only because of differences in farmer resources, cropping opportunities, market access and inherent land fertility but also because, at any one time, farm-households have different opportunities for non-farm wage employment or other income-earning activities. Often it is the nature and extent to which farm-households exploit these non-farm opportunities that most strongly influences farming practices and the aims and objectives of farm production.

Thus it is commonly observed that within homogeneous agro-climatic locations with similar market opportunities, neighbouring farmers with similar income or resource levels will farm in very different ways. Households that are in a position to exploit non-farm income opportunities, by dint of better qualifications, experience or enterprise, will tend not to have the time or inclination to manage their farming operations in as thorough a manner as their neighbours who are orientated less to wage employment. With these farm-households, the aims and objectives of farming tend to be less production-orientated and more social-orientated and security-orientated. Their neighbours who are less able to exploit non-farm opportunities will look on farming more in terms of production and income and will tend to give more time and attention to farming activities. The cultivation practices of these two types of farmers will differ, as will relevant interventions and recommendations.

For example a recommendation domain exercise was carried out in Swaziland with the expectation that different farming systems would be observed in the very different ecological conditions of the highveld, middleveld and lowveld areas in the country (Watson, 1983). However, it was found that the variations within the regions were much greater than the variations in cropping systems between the regions. The within-region variation stemmed from differences in internal household circumstances rather than from external circumstances (Low, 1984a). And in the Agricultural Technology Improvement Project in Botswana researchers concluded that the variation within villages was greater than variations between villages and recommendation domains have been identified on the basis of internal household characteristics such as asset ownership, wage income, access to draught and commitment to farming (ATIP, 1984, pp. 7-49).

Evaluation of technologies

One of the outcomes of applying an on-farm research approach to technology generation in a way which seeks to take the farmers' viewpoint into account is that researchers are coming to recognize that technologies which increase productivity per unit of land are not the only ones that can be beneficial to small farmers. Technologies that do not increase area yields but use time or cash more efficiently are often equally acceptable.

It is becoming apparent that technologies which save family labour time in particular are attractive to small family farm units. The rapid uptake of improved implements, herbicides and mechanization by small farmers in southern Africa and around the world, as well as farmers' own labour-saving strategies bear witness to this.

Household-economics theory implies that households seek to maximize the subjective return to the labour of their members and that what tasks are performed and by whom depends on the opportunity cost of members' time. The opportunity cost of labour time also often forms an important component in the evaluation of farm technologies by on-farm researchers. However, opportunity-time costs are generally determined in terms of alternative farm activities or of wages that can be earned off the farm. Thus, for example, the cost of the time of women in parts of the season when there is little crop work to be done is generally assumed to be near to zero.

Commenting on the unresponsiveness of farmers to advice on bush clearing in western Kenya which experimental results had shown to be productive, Tessema (1983, p. 12) remarks that 'Many were unwilling to carry out the work because they say it is a hard and difficult task even though it does not conflict with other operations, as it can be done in the dry season when there is little other activity'. Even in times of little farm activity the demands on family labour are many and, as the above example illustrates, it is wrong to assume that when there is little farm work to do the opportunity cost of family labour is negligible. In Malawi, for example, farmers indicated that they did not prepare land for cultivation in advance of the rains because tasks such as thatching or house building (which often takes two years to complete) were reserved for the winter months.

Taking a household-economics perspective will help to prevent researchers from falling into Tessema's trap, and will provide a basis for making some assessment of what value to place on family labour used outside farming and wage employment. The question researchers need to ask is what other tasks (farm and non-farm) are being performed by the relevant household members at the time. Answering this question will probably be easier than going on to the next stage and estimating the subjective value of a unit of the member's time in that activity. What value do you put on an hour spent looking after children, collecting firewood or thatching grass or drinking beer with friends? The important point though is that the answer is certainly not zero just because the activity does not have to do with farming.

Even when positive opportunity-time costs are assumed, the farm-based and household-economics approaches to evaluating farm technologies can give markedly different results. For example Table 13.2 presents a typical partial budget analysis based on data from Ghana in which opportunity costs of labour are included and a reasonable return on capital is obtained when extra management time and fertilizer are applied. Moving from the traditional to the new technology gives an increased net benefit (gross benefit less total variable costs) of 298 cedis. This additional net benefit is achieved at a cost of 642 cedis (1252–610), which implies a return to capital of 46 per cent (298/642 × 100). On this conventional analysis it is probably worth while moving to the new technology.

TABLE 13.2 *Farm-based partial budget analysis*

	Returns per hectare analysis	
	Traditional	New technology
Yield kg/ha	1300	2400
Adjusted yield (-15%)	1100	2040
Gross benefit at ¢1/kg	1100	2040
Cost of fertilizer	—	192
Labour input (man days)	61	106
cost at ¢10/day	610	1060
Total variable costs	610	1252
Net benefit per hectare	490	788

Source: Bruce et al. (1980), Table 6.2

Compare this approach with the following analysis of the same data based on the household-economics assumption that farm-households seek to minimize the costs of producing goods for own consumption in order to maximize returns to family labour time. Table 13.3 presents the analysis of the data in Table 13.2 based on a comparison of the costs of producing each unit of the crop, rather than on the returns to capital invested per hectare.

With the new technology each ton can be produced with three fewer man days of labour input, giving a saving of 30 cedis per ton. However since the new technology requires an extra cash outlay of 94 cedis, it is 64 cedis more costly per unit of produce than the traditional one. On a per ton basis, then, the traditional technology, which requires more labour and less cash, is the lower-cost alternative (at the given opportunity cost of labour time).

For subsistence producers, whose priority objective is often to grow own-food requirements (either because it is expensive to purchase their needs or because reliable retail supplies do not exist), the cost-of-production analysis is probably more relevant than a computation of the returns to capital invested per hectare.

TABLE 13.3 *Household-economics time-efficiency analysis*

	Costs per ton analysis	
	Traditional	New technology
Time costs/ton		
Man days required/ton[a]	55	52
time costs at ¢10/day	550	520
Cash cost/ton		
fertilizer cost/ton[b]	—	94
Total cost/ton	550	614

Notes:
    a) (man days per ha) ÷ (adjusted yield per ha)
    b) (fertilizer cost per ha) ÷ (adjusted yield per ha)

More important than the different answers given by each analysis, is the difference in the implications of each approach for changes in the value of time of household members (or household welfare). In the farm-based approach the new technology becomes *less* attractive as the opportunity cost of time is increased, since the new technology uses more labour per unit area of the enterprise cultivated and net returns per hectare are reduced. In the household-economics approach, the new technology becomes *more* attractive as the opportunity cost of time increases, because less time is needed to produce each unit of the consumption good produced and the value of this time-saving is increased.

The Lesotho experience (see above, pp. 130–1) supports the argument that, where labour hiring is not prevalent and scarce family labour time must be used in a subsistence-crop activity, increasing values of members' time (or household welfare) is likely to encourage the use of cash-expensive technology as long as it reduces the labour required per unit of production, regardless of the effect it may have on net returns per unit of land.

Clearly an understanding of *household* circumstances, aims and objectives is crucial to the evaluation and design of appropriate technology for small farmers. Incorporation of a household-economics perspective in farming-systems research methodology can improve the effectiveness of the approach and help researchers to perceive more clearly the implications of the two-way linkage that exists between farm income and household welfare.

Evaluation of farming-systems research

A recognition that farming-systems research can contribute to household welfare without necessarily increasing marketed production or even total farm production is crucial if the approach is to be realistically evaluated. Unfortunately the approach has been sold to donors and governments alike as a means of quickly generating farm technology that will have major production benefits in the short term.

While we can expect some short-term benefits where researchers identify new crops or varieties that better exploit existing resources or new inputs that relieve a key constraint, the output of early farming-systems research work in the region suggests that these types of 'finds' are not easy to come by. The types of technology coming out of farming-systems research in southern Africa to date can be grouped into three categories:

1) Adaptations of existing recommendations to fit farmer circumstances better. Often this involves revising recommendations towards what farmers are currently doing. An example is reduced fertilizer recommendations for late-planted commercial maize in Zambia and Zimbabwe. Current recommendations are based on early planting but farmers often plant late either as a risk hedge or, in Zambia, because they give preference to early planting of local maize which tastes and stores better.

2) Technologies aimed at alleviating constraints obliging farmers to make technical compromises in their crop management. Examples are:
a) the introduction of minimum tillage in Zimbabwe to alleviate oxen and labour shortages at planting time which cause delays in planting and the application of basal fertilizers.
b) herbicides in Swaziland to overcome the late planting and poor early weeding which is practised to make the most of household members returning from work or school over the Christmas vacation
c) the plough planter in Botswana designed to speed row planting to maximize the amount of land that can be cultivated given short and unreliable planting rains and to allow weed control with oxen cultivators.

3) Technologies requiring a redirection of station-based research such as the need to breed hybrid-maize varieties for Malawian farmers with better storing, pounding and cooking qualities. Or the need to develop shorter-season maize varieties in the recognition that farmers across the region, for a number of reasons, stagger their maize plantings over a three-month period.

Of the above types of output, only the second is likely to provide substantial production gains in the near term, and even here farm-households may prefer to take the gains in a form other than increased crop production. The real benefits of farming-systems research are more likely to be long term and gradual than short term and explosive. Given time the approach can be expected to improve the credibility of extension workers with farmers and of researchers with extension workers. This will foster better feedback from farmer to researcher, which in turn can be expected to direct both commodity and on-farm research more towards the real needs of small farmers.

In the southern African context however, the generation of appropriate technology will not guarantee short-term production increases. Hybrid-maize seed in Swaziland, fertilizers in Lesotho and herbicides in Zimbabwe are all appropriate in that they have been rapidly adopted by small farmers. As yet none have proved to generate substantial increases in production, though all can surely be said to have increased farm-household welfare.

Notes

1 An earlier version of this chapter was invited by the Rockefeller Foundation for presentation at the Rockefeller/Ford Foundation conference on Intra-household Processes and Farming Systems Analysis at Bellagio, Italy in March 1984 and has been published in a proceedings volume (Rockefeller Foundation, 1985).
2 Complexity may also exist in terms of the range and mix of farm and non-farm activities carried out by small farm-households. Such complexity may not be so readily apparent in a purely farm context but may still be very significant in the broader household context, where different members undertake a wide range of household production tasks.
3 This is not an isolated finding. Other studies in Swaziland (FMS, 1978) and Zimbabwe (CIMMYT, 1982) demonstrate the same differences between cattle owners and non-owners.

14 Household economics and agrarian development in other settings

In this book we have suggested that the household-economics approach provides a new perspective on agricultural development in southern Africa, and contributes to an understanding of the nature of the problem in that particular region. Since this has been the principal purpose of the study, only passing reference has been made to the rest of Africa and beyond. However, it is appropriate to conclude the book by considering the extent to which the approach and analysis presented in the preceding chapters are specific to the particular circumstances of southern Africa, or to what extent, and with what caveats, the approach may be applicable to the study of agrarian development in other settings. First, we will note that the circumstances in which the indigenous southern African farm-household finds itself are not unique. Second, we will show that in respect of the allocation of family time to farm production, household economics provides a consistent interpretation of behaviour over a wide range of circumstances. Finally, we will consider how the circumstances in southern Africa differ from the rest of the continent, and the implications that this has for the insights that a household-economics perspective can bring to the problem of declining food production in sub-Saharan Africa as a whole.

The common circumstances of Peruvian and southern African peasantry

Commenting on the Rannis-Fei two-sector development model Oshima (1964, p. 196) points out that in an open economy a large part of the industrial (modern) sector output will be exported, while farm products are imported. 'In this case, a large peasant economy, predominantly subsistence, can coexist with a highly industrialized sector with $MPP = W$ (marginal physical product equals the wage rate) in the economy as a whole. Instead of development we have a dual economy'.

Caballero (1982) suggests that economic development in Peru has followed such a pattern. More than two decades of industrial growth has created a modern market economy in Peru but, as in southern Africa, semi-subsistence farm production has stagnated and the economy exhibits a sharply dualistic character. In contrast with the semi-subsistence peasant economy, capitalist agriculture, located mainly in the coast and irrigated areas of the highlands, has grown rapidly. Medium-sized commercial farms have expanded and shifted from production for export to production to supply urban and agro-industrial demand.

Under these circumstances, the characteristics of the Peruvian peasant farmer described by Caballero are remarkably similar to those of his southern African counterpart. Although the highland peasant has participated in the market 'since the early epochs of the colonial period', this integration has not generated any overall increase in peasant farm production. As with indigenous farm-households in southern Africa, the percentage of Peruvian peasant families with wage incomes is high (between 33 and 56 per cent), and there is substantial dependency on purchased foods, which comprise the principal expenditure item, accounting for 48 per cent of monetary expenditure in one community.

Caballero's (1982) perception of the economic rationality of Peruvian peasant behaviour suggests that the farm-household model developed in this study would provide an appropriate analytical tool in the Peruvian setting:

> peasants do not take their surpluses to the market after having covered their necessities; in their resource allocation strategy production for the market is present from the beginning. They depend on the market not only for the occasional purchase of tools or 'luxury goods' which the domestic economy cannot produce, but also for articles basic for survival (food, clothing, tools). Social organisation is based on the family and the family organisation of the land (Caballero, 1982, p. 26).
>
> In other words [the Peruvian peasant] combines two types of economic calculus: that of the market, i.e. that of price relations, and the natural, i.e. that of the technical (transformation) relations between available resources and the goods that can be produced with them (Caballero, 1982, p. 31).

This strategy results in an important part of the average income of the Andean peasantry being derived from temporary migration. These wage earnings are used to purchase household requirements and also constitute an investment fund 'whose role must be seen within the vital cycle of the peasant family. This fund is mainly invested in commerce, transport, purchase of livestock, education and construction of a house; little is invested in agriculture or land purchases.' (Caballero, 1982, p. 30).

Caballero echoes the sentiments of many writers on economic development in southern Africa when he says that capitalist expansion in Peru has been able to introduce important changes into the Andean peasant economy such as widespread commoditization, expansion of the casual labour market and migration. But, at the same time, it has been unable to absorb peasants as proletarians and replace them by capitalist production units, because 1) wage employment has not grown faster than population; 2) the richer peasants do not re-invest their savings in the land and, 3) there are strong institutional and political barriers against the clearance of the peasants from their lands.

The economic (though not cultural or political) circumstances of Peruvian and southern African peasantry are markedly similar and these economic circumstances have provoked very similar production behaviour responses at the farm-household level, which have given rise to similar agricultural development problems. Nor is Peru the only country in Latin America where economic circumstances have resulted in similar farm-household production patterns to those observed in southern Africa. In the wake of Mexico's rapid industrial expansion, most peasants now generate more income by selling their labour than from the production of their farms (Centro de Investigaciones Agrarias, 1974), and much of the rainfed land previously opened up for cultivation is currently left idle or used for extensive cattle grazing (Barkin, 1980).

These trans-continental comparisons suggest that the household-economics approach has general relevance for the study of the relationship between market and non-market aspects of agrarian development. This is a relationship that assumes particular significance in the study of farm-household behaviour in dual economy settings, where market production takes the form of off-farm wage employment, rather than commercial farm production.

A unifying interpretation of family labour use in farm production

Although the economic circumstances of Mexico, Peru and southern Africa are different from those in many other parts of the world, the implications of household economics for the allocation of family labour in farm production can be shown to apply in a number of diverse circumstances. For example, White (1980, p. 22), commenting on the stimulus that the new interest in household economics is likely to give to collecting data on patterns of time allocation at the household level, points out that:

> Such data, even on a small scale, and with simple techniques of analysis, can provoke new conceptions of the 'rural employment problem' in Asia by showing that rural poverty is not characterized by open unemployment ('no work to do') nor even by underemployment ('not enough work to do') but rather by a lot of work to do, with very low returns.

Tripp (1982, p. 399) makes a similar observation in concluding his report of a household-allocation study in northern Ghana, when he says that although the time devoted to conventional farming activities is not terribly high, people are nevertheless fully occupied, and that the nature of these activities must be fully understood before one can hope to plan meaningful development programmes.

The effect of the time-consuming nature of household production on farming activities is illustrated by the time-allocation and farm-production strategy of a single-person household in a Bangladesh village. Cain (1980, p. 222) estimates that this 50-year-old man, who owns a small amount of land which is rented to sharecroppers, spent 77 per cent of his waking hours in work. Of the working hours, 93 per cent consisted of housework, including cooking, drying, winnowing and husking paddy, sweeping, fetching water and washing dishes and utensils. Cain notes that women or young children would normally perform these tasks, thus permitting the household head and other able males to cultivate the family land and engage in other income-producing work. In the case of the man who lives alone, however, the demands of necessary housework exhaust his time, forcing him to lease his land to sharecroppers.

These studies emphasize the importance of home production in the time allocation of rural households, and help to dispel the notion that family time not spent in farm production has either a zero opportunity cost or a very low one. The recognition that farm-household labour may be employed in a diverse range of market or non-market production activities, of which farm production is but one, provides an explanation for the family-labour substitution strategies commonly employed on family farms around the world. In Mexico, for example, Roberts (1982, p. 310) notes that in one area households prefer to hire labour, even though they could provide these inputs internally, 1) because of the comparative advantage of women in other household tasks and, 2) because male labour is often employed in off-farm activities throughout the year. In another area Roberts (1982, p. 308) concludes that 'Mechanization, primarily in land preparation, appears to have substituted for household labour rather than hired labour'. Farrington and Abeyratne (1982) found the same substitution pattern in a study of mechanization in Sri Lanka.

Goldman and Squire (1982, p. 773) report similar family-labour substitution behaviour on the part of Malaysian farm-households to the introduction of short-maturing rice varieties and a move from single to double cropping:

> The net labour using characteristic of the new technology only partially explains the ultimate impact of the level and distribution of net farm income. Between 1969 and 1973 net farm income grew almost fivefold. This growth might have been even larger had Muda farm families not made intensive use of hired labourers. Although the share of family labour in value of output grew over the period, there was also a substantial increase in hired labour use in the face of an apparently abundant supply of family labour.

Goldman and Squire (1982, p. 773) suggest that the low intensity of labour use by farm families was probaby caused by the wealth effect of the project, which induced a high demand for leisure at the margin. However, as we have noted above (p. 131), the household-economics interpretation would be that the increased returns to family labour induced a substitution away from the relatively scarce resource of family time, towards a time-saving, more expensive (in money terms) production technology involving hired labour. Thus, on a household-economics interpretation, even though returns to family labour in farming are relatively high, the marginal returns to time in non-farm activities encourage the adoption of family labour-saving production inputs.

Reyna (1976) describes a very different strategy for saving family labour time in Chad. There the Barma seek to extend households by adding to the original married couple: 1) another wife(s); 2) a married son(s); 3) a married brother(s); 4) a divorced sister or daughter. Reyna shows that this method of recruiting adults to households (termed extending-strategy) is a cultural means, engineered by enterprising individuals, to provision households with more abundant labour supplies relative to consumption needs. Compared with nuclear households, individuals in extended households thereby spend less time in attaining subsistence requirements. Reyna (1976, p. 193) argues that the 'extended family households, from the vantage of the individual labourer, because they have reduced labour time input (by 13%), have decreased production costs. The individual's saved labour can be used to satisfy other utilities'. And back in southern Africa, in the Mangwende communal area of Zimbabwe, where a large proportion of male adults migrate to wage employment on commercial farms or to commerce and industry in Harare, the wives remaining on the land have made up for this loss of family labour by forming farming groups. This development of farming groups, which is being encouraged by the extension service, has been most enthusiastically taken up by women farmers who form the bulk of the membership.

Thus, in the diverse rural situations of Mexico, Sri Lanka, Malaysia, Chad and Zimbabwe, the inclination to adopt various strategies (labour hire, mechanization, extended families or farming groups) to save or make up for the loss of family labour in farm production has been observed. Household economics provides a unifying interpretation for these observations in terms of the high premium placed on family time in non-farming household activities. As we will argue, this has particular implications for agricultural development in Africa, where the possibility of hiring labour to substitute for family time in farm production is much more limited than in most other regions of the Third World.

A pan-African perspective

The African land-tenure system

In one respect the rural situation in sub-Saharan Africa differs from most other regions of the world, namely in the absence of a class of landless labourers (Byerlee and Eicher, 1972, p. 4). This is a function of the usufruct land-tenure system that prevails throughout the continent. In terms of our household-economics analysis of farm production, it is an important distinction because it means that hired labour, which is a common means of releasing family time from farm production, is less readily obtained by most farm-households.[2] Although this is a characteristic that southern Africa has in common with most of the rest of the continent, the hired labour market is further restricted in southern Africa by the availability of non-farm employment opportunities. In Malawi, as in Swaziland, surveys indicate that only about 3 per cent of total farm-household labour input to farming is hired.

The implication, from the farm production point of view, is that the conservation of the scarce resource of family labour time must be achieved by means other than hiring agricultural wage labour. One way of reducing the input of family time per unit of output is to reduce the amount of labour applied per unit of land. Labour-extensive production strategies are common throughout Africa, and have been seen as a rational response to a relatively land-abundant environment. However, we have seen that labour-extensive strategies continue to be employed in situations where land is extremely scarce, as in densely populated Lesotho for example. We quoted the World Bank above (p. 148) to the effect that, in the absence of labour to hire, households in Lesotho use fertilizer as 'a substitute for good husbandry', i.e. as a substitute for family labour time in farm production. Contrast the use of the fertilizer technology in Lesotho with the use of new short-season rice varieties and double cropping in Malaysia, which we commented on above (p. 182). This technology required a large increase in labour input, which was supplied by hired and family labour. However family labour, although abundant, did not increase as much as it might have done. In the Malaysian case, hired labour was used to save family time so that the production effect of the technology was not greatly compromised, although net farm returns were reduced. In the

Lesotho case, the saving of family labour by using fertilizer as a substitute for more intensive husbandry conflicts directly with the potential impact of the 'yield (per hectare) increasing' fertilizer technology (and perplexes World Bank evaluation missions).

Different rates of market development

The Lesotho example is extreme perhaps, but it illustrates how the impact of yield-increasing, labour-using, technology may be limited on family farms where a landless labouring class does not exist. The use of a market goods-intensive technology to save family labour in Lesotho is facilitated by the availability of cash income from wage employment, and can be expected to be less common in situations where off-farm wage opportunities have not expanded as fast as they have done in southern Africa. However, even where market production takes the form of cash cropping on the farm rather than off-farm wage employment, trade offs exist between the allocation of time to market farm production, on the one hand, and non-market farm and household production on the other. Evidence from Nigeria (Okurume, 1970) and Tanzania (Collinson, 1970) indicates that farmers move towards less labour-intensive subsistence crops such as cassava in order to accommodate cash cropping.

In the rest of Africa, with the exception of a few West African countries such as Ivory Coast and Nigeria, there is less of a tendency for household members to specialise in market production and to meet subsistence needs with market-intensive technology, because of the lack of development and reliability of markets for consumer goods, crop inputs or foodstuffs. Thus household time is preferentially allocated to essential non-market household activities, including the provision of a secure food supply. In these situations, risk and uncertainty play a more important role than has been suggested in this study. Nevertheless, while the conflict between market and non-market production may be less pronounced where markets are poorly developed, the conflicts between the allocation of family time spent on non-market production on the farm versus the household remains. Furthermore, as the market develops, we can expect to observe increasing conflict between market and non-market (including subsistence) production. Aboyade (1983) makes this point. Speaking about West Africa, he comments that the introduction of an urban wage sector for general labour 'only widens the rural family's horizon further and raises the opportunity cost of its farming effort'.

Permanent versus oscillating migration

Southern Africa does not only differ from much of the rest of Africa in the extent of modern-sector development and off-farm job opportunities. It also differs in the nature of these opportunities. This difference, together with political factors, has led to the institutionalization of a significant proportion of labour migration in southern Africa, whereby rural males are recruited to work on South African mines for fixed periods of about a year and are then returned to their rural homes. Thus Stahl and Bohning (1981, p. 148) comment that the southern African migrant was 'forced in the past by economic circumstances to keep his family living and working in the rural hinterland and to return thereto, and [is] forced today by the laws of apartheid to do the same'. Lyby (1980, p. 40) argues that the migrant labour system in southern Africa 'is based on forced oscillating migration: there being no way in which a migrant can ever hope to settle permanently near his place of work'.

While there is no question that the institutionalization of migration to the South African mines has had a substantial influence on the nature of development in the region and sets it apart from the rest of the continent, it does not follow that our analysis of the development process, and of rural out-migration in particular, has little relevance elsewhere. The tendency to view migration in southern Africa solely in terms of the political and institutional framework that characterizes recruitment to South African mines is misleading. In the first place it is by no means clear that the institutionalization of South African mine migration has been dictated by the needs of the modern mining sector alone. In Chapter 5 we noted that political economists such as Hyden (1980) and Meillassoux (1981) argue that the indigenous peasant economy has the ability to affect the mode of operation of the market economy. On these grounds the following argument could be made in respect of the development of South African mine labour procurement operations.

Since the indigenous tenure system in southern Africa requires a household presence to be maintained in order to retain access to non-market benefits and allows for temporary absences of some household members without forfeit of most of these benefits, temporary migration is compatible with, and does not threaten the survival of, indigenous modes of production. Faced with a great need for labour and the tendency for labour to remain only for limited periods, the gold mining industry was obliged to cast its net wide in search of recruits and, at an early stage, established recruiting agencies such as the Native Recruiting Corporation (NRC, formed in 1912) and the Witwatersrand Native Labour Association (WNLA, formed as the Rand Labour Association in 1987 and renamed in 1901). These agencies operated in neighbouring countries and recruited, arranged transport, and organized payment schemes (such as deferred pay and remittances). It is through these agencies that the mines were able to obtain their labour requirements, and international oscillating migration has become institutionalized. While these institutions now contribute to the persistence of oscillating migration in the region, it is important to recognize that they satisfy both modern and indigenous sector needs.

In the second place, institutionalized migration is not the only form of oscillating migration found in southern Africa. While migration to the South African mines is predominant in Botswana, Ciskei, Lesotho and Transkei, it forms only a minor proportion of oscillating migration in other countries, such as Swaziland and Zimbabwe where most communal area farm-households have members working and living away from home. In the latter two countries internal migration to local industries and urban complexes constitutes the major part of rural out-migration, and is predominantly of an oscillating character. For example, only 12 per cent of those Swazis engaged in wage employment in 1979 were employed in South African mines. And de Vletter (1981, p. 55) notes that in Swaziland:

> The most dominant [migration] flow is clearly internal, even in many areas adjacent to the South African border. Internal flows were mainly to the urban areas and accounted for approximately 40% or more of the rural homestead absentees, while about one third were situated in other rural areas... Our

findings showed that virtually all external and internal migrants retained their home base in the rural areas . . . and that at least 50 per cent of the internal migrants could not be considered proximate to their homesteads, i.e. the distance between home and place of work would not enable the worker to return daily.

This pattern of oscillating migration within Swaziland is clearly not determined by the type of institutional or political factors that characterize migration to South Africa.

In the third place, oscillating migration needs to be seen in its proper geographic and historical context. Spengler (1964, p. 295) notes that oscillating migration takes place throughout Africa: 'Migration in Africa,' he notes, 'differs from migration in much of the world in that so small a fraction of the migrants settle permanently in the places where they find employment'. Oscillating migration is not confined to southern Africa: it is as much a feature in West Africa as it is in East Africa and has been associated with indigenous enterprise in Ghana and Uganda as much as with settler development in Kenya and Zimbabwe.

Neither is oscillating migration a recent phenomenon. In colonial times it was originally thought that oscillating migration represented a transitory stage in a young economy's development out of primitive conditions (Elkan, 1960, p. 4). However its persistence occupied the minds of colonial administrators, whose main concern was to devise methods by which the stabilization of labour could be promoted (Powesland, 1954, p. 133).

The need for a stabilized work force was viewed in terms of production efficiency in the modern sector. Low levels of productivity in African industry were explained in terms of the lack of skill of the majority of the work force, and the difficulty of developing the necessary skills where labour only remained for short periods. Thus a vicious circle was envisaged in which:

> Because [the worker] is frequently absent from his work he fails to maintain his skill at the highest level of which he is capable, and his employer has to maintain a larger roll of employees to allow for the proportion of workers who may be absent at any one time. The worker's pay is therefore reduced, and this, from his point of view, confirms his need to spend part of his time working on his farm (Powesland, 1954, p. 113).

As we noted in Chapter 10, the recent radical political-economy literature places a different perspective on the basic cause of oscillating migration. In order to provide labour for capitalist development, workers are said to have been forced from their lands (by asset confiscation, taxation and trade restrictions) and the pattern of oscillating migration is seen to be a direct result of low wages, which are deliberately kept at levels which are insufficient to support whole families at places of work.

The weakness of both the colonial and radical analyses is that they pay insufficient attention to the indigenous factors influencing migration patterns. Colonial analysis concentrated on conditions of employment in the modern sector, and political economists have concentrated on institutional factors at the state level.

Elkan points out the fallacy of accounting for the phenomenon of oscillating migration solely in terms of what happens to workers while they are in employment. He observes that a migrant's income is not only made up of his wages but also of the income which his family draws from farming in the countryside. The 'income from farming,' he notes, 'may hardly suffice to support a family at all. Yet even here [in Uganda] people cling to their farms tenaciously, because if they did not they would forgo part of their income' (Elkan, 1960, p. 135). Acharya (1978, p. 14) also recognizes that the rural base has certain advantages. He attributes oscillating migration to the fact that the relative abundance of land in Africa allows a low-level subsistence livelihood to be reaped 'easily' relative to South Asian economies. This tends to ensure a high 'reservation price' for rural labour, which fosters tendencies towards oscillating migration.

Chapman and Prothero (1977, p. 5) summarize a review of the literature on oscillating or 'circular' migration by remarking that 'circulation rather than being transitional or ephemeral, is a time-honoured and enduring mode of behaviour, deeply rooted in a great variety of cultures and found at all stages of economic change'. Despite these caveats about the non-peculiarity of migration in southern Africa today, it is clear that oscillating migration, though by no means confined to southern Africa, is more extensive there than elsewhere on the continent and that, with the exception of Zambia, urbanization or permanent rural out-migration has been less extensive. Together with data on the characteristics of internal versus external migrants in Swaziland, our analysis can offer some insight into these differences.

It was found by de Vletter et al. (1981) that in Swaziland external and internal migrants had markedly different characteristics. While most external (i.e. South African mine) migrants said they would prefer to work in Swaziland given the right conditions, two-thirds said that they would not consider local work because wages were too low and the work was too hard. Most (80 per cent) of these migrants were junior members of their households and under 30 years of age. By contrast only half the internal migrants were less than 30 years of age and, for many of these senior household members, proximity to home was more important in job selection than wage levels (de Vletter et al., p. 50). Internal migrants indicated that they spent their money on basic family support: food, household goods, clothing and school fees. External migrants also emphasized the importance of family support, but gave equal or greater emphasis to the purchase of cattle, with 50–60 per cent stating that they intended to buy cattle (de Vletter et al., p. 72).

It is clear that the internal migrants, who are older and have greater family responsibilities, conform most closely to the household-economics analysis we have presented in this study. The younger external migrant, with fewer family responsibilities, has been attracted to the mines by higher wages and also, according to van Drunen (1978), by the technological and cosmopolitan nature of the mine environment. For many of these migrants, mine employment offers a means of temporary escape from their subordinate roles in the rural household, where they have claim to little more than basic support for their labour inputs (Rozen-Prinz and Prinz, 1978). At the same time, it provides the means for attaining individual wealth (in cattle especially), and thus hastens the day when a permanent break with the parental household can be made.[3]

In southern Africa contract mine employment has attracted many young rural males who would otherwise have been most inclined to seek distant urban employment. In this sense mine migration has acted as a 'safety valve' in terms of urbanization and urban unemployment. Moreover it has helped to maintain rural links by ensuring regular home visits, which might be less easily made or afforded by the urban job seeker.

In some countries such as Lesotho and Transkei, where internal job opportunities are very limited, institutionalized oscillating migration is the norm for all classes of migrants, and the maintenance of a rural home base is as much a necessary condition of migration as a conscious choice. In other countries, where internal job opportunities are more plentiful, as in Swaziland and Zimbabwe, the maintenance of a rural home base is especially important for the older migrant with family responsibilities and they choose lower-paying, closer-situated, internal migration on this account. In the absence of institutionalized oscillating migration to the mines, it is likely that there would have been a much greater flow of young urban job seekers with weak incentives to maintain rural ties than has been the case to date. Thus the institutionalization of oscillating migration in southern Africa probably does help to account for the lesser extent of permanent urban migration there than elsewhere in Africa. Even so, the maintenance of a rural home base is still an important factor for many urban migrants throughout the continent. In Sierra Leone, for example, two-thirds of urban migrants return to their rural base within five years (Byerlee, Tommy & Fatoo, 1976). And Johnson and Whitlaw (1974) found that 60 per cent of a sample of 1140 low-income and middle-income married male wage earners in Nairobi have a wife in rural areas. An appreciation of the nature of these rural–urban links at the farm-household level can help us to move towards a fuller understanding of the agricultural development problem in Africa.

Implications for agricultural development in Africa

In this study we have shown how a household-economics perspective can contribute to an understanding of the stagnation of indigenous agriculture in southern Africa. And in the last two sections we have suggested that, despite differences in the nature and extent of modern market development in southern Africa compared with the remainder of the continent, the southern African analysis is not irrelevant to the wider problem of agricultural development in Africa as a whole.

The harmful effects of the out-migration of part of a farm-household's labour force is seen clearly in terms of the oscillating nature of migration in southern Africa. But even where migration is of a more permanent character, the concepts we have put forward of 'complex co-operation' and comparative advantage at the farm-household level suggest that, contrary to orthodox thinking, withdrawal of labour from the African countryside tends to result in residual farm work forces which have lower productive potential than they would otherwise have had. This conclusion stems from the realization that urban migration will tend to be undertaken by the younger, more able, better-educated members of farm-households. Not only are those members left behind disadvantaged from the farm production point of view, in that they benefit less from complex co-operation, but they often have other non-farm (household maintenance) duties to perform, which place a premium on their time and lead them to seek labour-saving cultivation strategies. Indeed, our argument suggests that those members who remain in the rural areas do so, not only because they have a comparative disadvantage in urban employment, but also because of the relative cost-advantage of maintaining a home in the countryside compared with the town.

The ubiquitous usufruct land-tenure system in Africa impinges on this situation in two respects. First, the nature of the use rights provided under traditional African tenure, and the costs of maintaining these rights, encourage most households to retain rural ties in one form or another. Where this involves the continued presence of some household members on the land, it implies that a significant proportion of the available resources are preempted by groupings that do not look on their land holdings primarily as productive assets, but rather as a form of long-term security and a source of household requisites that require little or no money expenditure, and can be cheaply procured with low-opportunity cost labour. Second, the availability of land-use rights to all means that there is typically no landless labouring class to provide a ready substitute for family labour in farm production.

The implications of this thinking for the impact of new agricultural technology have been discussed in Chapters 8, 11 and 13. We have particularly noted that subsistence crop technologies have been adopted in southern Africa to save family time in subsistence farm production. Under existing produce and food price structures, the adoption of these technologies has not resulted in increases in marketed output. Elsewhere in Africa, marketing difficulties and input supply problems are generally recognized to have hindered the production of food surpluses for urban consumption. But cheap urban food policies in these countries have also created price structures that restrict the incentives to produce in excess of subsistence requirements. Cheap urban food policies have not only reduced market incentives in this way, they have also made real urban wages relatively attractive and have helped to encourage townward migration of part of the farm-household's labour force. This has reduced the quantity and quality of farm labour complements.

The decline of per capita food production in Africa over the last two decades reflects a situation where urban populations have increased substantially, (and prematurely in terms of the Lewis (1954) development model). Rural production has barely continued to provide for rural food needs, let alone generate surpluses to feed the growing urban populations. As the World Bank (1981) has pointed out, these growing urban populations have been provided for by international imports or by modern-sector production. On the basis of the Nigerian experience Aboyade (1983) suggests that in the African environment the common stretegies of importing food deficits and of maintaining low urban food prices may temporarily fill the food gap but are more likely to fuel it in the longer term.

In the wake of the success of the 'green revolution' in solving Asia's food crisis of the 1960s, donors and governments alike have looked for technological answers to the African food production problem. In this book we have argued that the potential of the labour-using types of improved food production technology that worked in Asia and have been transferred to Africa with vast amounts of donor assistance have been severely limited by the socio-economic circumstances prevailing in Africa, where:
  1) real urban wages have been inflated by cheap food policies;
  2) usufruct land-tenure has encouraged most households to retain rural links, often for non-farm production reasons;

3) in the face of relatively high real urban wages, and given the advantages of retaining a rural base, the most able household members have migrated townwards, leaving farm labour forces depleted in quality and quantity;

4) because of the non-farm demands on their time and low market food prices, the remaining farm labour complements have not been able or inclined to devote sufficient attention to food crop production to generate surpluses for the market, and the labour-using types of improved food crop technologies that have been introduced have not been of much help in this regard.

There are many and various reasons why the green revolution has bypassed Africa[4]. The technical difficulties, such as a harsh agro-climatic environment, poor soils, disease prevalence and lack of infrastructure and training, so often given as principal reasons in tropical Africa, apply to a much lesser extent in southern Africa. From a household-economics perspective we have argued that a combination of socio-economic factors, such as relatively low food prices, expansion of wage employment opportunities and traditional land-tenure arrangements, have significantly contributed to the lack of production on indigenous farms in southern Africa.

These socio-economic factors are common to Africa as a whole, though they are often overshadowed by the technical and infrastructural difficulties upon which development efforts through the 1970s have concentrated. However, according to Mellor (1985), socio-economic factors are at the core of Africa's food crisis:

> Africa's poor record on food production is largely due to the labor constraint combined with rapid urbanization, rising urban incomes and rising remittance to rural areas. These all serve to reduce labor input into agriculture, slowing the expansion of area cultivated as well as of yields per acre. These same forces have a much less negative impact on agriculture under the labor surplus regimes of Asia.

While this does not mean that the type of biological scientific research that solved Asia's food crisis of the 1960s has little relevance in Africa, it *does* mean that it is likely to be more difficult to *focus* research towards technologies that are acceptable to African farm-households, for whom increases in yields per area of land may not be the overriding concern. It also means that technology alone will have limited impact while the broad socio-economic environment facing farm-households remains unfavourable for marketed production.

This book has argued that the adoption of a household-economics perspective can contribute to our understanding of the nature of the socio-economic characteristics that make African farming and urbanisation different, as well as provide guidance to researchers and development planners seeking to learn from and improve upon the disappointing performance of agrarian development efforts in southern Africa over the last two decades.

Negative lessons can help us to recognise and understand a problem and thus contribute towards the search for appropriate solutions. That has been the major objective of this book. Let us end by taking note of a positive lesson which may be equally instructive (and more encouraging) in guiding future action. Since independence there has been an impressive increase in the proportion of formal marketings of maize coming from small scale farmers in Zimbabwe: from 10% in 1980 to 40% in 1985. These increases have been associated with a broad range of complementary changes.

While the effect of an end to the disruptions of the war, as well as the psychological influence of post-war purpose and patriotism, cannot be repeated elsewhere, there have also been a number of more replicable changes. These include an increase in the maize price relative to other crops and to wages, reductions in commercial farm workforces, expansion of credit and of marketing facilities in rural areas, an explosion in rural retail trade, some land tenure changes and a marked downturn in the rate of industrial sector development since 1975. All these changes impinge on the socio-economic environment facing farm-households and have encouraged households to market a larger proportion of their production as well as use improved technologies, such as hybrid seed (previously available and developed for the modern commercial sector), to increase total production.

The response has not been uniform across all households, even in the agro-ecologically favourable areas. Nevertheless, this positive experience provides hope and encouragement for the future. Whether and to what extent such changes will bring about the coexistence of a commercial small farm sector with an expanding modern industrial urban sector, and what the implications may be for the non-market and social security functions of traditional land tenure, remain to be seen.

Notes

1 See also Benjamin, 1980, Table 4.
2 This does not mean that hired labour is not used on African farms. Rather it implies that labour availability tends to be seasonal and is particularly difficult to obtain during periods when farm work demands are heaviest. For example Bruce, Byerlee and Edmeades (1980, p. 8) observe that in Ghana hired labour was available (from migrants and schoolchildren) in particular seasons, but it was not available to alleviate the weeding-labour bottleneck experienced by most farm-households.
3 Asian household studies on the allocation of children's time have indicated that children (especially males) have a net positive economic value to their parents aside from the security in old age that they provide them (Cain, 1980, p. 218), and that households with relatively large numbers of children ensure themselves a lengthy period of economic success. Nag, White and Peet (1980, p. 269) point out that the length of this period of success depends on the parents' ability to produce children who survive, and their ability to retain control of their childrens' labour by postponing their dispersal from the household. When adult children obtain wage employment away from the home, there is an inherent conflict at the household level between the support this employment provides and the increased chances that such employment will lead to the early loss of the worker from the household. This dilemma is common to most households in most societies, although in some societies parents will have more control over their children's labour than in others. At least household economics contributes to an appreciation of this dilemma, by recognizing that migration is often not an individual decision and, even when it is, has implications for the remaining members of a migrant's household.
4 Lack of foreign aid is not one of them. In 1980 net official aid was US$13.70 per capita in Africa compared with an average of US$9.60 for all developing countries.

Appendix 1
Characteristics of survey areas

TABLE A1.1 *Details of the Swaziland rural development areas covered by the farm management surveys*

	Northern	Southern	Mahamba–Zombodze	Central	Mahlangatsha
Year surveyed	1978/79	1978/79	1977/78	1977/78	1976/77
Initial year of development	1972	1973	1978	1973	1973
Altitude (metres)	330–1000	760–1060	850–1285	610–1070	1070–1340
Annual rainfall (millimetres)	955	878	856	911	1016
Arable area (ha)	5290	3075	5790	4420	3330
Grazing area (ha)	9250	8220	14020	14400	19340
No. of households	1640	950	2453	1411	614
Average holding size (ha) (survey data)	1.4	1.8	1.1	1.3	2.2

Appendix 2
Farm Management Survey data collection and analysis

In the farm management surveys, data are collected from a random sample of about eighty farmers within the sampling frame of a rural development area using the population census enumeration areas. Two types of data are collected: stock data and flow data. Stock data are collected at the beginning and end of each season and are analyzed by hand. Stock data include family members by age and sex, off-farm workers, field sizes, livestock numbers and equipment ownership. Field sizes are estimated using a measuring wheel and triangulation.

Flow data are composed of farm inputs and outputs. These data are collected on a weekly record sheet which is composed of a two-page questionnaire. Farm work is recorded on the first page. Information is gathered on the plot and crop, the type of work done, the equipment used, the material inputs applied, the person(s) doing the work and the time spent on the specified operation. The second page is used to obtain information on farm and non-farm receipts or expenditures. The form of payment is recorded: whether cash, credit or kind. Farm production generated is also recorded.

The forms are returned to headquarters weekly where they are checked, coded and punched in the subsequent week. Errors and inconsistencies are checked for, manually as well as mechanically and if any are found the forms are returned for field checking the following week. At year end the yields from randomly selected fields are estimated by weighing the total harvest from each selected field. In the case of cotton and tobacco, the sales records of each farm are related to the cotton or tobacco area cultivated on that farm.

For coding purposes two basic forms of input/output are identified: 1) Labour and power; and 2) Others (mainly materials). Each input/output type relates to a farm, a subject (enterprise), and a sub-subject (field size when the subject is a crop). Each input/output relating to a subject/sub-subject may be described by type, operation (in the case of labour and power input/outputs), time, quantity and value (which may be in terms of cash or kind). This coding format is shown below, with an example of an input of 5 kg of own seed on to field number 3 on which 0.25 hectares of maize is planted. A corresponding entry will be made for the second input/output relating to the same operation on the same field, i.e. labour used to sow the seed by type, operation (e.g. hand sow), time (same as for first input) and quantity (in hours), relating to the same field.

Appendix 2 Farm-Management Survey data collection and analysis

Farm No.	Subject	Field No.	Sub-subject (fld size)	type	oper	First Input/Output Time mo wk	qty	knd	value
1	Maize	3	0.25	own seed		11 2	5		

Programmes have been written to obtain the following farm-by-farm analyses from this coding format:

  1) Cropping patterns:
— total and percentage areas under different crops;
— field analysis – numbers and sizes.

  2) Labour analyses:
— labour hours by operational category for all farm work;
— labour hours by month and type of labour for all farm work;
— labour hours by month and type of labour for each enterprise;
— per hectare labour hours by operational category for each crop enterprise;
— per hectare labour hours by month and type of labour for each crop enterprise.

  3) Non-farm income and expenditure by item;

  4) Cropping income and expenditure by item;

  5) Farm, non-farm and total income and expenditure;

  6) Per crop inputs and outputs by quantity and value and crop gross margins;

  7) Livestock analysis (stock removals and births and cash expenditure and income by livestock category).

For categories 2) and 6) the data for each farm are also broken down by field. These data were combined with hand-collated information on household composition, as well as livestock and equipment ownership, to make up two basic S.P.S.S.* system files: a farm-level file and a field-level file. The field-level file was used for regression analysis, and the farm-level file for all other FMS-related analyses presented in Part II.

* Nie, N.H., Bent, D.H. and Hull, C.H., *Statistical Package for the Social Sciences*, Version IV.

Appendix 3
Statistical supplement

TABLE A7.1 *Standard errors of the means: arable areas allocated and cropped per farm by de jure and de facto household workforce*

	No. 16–64 years of age			No. 16–64 years of age on farm		
	0–3	4–5	6+	0–2	3–4	5+
Area allocated						
5 RDAs	.07	.09	.11	.07	.09	.14
Northern	.13	.16	.22	.13	.18	.30
Southern	.13	.13	.30	.11	.18	.22
Zombodze	.10	.16	.17	.11	.15	.18
Central	.12	.27	.17	.12	.21	.20
Mahlangatsha	.29	.18	.42	.17	.19	.55
Area cropped						
5 RDAs	.06	.09	.10	.06	.08	.12
Northern	.11	.12	.21	.11	.16	.29
Southern	.12	.12	.14	.10	.11	.17
Zombodze	.10	.15	.16	.10	.14	.18
Central	.09	.32	.16	.08	.20	.20
Mahlangatsha	.17	.17	.36	.15	.20	.44

TABLE A7.2 *Standard errors of the means: farms spending less than E10 on power, maize yield and gross margin/hr by labour hours in cropping*

	Crop labour: hrs/farm		
	0–199	200–399	400+
Maize yield/hr			
5 RDAs	.82	1.19	.61
Northern	1.09	1.14	.57
Southern	1.60	.21	.65
Zombodze	1.69	5.18	4.31
Central	2.71	2.07	—
Mahlangatsha	1.08	1.87	.97
Maize GM/hr			
5 RDAs	6.31	8.82	4.77
Northern	9.88	7.44	4.43
Southern	11.18	4.38	4.62
Zombodze	15.02	3.70	41.19
Central	18.58	19.42	—
Mahlangatsha	6.64	13.32	6.29

TABLE A7.11 *Standard errors of the means: area cropped and cattle held by household size*

	Household size		
	1–5	6–8	9+
Area cropped (ha)			
5 RDAs (n = 376)	.06	.07	.09
Northern (n = 78)	.09	.13	.21
Southern (n = 77)	.15	.15	.11
Zombodze (n = 76)	.12	.11	.15
Central (n = 79)	.09	.10	.20
Mahlangatsha (n = 66)	.14	.21	.24
No. of cattle held (head)			
5 RDAs	.51	.71	.87
Northern	.66	1.77	2.40
Southern	.83	1.60	1.20
Zombodze	.62	1.18	1.18
Central	1.82	1.57	1.66
Mahlangatsha	1.67	1.55	2.23

TABLE A7.14 *Correlation coefficients and number of observations: household size with crop production and wage income*

	Survey areas				
	Northern RDA	Southern RDA	Zombodze RDA	Central RDA	Mahlangatsha RDA
Household size with:					
Maize area cropped	.67	.42	.33	.40	.43
no. of observations	78	77	76	79	66
Crop income	.22	.16	.33	−.06	.08
no. of observations	78	77	76	79	66
No. of wage earners	.41	.59	.36	.67	.53
no. of observations	78	77	76	79	66

TABLE A7.18 Standard errors of the means: net voluntary cattle disposals by domestic development group (Cattle Marketing Survey 1980)

	Establishment Group 1	Expansion Group 2	Consolidation Group 3	Fission Group 4	Decline Group 5
Classification criteria					
Household size	1-6	7-10	11+	7-10	1-6
Any pre-school children	Yes	—	—	—	No
More children than others	—	Yes	—	No	—
Net voluntary cattle disposal rate (percentage)	3.8	2.5	1.8	2.6	3.0

198 Appendix 3 Statistical supplement

TABLE A7.19 Standard errors of the means: domestic development groups – resource structures and production characteristics

	Establishment Group 1	Expansion Group 2	Consolidation Group 3	Fission Group 4	Decline Group 5	FH Group 6
Resources						
R1 Allocated area (ha)	.11	.09	.17	.13	.09	.11
R2 Equipment value (E)	5.4	2.0	2.6	2.1	1.1	1.4
R3 Cattle held (head)	.90	.95	1.48	1.48	.81	1.04
R4 No. of farm workers	.16	.19	.31	.18	.18	.24
R5 No. of wage earners	.09	.11	.19	.16	.11	.21
Production						
P1 Cultivated area (ha)	.08	.08	.14	.11	.08	.09
P2 Maize area	.08	.07	.13	.10	.08	.10
P3 Percentage of P2 in hybrid vars	7.2	5.4	5.0	5.0	5.5	5.4
P4 Cash crop area (ha)	.05	.01	.01	.02	.01	.01
P5 Maize income (E)	1.0	4.5	3.4	5.1	2.4	.72
P6 Other crop income (E)	4.6	6.4	3.8	3.0	1.8	5.0
P7 Crop labour in (hrs)	31	28	39	36	15	42
P8 Crop labour intensity (hrs/farm worker)	25	13	10	12	7	11
P9 Crop labour intensity (hrs/ha)	29	32	22	19	25	26
P10 Percentage of workers in wage employment	3.8	2.4	2.0	2.4	3.7	3.1
P11 Farm expenditure per farm worker (E/head)	4.6	3.7	1.3	2.4	1.8	1.1
P12 Power expenditure per farm worker (E/head)	2.7	1.4	1.0	0.9	1.9	1.5

References

Aboyade, O. (1983), 'Growth strategy and the agricultural sector', paper presented at the IFPRI Conference on Food Policy in Africa, Victoria Falls, September 1983

Acharya, S.N. (1978), 'Perspectives and problems of development in low income sub-Saharan Africa', in *Two Studies of Development in Sub-Saharan Africa*, World Bank Staff Working Paper No. 300, Washington, DC: World Bank

Adams, M. (1978), *Annual Report: Mahlangatsha RDA*, mimeo, Mbabane: Ministry of Agriculture and Cooperatives

Agricultural Research Division (1974), *Advisory Bulletin No. 1*, University of Botswana and Swaziland, Luyengo, Swaziland

Agrotec (1980), *Study of Livestock Marketing and Meat Production*, Mbabane: Ministry of Agriculture and Cooperatives

Ahn, C., Sing, I.J. and **Squire, L.** (1980), *A Model of an Agricultural Household in a Multicrop Economy, The Case of Korea*, Studies in Employment and Rural Development No. 58 Washington, DC: World Bank

Aklilu, B. (1980), 'The diffusion of fertilizer in Ethiopia: pattern, determinants, and implications', *Journal of Developing Areas*, vol. 14 no. 3, pp. 387–99

Alverson, H. (1979), *The Social and Economic Context of Agriculture in Botswana: Some Indicators*, Gaberone: Institute of Development Management, Research Paper No. 6

Arrighi, G. (1970), 'Labour supplies in historical perspective: a study of the proletarianization of the African peasantry in Rhodesia', *Journal of Development Studies*, vol. 6, no. 3, pp. 197–234

ATIP (1984), *Agricultural Technology Improvement Project Annual Report Number 2*, Mid America International Agricultural Consortium, Gaberone: Dept of Agricultural Research, Ministry of Agriculture

Bale, M.D. and **Lutz, E.** (1981), 'Price distortions in agriculture: an international comparison', *American Journal of Agricultural Economics*, vol. 63, pp. 8–22

Ballah, S.S. (1979), 'Farm size, productivity and technical change in Indian agriculture', in R. Berry and C. Cline (eds), *Agrarian Structure and Productivity in Developing Countries*, Baltimore: Johns Hopkins University Press

Barber, W.J. (1961), *The Economy of British Central Africa*, London: Oxford University Press

Barclay-Smith R.W. (1980), *Crop Production and Extension, Swaziland: Project Findings and Recomendations*, Terminal Report of the UNDP Project AG:SWA/72/015, Rome: UNDP

Barker, R. (1965), *Swaziland*, London: HMSO

Barkin, D. (1980), *Mexican Agriculture and the Internationalization of Capital*, Social Science Research Report No. 68, School of Social Science, University of California, Irvine

Barnum, H.N. and **Squire, L.** (1979), 'An econometric application of the theory of the farm-household', *Journal of Development Economics*, vol. 6, no. 1, pp. 79–102

Barrett, V. et al. (1982), *Animal Traction in Eastern Upper Volta: A Technical, Economic and Institutional Analysis*, East Lansing: Dept of Agricultural Economics, Michigan State University, International Development Paper No. 4

Bauer, P.T. (1974), 'Some economic aspects and implications', in J. Barratt, S. Brand, D.S. Collier and K. Glaser (eds), *Accelerated Development in Southern Africa*, London: Macmillan, pp. 217–34

Becker, G.S. (1965), 'A theory of the allocation of time', *Economic Journal*, vol. 75, pp. 493–517

Becker, G.S. (1976), *The Economic Approach to Human Behavior*, Chicago: University of Chicago Press

Behnke, R. and **Kerven, C.** (1983) 'FSR and the attempt to understand the goals and motivations of farmers', *Culture and Agriculture*, vol. 19, pp. 9–16

Bell, R.T. (1972), 'Migrant labour: theory and policy', *South African Journal of Economics*, vol. 40, no. 4, pp. 337–59

Bembridge, T.S. (1980), 'Rural development: increasing livestock production in South Africa's black states', *Africa Insight*, vol. 10, pp. 66–72

Benjamin, A. (1980), *An Economic Evaluation of Maize Production in Three Valleys of the Peruvian Andes*, Economics Program, International Maize and Wheat Improvement Center (CIMMYT), Mexico

Berg, E. (1980), *Alternative Strategies for Zimbabwe's Growth*, Center for Research on Economic Development, University of Michigan

Berry, S.S. (1970), 'Economic development with surplus labour: further complications suggested by contemporary African experience', *Oxford Economic Papers*, vol. 22, no. 2, pp. 275–87

Billing, K.J. (1978) 'Labour migration in Rhodesia – future extension and development strategies for Zimbabwe', MSc. (Agricultural Extension) dissertation, University of Reading

Binswanger, H.P., Evenson, R.E., Florencio, C.A. and **White, N.F.** (eds) (1980), *Rural Household Studies in Asia*, Singapore: Singapore University Press

Bonnerie, H. (1983), *The Impact of Migration in Zimbabwe: Preliminary Findings*, Centre for Udviklingsforskning, Wageningen, Netherlands

Booth, A.R. (1981), *The Development of the Swazi Labor Market, 1900–1968*, mimeo, Ohio University, USA

Botswana Government (1979), *1977/78 Farm Management Survey*, Gaberone: Planning and Statistics Division, Ministry of Agriculture

Brand, S.S. (1974), 'Agriculture in economic development in southern Africa', in J. Barratt, S. Brand, D.S. Collier and K. Glaser (eds), *Accelerated Development in Southern Africa*, London: Macmillan, pp. 257–78

Brown, L.H. (1977), 'The ecology of man and domestic livestock', in D.J. Pratt and M.D. Gwynne (eds), *Rangeland Management and Ecology in East Africa*, London: Hodder & Stoughton, pp. 34–40

Bruce, K., Byerlee, D. and **Edmeades, G.E.** (1980), *Maize in the Mampong-Sekodumasi Area of Ghana: Results of an Exploratory Survey*, Economics

Program, International Maize and Wheat Improvement Center (CIMMYT), Mexico
Bundy, C. (1979), *The Rise and Fall of the South African Peasantry*, London: Heinemann
Bwalya, M.C. (1980), 'Rural differentiation and poverty reproduction in northern Zambia: the case of Mpika District', in *The Evolving Structure of Zambian Society*, Edinburgh: Centre of African Studies, University of Edinburgh
Byerlee, D.B. (1983), *The Increasing Role of Wheat Consumption and Imports in the Developing World*, Economics Program Working Paper No. 05/83, International Maize and Wheat Improvement Center (CIMMYT), Mexico
Byerlee, D. and **Eicher, C.K.** (1972) *Rural Employment, Migration and Economic Development: Theoretical Issues and Empirical Evidence from Africa*, Rural African Employment Study, Paper No. 1, Michigan State University, East Lansing
Byerlee, D., Harrington, L. and **Winkelmann, D.L.** (1982) 'Farming systems research: issues in research strategy and technology design', *American Journal of Agricultrural Economics*, vol. 64, pp. 897–904
Byerlee, D., Tommy, J.L. and **Fatoo, H.** (1976) *Rural-Urban Migration in Sierra Leone: Determinants and Policy Implications*, African Rural Economy Working Paper No. 13, Dept of Agricultural Economics, Michigan State University, East Lansing
Caballero, J.M. (1982), *Agriculture and the Peasantry Under Industrial Take-Off Pressures: Lessons from the Peruvian Experience*, Centre of Latin American Studies, Cambridge University
Cain, M.T. (1980), 'The economic activities of children in a village in Bangladesh', in Binswanger, H.P. et al. (eds) (1980)
Caldwell, J.S. (1983), 'An overview of farming systems research and development: origins, applications and issues', in C.B. Flora (ed), *Proceedings of Kansas State University's 1982 Farming Systems Research Symposium – farming systems in the field*, Paper No. 5, Kansas State University, Manhattan, Kansas
Centro de Investigacions Agrarias (1974), *Estructura Agraria y Desarrollo Agricola en Mexico*, Fondo de Cultura Economica, Mexico
Chapman, M. and **Prothero, R.M.** (1977), 'Circulation between home places and towns: a village approach to urbanization', Paper presented at a working session on urbanization in the Pacific, Association for Social Anthropology in Oceania, Monterey, California
Chayanov, A.V. (1966) *The Theory of Peasant Economy*, (D. Thorner, B. Kerblay, and R.E.F. Smith, (eds)) Irwin, Illinois, American Economic Association
Chipande, G. (1983), 'Smallholder agriculture in a rural development strategy', PhD dissertation, University of Glasgow
CIMMYT (1978), *Demonstration of An Interdisciplinary Approach to Planning Adaptive Agricultural Research Programs in the Serenje Province, Zambia, 1978*, Economics Program, International Maize and Wheat Improvement Center (CIMMYT), Mexico
CIMMYT (1981), *World Maize Facts and Trends*, International Maize and Wheat Improvement Center (CIMMYT), Mexico

CIMMYT (1982), *Demonstrations of an Interdisciplinary Approach to Planning Adaptive Agricultural Research Programmes*, Report No. 5, November 1982, Ministry of Agriculture, Zimbabwe/Department of Land Management, University of Zimbabwe/CIMMYT

Clarke D.G. (1977), *Foreign Migrant Labour in South Africa*, mimeo, World Employment Programme Working paper, WEP2-26/WP 16, Geneva: ILO

Cleave, J.H. (1970), 'Labor in the development of African agricutlure: the evidence from farm surveys', PhD dissertation, Stanford University

Cole, D.P. (1979), *Pastoral Nomads in a Rapidly Changing Economy: The Case of Saudi Arabia*, Pastoral Network Paper No. 7e, London: Overseas Development Institute

Collinson, M.P. (1970), 'A survey of innovations in traditional agriculture in Tanzania', East African Agricultural Economics Conference Paper

Collinson, M.P. (1982), *Farming Systems Research in Eastern Africa: The Experience of CIMMYT and some National Agricultural Research Services, 1976-81*, MSU International Development Paper No. 3, Dept of Agricultural Economics, Michigan State University, East Lansing

Crush, J.S. (1979), 'The parameters of dependence in southern Africa: a case study of Swaziland', *Journal of Southern African Affairs*, vol. 4, no. 1, pp. 55-66

Crush, J.S. (1980), 'The genesis of colonial land policy in Swaziland', *South African Geographic Journal*, vol. 62, no. 1, pp. 73-88

Daniel, J.C.McI. (1964), 'The Swazi rural economy', in Holleman, J.F. (ed.) (1964), pp. 204-50

Daniel J.B. McI. (1966), 'Some government measures to improve African agriculture in Swaziland', *Geographical Journal*, vol. 132, pp. 506-15

Dean, E. (1966), *The Supply Responses of African Farmers: Theory and Measurement in Malawi*, Amsterdam: North Holland

Deboeck, G. and **Kinsey, B.** (1980), *Managing Information for Rural Development: Lessons from Eastern Africa*, World Bank Staff Working Paper No. 379, Washington, DC: World Bank

Doran, M.H., Low, A.R.C. and **Kemp, R.L.**(1979), 'Cattle as a store of wealth in Swaziland: implications for livestock development and overgrazing in eastern and southern Africa', *American Journal of Agricultural Economics*, vol. 61, pp. 41-7

van Drunen, L.J.M. (1978), 'Lesotho village life and migrant labour: a case study of the impact of pressures of migrant labourers and returned migrants on rural life', MA thesis, Rijksuniversiteit, Utrecht

Eckert, J. and **Wykstra, R.** (1980), *South African Mine Wages in the Seventies and their Effects on Lesotho's Economy*, Research Report No. 7, Lesotho Agricultural Sector Analysis Project, Colorado State University

Economics Section (1980), *Cattle Marketing Survey*, mimeo, Mbabane: Ministry of Agriculture and Cooperatives

Eicher, C.K. (1982), 'Facing up to Africa's food crisis', *Foreign Affairs*, vol. 61, no. 1, pp. 151-74

Eicher, C.K. and **Baker, D.C.** (1982) *Research on Agricultural Development in sub-Saharan Africa: A Critical Survey*, MSU International Development paper No. 1, Michigan State University

Elkan, W. (1960), *Migrants and Proletarians: Urban Labour in the Economic*

Development of Uganda, London: Oxford University Press

Elkan, W. (1980), 'Labour migration from Botswana, Lesotho and Swaziland', *Economic Development and Cultural Change*, vol. 28, no. 3, pp. 583-96

Elling, M. (1981), *Background to Agricultural Development in Central Province Zambia*, FAO Agriplan Project, Rome

Evenson, R.E. (1978), 'Time allocation in rural Philippine households', *American Journal of Agricultural Economics*, vol. 60, pp. 323-30

Evenson, R.E., Popkin, B.M. and **Quizon, E.** (1980), 'Nutrition, work and demographic behaviour in rural Philippine households: a symposium of several Laguna household studies', in Binswanger, H.P. et al. (eds) (1980)

Farrington, J. (1976), 'A note on planned versus actual farmer performance under uncertainty in underdeveloped agriculture', *Journal of Agricultural Economics*, vol. 27, no. 2, pp. 257-60

Farrington, J. (1977), 'Research-based recommendations versus farmers' practices: some lessons from cotton spraying in Malawi', *Experimental Agriculture*, vol. 13, no. 1, pp. 9-15

Farrington, J. and **Abeyratne, F.** (1982), *Farm Power in Sri Lanka*, Development Study No. 22, Department of Agricultural Economics and Management, University of Reading

Fearn, R.M. (1981), *Labor Economics: The Emerging Synthesis*, Cambridge, Mass: Winthorp

Feder, G.F. and **O'Mara, G.T.** (1981), 'Farm size and the diffusion of green revolution technology', *Economic Development and Cultural Change*, vol. 30, no. 1, pp. 59-76

Fisk, E.K. (1964), 'Planning in a primitive economy: from pure subsistence to the production of a market surplus', *The Economic Record*, vol. 40, no. 90, pp. 156-74

Fisk, E.K. (1975), 'The response of non-monetary production units to contact with the exchange economy', in L.G. Reynolds, (ed.), *Agriculture in Development Theory*, New Haven: Yale University Press, pp. 53-83

Flaxen, D.W. (1972), *The Swaziland Rural Homesteads Survey*, Mbabane: Central Statistics Office

FMS (Farm Management Surveys) (1975/6-1978/9), *Reports Nos 2-6*, mimeo, Mbabane: Monitoring and Evaluation Unit, Rural Development Areas Programme

Fortes, M. (1970), *Time and Social Structure and Other Essays*, London: Athlone Press

Fowler, M.H. (1980), *Maize in Swaziland: A Review of its Production and Marketing in Recent Years*, mimeo, Mbabane: Ministry of Agriculture

Fowler, M.H. (1981), *Overgrazing in Swaziland: A Review of the Technical Efficiency of the National Herd*, ODI Pastoral Network Paper No. 12d

Fransman, M.J. (1978), 'The state and development in Swaziland, 1960-1977', PhD thesis, University of Sussex

Fry, J. (1980), 'Trends in wage differentiation in Zambia;, in *The Evolving Structure of Zambian Society*, Edinburgh: Centre of African Studies, University of Edinburgh

Gemmill, G.T. (1971), *The Economics of Farm Mechanization in Malawi*, Lilongwe: Bunda College of Agriculture

Gerhart, J. (1975), *The Diffusion of Hybrid Maize in Western Kenya*, International Maize and Wheat Improvement Center (CIMMYT), Mexico

Ghez, G.R. and **Becker, G.S.** (1975), *The Allocation of Time and Goods over the Life Cycle*, New York: Columbia University Press

Gilbert, E.H., Norman, D. and **Winch, F.E.** (1980), *Farming Systems Research: A Critical Appraisal*, East Lansing: Michigan State University Rural Development Paper No. 6

Goldman, R.H. and **Squire, L.** (1982), 'Technical change, labour use and labour distribution in the Muda irrigation project', *Economic Development and Cultural Change*, vol. 30, no. 4, pp. 754–75

Gordon, H.S. (1954), 'The economic theory of a common-property resource: the fishery', *Journal of Political Economy* vol. 62, no. 2, pp. 124–42

Griliches, Z. (1957), 'Hybrid corn: an exploration in the economics of technological change', *Econometrica*, vol. 25, pp. 501–23

Gronau, R. (1973), 'The intrafamily allocation of time: the value of housewives' time', *American Economic Review*, vol. 68, no. 4, pp. 634–51

Gronau, R. (1974), 'The effect of children on the housewife's value of time', in Schultz, T.W. (ed.), (1974), pp. 457–88

Gugler, J. (1982), 'Overurbanization reconsidered', *Economic Development and Cultural Change*, vol. 31, no. 1, pp. 173–89

Guillet, D. (1981), 'Surplus extraction, risk management and economic change among Peruvian peasants', *Journal of Development Studies*, vol. 18, no. 1, pp. 3–23

Gulhati, R. (1980), *Eastern and Southern Africa: Past Trends and Future Prospects*, World Bank Staff Working paper No. 413, Washington DC: World Bank

Guma, T. and **Gay, J.** (1978), *Socio-Economic Technical Report of Attitudes of Village Farmers about Farming*, Senqu River Agricultural Extension Project LES/72/003, Mohale's Hoek

Hay, M.J. (1972), 'Economic change in Luoland: Kowe, 1890–1945', PhD thesis, University of Wisconsin

Heyer, J. (1981), 'Agricultural development policy in Kenya from the colonial period to 1975', in J. Heyer, P. Roberts and G. Williams (eds), (1981)

Heyer, J., Roberts, P. and **Williams, G.** (eds) (1981), *Rural Development in Tropical Africa*, London: Macmillan

Holleman, F.D. (1949), *Het Bantoe Grondenrecht in die Unie van Suid Afrika en omgering*, Amsterdam

Holleman, J.F. (ed.) (1964), *Experiment in Swaziland*, Cape Town: Oxford University Press

Horowitz, M.M. (1979), *The Sociology of Pastoralism and African Livestock Projects*, Washington, DC: USAID Program Evaluation Discussion Paper No. 6

Houghton, D.H. (1961), 'Land reform in the Bantu Areas and its effects upon the urban labor market', *South African Journal of Economics*, vol. 29, no. 3, pp. 165–75

Houghton, D.H. (1964), 'The problems of labour in African development', in E.A.G. Robinson (ed.) (1964), pp. 312–39

Hughes, A.J.B. (1964), 'Incomes of rural homestead groups', in J.F. Holleman (ed.) (1964), pp. 251-74
Hughes, A.J.B. (1972), *Land Tenure, Land Rights and Land Communities on Swazi Nation Land in Swaziland: A Discussion of Some Inter-relationships Between the Traditional Tenurial System and Problems of Agrarian Development*, Monograph No. 7, Institute for Social Research, University of Natal, Durban.
Hughes, A.J.B. (1974), *Development in Rhodesian Tribal Areas: An Overview*, Harare: Tribal Areas of Rhodesia Foundation
Hunt, D.M. (1979), 'Chayanov's model of peasant household resource allocation', *Journal of Peasant Studies*, vol. 6, pp. 247-85
Hyden, G. (1980), *Beyond Ujamaa in Tanzania: Underdevelopment and an Uncaptured Peasantry*, Berkeley: University of California Press
Hyden, G. (1984), 'The political economy of smallholder agriculture in Africa', paper presented at Rockefeller/Ford Foundation Conference on Intra-household Processes and Farming Systems Analysis, Bellagio, Italy, March 1984
IBRD (1975a), *Rural Development*, Sector Policy Paper, Washington DC: IBRD
IBRD (1975b), *Republic of Zambia Agricultural and Rural Sector Survey*, Vol. I, Main Report, Washington DC: IBRD
IBRD (1980a), *Swaziland Agricultural Sector Memorandum*, Washington, DC: IBRD
IBRD (1980b), *Lesotho Agricultural Sector Review*, Washington DC: IBRD
IBRD (1981), *Accelerated Development in sub-Saharan Africa: An Agenda for Action*, Washington DC: IBRD
IBRD (1983), *Zimbabwe Agriculture Sector Study*, Vol. I, Main Text, Washington DC: IBRD
Imboden, N.(1980), *Managing Information for Rural Development Projects*, Paris: OECD
Jarvis, L.S. (1980), 'Cattle as a store of wealth in Swaziland: comment', *American Journal of Agricultural Economics*, vol. 62, pp. 606-13
Johnson, G. and **Whitlaw, W.E.** (1974), 'Urban-rural income transfers in Kenya: an estimated remittance function', *Economic Development and Cultural Change*, vol. 22, no. 3, pp. 473-9
Johnston, B. (1978), *Agricultural Production Potentials and Small Farmer Strategies in Sub-Saharan Africa*, in World Bank Staff Working Paper No. 300, Washington DC: World Bank
Kerven, C. (1979), *Rural Urban Migration and Agricultural Productivity in Botswana*, Ministry of Finance and Development Planning, Gaberone
Klepper, T. (1980), 'The state and peasantry in Zambia', in *The Evolving Structure of Zambian Society*, Edinburgh: Centre of African Studies, University of Edinburgh.
Knight, J.B. (1978), 'Labour allocation and unemployment in South Africa', *Oxford Bulletin of Economics and Statistics*, vol. 40, no. 2, pp. 93-129
Knight, J.B. (1982), 'The nature of unemployment in South Africa', *South African Journal of Economics*, vol. 49, no. 1, pp. 1-12
Knight, J.B. and **Lenta, G.** (1980), 'Has capitalism underdeveloped the labour reserves of South Africa?', *Oxford Bulletin of Economics and Statistics*, vol. 42, no. 3, pp. 158-97

Kowet, D.K. (1978), *Land, Labour Migration and Politics in Southern Africa: Botswana, Lesotho and Swaziland*, Uppsala: Scandinavian Institute of Africa Studies

Krishna, R. (1970), 'Comment – models of the family farm' in C.R. Wharton (ed.), *Subsistence Agriculture and Economic Development*, London: Frank Cass pp. 185–90

Kuper, H. (1961), *An African Aristocracy: Rank Among the Swazi*, London: Oxford University Press

LASA (1978), *Lesotho's Agriculture: A Review of Existing Information*, Research Report No. 2, Lesotho Agricultural Sector Analysis Project, Colorado State University

Lancaster, K.J. (1966), 'Change and innovation in the technology of consumption', *American Economic Review*, vol. 46, no. 2, pp. 14–23

Lau, L.J., Lin, W. and Yotopoulos, P.A. (1978), 'The linear logarithmic expenditure system: an application to consumption-leisure choice', *Econometrica*, vol. 46, no. 4, pp. 842–68

Leibowitz, A.S. (1972), 'Women's allocation of time to market and nonmarket activities: differences in education', PhD dissertation, Columbia University

Lele, U. (1979), 'A revisit to rural development in eastern Africa', *Finance and Development*, vol. 16, pp. 31–5

Lele, U. (1981), 'Rural Africa: modernization, equity and long term development', *Science*, vol. 211, pp. 547–53

Lenta, G. (1978), *Development or Stagnation? Agriculture in Kwazulu*, Occasional Paper No. 7, Dept of Agricultural Economics, University of Natal, Durban

Lewis, J.V.D. (1975), *The Status of the Ox-drawn Plough in Dukolomba*, Mali Livestock Project, State University of New York

Lewis, W.A. (1954), 'Economic development with unlimited supplies of labour', *The Manchester School*, vol. 22, no. 2, pp. 139–91

Linder, S.B. (1970), *The Harried Leisure Class*, New York: Columbia University Press

Lipton, M. (1977), *Why Poor People Stay Poor*, London: Temple Smith

Lipton, M. (1978), *Employment and Labour Use in Botswana*, Gaberone: Ministry of Finance and Development Planning

Lipton, Merle (1977), 'South Africa: two agricultures?', in F. Wilson, A. Kooy and D. Hendrie (eds), *Farm Labour in South Africa*, Cape Town: David Philip

Low, A.R.C. (1974), 'Decision taking under uncertainty: a linear programing model of peasant farmer behaviour', *Journal of Agricultural Economics*, vol. 25, no. 3, pp. 311–21

Low, A.R.C. (1978), 'Linear programing and the study of peasant farmer situations – a reply', *Journal of Agricultural Economics*, vol. 29, no. 2, pp. 189–90

Low, A.R.C. (1980), *The Estimation and Interpretation of Pastoralists' Price Responsiveness*, Pastoral Network Paper No. 10c, London: Overseas Development Institute

Low, A.R.C. (1981), 'The effect of off-farm employment on farm incomes and production: Taiwan contrasted with southern Africa', *Economic Development and Cultural Change*, vol. 29, no. 4, pp. 741–7

Low, A.R.C. (1982a), 'A comparative advantage theory of the subsistence farm-household: applications to Swazi farming', *South African Journal of Economics*, vol. 50, no. 2, pp. 136-57

Low, A.R.C. (1982b), 'Agricultural development in southern Africa: a household economics perspective', PhD thesis, Department of Agricultural Economics and Management, University of Reading

Low, A.R.C. (1984a), 'On-farm research and household economics', paper presented at Rockefeller/Ford Foundation Conference on Intrahousehold Processes and Farming Systems Analysis, Bellagio, Italy, March 1984

Low, A.R.C. (1984b), 'Agricultural development in southern Africa: theory, lessons and the food crisis in Africa', *Development Southern Africa*, vol. 1, pp. 294-318

Low, A.R.C., Kemp, R.L. and **Doran, M.H.** (1980a), 'Cattle wealth and cash needs in Swaziland: price response and rural development implications', *Journal of Agricultural Economics*, vol. 31, no. 2, pp. 225-36

Low, A.R.C., Kemp, R.L. and **Doran, M.H.** (1980b), 'Cattle as a store of wealth in Swaziland: reply', *American Journal of Agricultural Economics*, vol. 62, pp. 614-17

Low, A.R.C. and **Fowler, M.H.** (1979), *Ex-Post Evaluation of Mahlangatsha RDA (1973-1978)*, mimeo, Mbabane: Monitoring and Evaluation Unit, Ministry of Agriculture and Cooperatives

Lyby, E. (1980), 'Migration and underdevelopment: interviews with migrants on South African mines', *South African Labour Bulletin*, vol. 5, pp. 27-43

McInerney, J.P. (1978), *The Technology of Rural Development*, World Bank Staff Working Paper No. 295, Washington, DC: World Bank

Maina, M.M. and **Strieker, G.G.** (1971), *Customary Land Tenure and Modern Agriculture of Swazi Nation Land: A Programme of Partnership*, Mbabane: Ministry of Agriculture

Malawi Government (1970), *Compendium of Statistics for Malawi: 1970*, Zomba: National Statistics Office

Marter, A. (1978), *Cassava or Maize*, Lusaka: Rural Development Studies, Bureau, University of Zambia

Marter, A. and **Honeybone, P.** (1976), *The Economic Resources of Rural Households and the Distribution of Agricultural Development*, Lusaka: Rural Development Studies Bureau, University of Zambia

Marwick, B.A. (1940), *The Swazi: An Ethnographic Account of the natives of the Swaziland Protectorate*, Cambridge, Cambridge University Press

Mashasha, F.J. (1977), 'The road to colonialism: concessions and the collapse of Swazi independence. 1875-1926', PhD thesis, Oxford University

Matlon, P.J. (1979), *Income Distribution Among Farmers in Northern Nigeria: Empirical Results and Policy Implications*, African Rural Economy Paper No. 18, East Lansing: Michigan State University

Meadows, S.J. and **White, J.M.** (1979), *Structure of the Herd and Determinants of Offtake Rates in Kajiado District in Kenya 1962-1977*, Pastoral network paper No. 7d, Overseas Development Institute, London

Meillassoux, C. (1981), *Maidens, Meal and Money: Capitalism and the Domestic Community*, Cambridge: Cambridge University Press

Mellor, J.W. (1963), 'The use and production of labour in early stages of agricultural development', *Journal of Farm Economics*, vol. 45, pp. 517–34

Mellor, J.W. (1985) 'The Changing World Food Situation', Food Policy Statement, International Food Policy Research Institute, Washington.

Mettrick, H. (1978), *Oxenization in The Gambia: An Evaluation*, London: Overseas Development Administration

Michael, R.T. and **Becker, G.S.** (1973), 'On the new theory of consumer behaviour', *The Swedish Journal of Economics*, vol. 75, pp. 378–95

Mines, R. and **de Janvry, A.** (1982), 'Migration to the United States and Mexican rural development: a case study', *American Journal of Agricultural Economics*, vol. 64, pp. 444–54

Minford, P. and **Ohs, P.** (1976), 'Supply response of Malawi labour', *Eastern Africa Economic Review*, vol. 8, pp. 15–34

Miracle, M.P. (1968), 'Subsistence agriculture: analytical problems and alternative concepts', *American Journal of Agricultural Economics*, vol. 50, pp. 292–310

Morse, C. et al. (1960), *Basutoland, Bechuanaland and Swaziland: Report of an Economic Survey Mission*, London: HMSO

Mudahar, M.S. (1980), *Principal Policy Issues Facing the Fertilizer Sector in Africa: A Perspective*, Draft Paper, IFDC, Alabama

Murray, C. (1980), 'From granary to labour reserve: an economic history of Lesotho', *South African Labour Bulletin*, vol. 6, pp. 3–20

Muth, R.F. (1966), 'Household production and consumer demand functions', *Econometrica*, vol. 34, pp. 699–708

Nag, M., White, B.N.F. and **Peet, C.R.** (1980), 'An anthropological approach to the study of the economic value of children in Java and Nepal', in Binswanger, H.P. et al. (eds) (1980)

Nakajima, C. (1970), 'Subsistence and commercial family farms: some theoretical models of subjective equilibrium', in Wharton, C.R. (ed.), *Subsistence Agriculture and Economic Development*, London: Frank Cass

Natrass, J. (1976), 'Migrant labour and South African economic development', *South African Journal of Economics*, vol. 44, no. 1, pp. 65–83

Nerlove, M. (1974), 'Toward a new theory of population and economic growth', in Schultz, T.W. (ed) (1974)

Nie, N.H., Bent, D.H. and **Hull, C.H.** (1970), *Statistical Package for Social Sciences: Version IV*, New York: McGraw Hill

Norman, D.W. (1983), *Helping Resource Poor Farmers: The Agricultural Technology Improvement Project, Botswana*, Workshop for US Technicians Preparing for Overseas Assignments, Manhattan, Kansas, ATIP MP 83-2

Norman, D.W., Simmons, E.B. and **Hays, H.M.** (1982), *Farming System in the Nigerian Savanna: Research and Strategies for Development*, Boulder: Westview Press

ODA (1981), *A Note on the RDA Programme: Swaziland*, London: Overseas Development Administration

Odell, M.L. and **Odell, M.J.** (1980), *The Evolution of a Strategy for Livestock Development in the Communal Areas of Botswana*, Pastoral Network Paper No. 10b, London: Overseas Development Institute

OECD (1980), *Development Cooperation*, Paris: OECD

Okigbo, B.N. (1981), 'Agriculture and food production in tropical Africa', mimeo, IITA, Ibadan, Nigeria
Okurume, G.E. (1970), 'Foreign trade and the subsistence sector in a peasant export economy, PhD dissertation, Yale University
Oshima, H.T. (1964), 'The Ranis-Fei model of economic development: comment', in C. Eicher, and L. Witt (eds), *Agriculture in Economic Development*, New York: McGraw Hill
Palmer, R. and **Parsons, N.** (eds) (1977), *The Roots of Rural Poverty in Central and Southern Africa*, London: Heinemann
Palmer-Jones, R.W. (1977), 'A comment on planned versus actual farmer performance under uncertainty in underdeveloped agriculture', *Journal of Agricultural Economics*, vol. 28, no. 2, pp. 177-9
Palmer-Jones, R.W. (1979), 'Linear programing and the study of peasant farming: a rejoinder', *Journal of Agricultural Economics*, vol. 30, no. 2, pp. 199-204
Peterson, W.L. (1979), 'International farm prices and social cost of cheap food policies', *American Journal of Agricultural Economics*, vol. 61, pp. 12-21
Peterson, W.L. (1983), 'International farm prices and the social cost of cheap food policies; a reply', *American Journal of Agricultural Economics*, vol. 65, pp. 827-8
Petit, M. (1975), 'Farmers' adoption of technical innovations', *European Review of Agricultural Economics*, vol. 3, pp. 293-322
Pike, J.G. (1968), *Malawi: A Political and Economical History*, London: Pall Mall
Pim, A.W. (1932), *Financial and Economic Situation of Swaziland*, cmd. 4140, London: HMSO
Pim, A.W. (1935), *Basutoland: Financial and Economic Position*, cmd. 4907, London: HMSO
Powesland, P.G. (1954), 'African attitudes and economic change: some indications from Uganda', in *The Collaboration of the Natives to the Economic Development of Africa*, International Days for African Studies, International Fair, Ghent (published by the Department of Agriculture of the Ministry of the Colonies, Brussels)
RDA Management Unit (1981a), *Inputs - 1980/81 Season*, mimeo, Mbabane: Ministry of Agriculture and Cooperatives
RDA Management Unit (1981b), *Crop Record - Season 1980/81*, mimeo, Mbabane: Ministry of Agriculture and Cooperatives
RDA Monitoring and Evaluation Unit (1980), *Rural Development Areas Maize Production and Marketing Survey, 1979*, mimeo, Mbabane: Ministry of Agriculture and Cooperatives
Reyna, S.P. (1976), 'The extending strategy: regulation of the household dependency ratio', *Journal of Anthropological Research*, vol. 32, pp. 182-98
Richards, A.I. (1954), *Economic Development and Tribal Change*, Cambridge: Cambridge University Press
Richards, A.I., Sturrock, F. and **Fortt, J.M.** (eds) (1973), *Subsistence to Commercial Farming in Present Day Buganda: An Economic and Anthropological Survey*, Cambridge: Cambridge University Press
Roberts, A. (1976), *A History of Zambia*, London: Heinemann
Roberts, K.D. (1982), 'Agrarian structure and labour mobility in rural Mexico', *Population and Development Review*, vol. 8, pp. 299-322

Robertson, A.F. (1976), *A Study of the Domestic Development Cycle and the Agricultural Performance of Small Farms*, mimeo, Cambridge University, Cambridge

Robertson, H.M. (1935), '150 years of contact between white and black', *South African Journal of Economics*, vol. 3, no. 1, pp. 3–25

Robinson, E.A.G. (ed.) (1964), *Economic Development for Africa South of the Sahara*, London: Macmillan

Rockefeller Foundation (1985), *Understanding Africa's Rural Households and Farming Systems*, Boulder: Westview Press.

Rozen-Prinz, B.D. and **Prinz, F.A.** (1978), *Migrant Labour and Rural Homesteads: An Investigation into the Sociological Dimensions of the Migrant Labour System in Swaziland*, mimeo, World Employment Programme Research Working Paper, ILO, Geneva

Rutman, G. (1971), 'Asset deterioration, the nature of property rights and the "traditional" economic system', *South African Journal of Economics*, vol. 39, no. 1, pp. 79–87

Schapera, I. (1947), *Migrant Labour and Tribal Life: A Study of the Conditions in the Bechuanaland Protectorate*, London: Oxford University Press

Schuh, E.G. (1974), 'The current state of economic theory for the explanation of subsistence agriculture', paper prepared for the research seminar on development alternatives for low-income groups in Brazilian agriculture, Piracicaba, Brazil

Schultz, P.T. (1976), 'Notes on the estimation of the micro economic determinants of migration', paper prepared for the research workshop on rural-urban labour market interactions, Washington DC

Schultz, T.W. (ed.) (1974), *Economics of the Family: Marriage, Children and Human Capital*, Chicago: University of Chicago Press

Schutjer, W. and **Van Der Veen, H.G.** (1977), *Economic Constraints on Agricultural Technology Adoption in Developing Nations*, USAID Occasional Papers No. 5, Washington DC: USAID

Sen, A.K. (1966), 'Peasants and dualism with or without surplus labour', *Journal of Political Economy*, vol. 74, no. 5, pp. 425–50

Shanin, T. (1972), *The Awkward Class: Political Sociology of Peasantry in a Developing Society: Russia 1910–1925* Oxford: Clarendon Press

Shapiro, K.H. (1978), 'Water, women and development in Tanzania', Paper presented to 3rd Annual Conference of the International Water Resources Association, São Paulo, Brazil

Sharir, S. (1975), 'The income leisure model: a diagrammatic extension', *The Economic Record*, vol. 51, no. 133, pp. 93–8

Shumba, E. (1983), *The Crop-Livestock Interrelationship and Farmer Adaptation to Problems of Reduced Cattle Numbers and Lack of Dry Season Feed in Communal areas of Zimbabwe*, CIMMYT technical networkshop, Ezulwini, Swaziland, October 1983

Shumba, E. (1985), *A Diagnostic Survey of Mangwende Communal Area, Zimbabwe for On-Farm Research Planning*, Research Report No. 6, Research & Specialist Services, Harare

Sibisi, H. (1980), *Traditional Securities and the Response to 'Modern' Economic Opportunities*, mimeo, Mbabane: Ministry of Agriculture and Cooperatives

Sibisi, H. (1981), *Keen Farmers on Swazi Nation Land: A Case Study*, Mbabane:

Economic Planning and Analysis Section, Ministry of Agriculture and Cooperatives
Simson, H. (1979), *Zimbabwe: A Country Study*, Research Report No. 53, Uppsala: Scandinavian Institute of African Studies
South African Government (1955), *Commission for the Socio-Economic Development of the Bantu Areas Within the Union of South Africa (Tomlinson Commission)*, Report U.G. 61/1955, Pretoria: Government Printer
Spengler, J.J. (1964), 'Population movements and problems', in E.A.G. Robinson (ed.) (1964), pp. 281-311
Spiegel, A.D. (1980), 'Rural differentiation and the diffusion of migrant labour remittances in Lesotho', in P. Mayer (ed.), *Black Villagers in an Industrial Society: Anthropological Perspectives on Labour Migration in South Africa*, Cape Town: Oxford University Press, pp. 109-68
Spiegel, A.D. (1981), 'Rural differentiation and the diffusion of migrant labour remittances in Lesotho', *Social Dynamics*, vol. 6, pp. 1-13
Spray, P. (1975), *A Tentative Economic History of Lesotho from 1800*, Institute of Development Studies, University of Sussex
Squire, L. and van der Tak, H.G. (1975), *Economic Analysis of Projects*, Baltimore: Johns Hopkins University Press
Stahl, C.W. (1981), 'Migrant labour supplies, past, present and future: with special reference to the gold mining industry', in W.R. Bohning (ed), *Black Migration to South Africa*, Geneva, ILO
Stahl, C.W. and Bohning, W.R. (1981), 'Reducing dependence on migration in southern Africa', in W.R. Bohning (ed.), *Black Migration to South Africa*, Geneva: ILO
Stark, O. and Levhari, D. (1982), 'On migration and risk in LDCs', *Economic Development and Cultural Change*, vol. 31, no. 1, pp. 191-6
Steyn, A.F. (1974), 'Some aspects of African society influencing development', in J. Barratt, S. Brand, D.S. Collier, and K. Glasser (eds) *Accelerated Development in Southern Africa*, London: Macmillan, pp. 299-347
Strauss, J. (1982), *Socio-Economic Determinants of Food Consumption and Production in Rural Sierra Leone: Application of an Agricultural Household Model with Several Commodities*, MSU International Development Paper, Dept of Agriculture Economics, Michigan State University, East Lansing
Strauss, J. et al. (1981), *Joint Determination of Food Production and Consumption in Rural Sierra Leone: Estimates of a Household-Farm Model*, working paper No. 17, MSU Rural Development series, Michigan State University, East Lansing
Sumner, D.A. (1982), 'The off-farm labor supply of farmers', *American Journal of Agricultural Economics*, vol. 64, pp. 499-509
Swaziland Government (1973), *Agricultural Sample Census: (Swazi Nation Land) 1971/72*, Mbabane: Central Statistics Office
Swaziland Government (1976), *Annual Statistical Bulletin*, Mbabane: Central Statistics Office,
Swaziland Government (1979), *Report of the Swaziland Population Census*, Vol. 1, Mbabane: Central Statistics Office
Tessema, S. (1983), *Animal Feeding in Small Farm Systems*, CIMMYT technical networkshop, Ezulwini, Swaziland, October 1983
Thornton, D.S. (1982), *The Study of Rural Development: Changing Perspective*, Development Study No. 24, Department of Agricultural Economics and Farm Management, University of Reading

Todaro, M.P. (1969), 'A model of labor migration and urban unemployment in less developed countries', *American Economic Review*, vol. 59, no. 1, pp. 138-48

Tripp, R.B. (1982), 'Time allocation in northern Ghana: an example of the random visit method', *Journal of Developing Areas*, vol. 16, no. 3, pp. 391-400

Umphawi, A.C. (1984), *Blantyre ADD 1982/3 Evaluation Working Paper*, mimeo, Lilongwe: Ministry of Agriculture

United Nations (1980), *Demographic Yearbook*, New York: UN Department of International Economic and Social Affairs

Upton, M. (1979), 'The unproductive productive function', *Journal of Agricultural Economics*, vol. 30, no. 2, pp. 179-94

Upton, M. and **Casey, H.** (1974), 'Risk and some pitfalls in the use of averages in farm planning', *Journal of Agricultural Economics*, vol. 25, no. 2, pp. 147-52

USAID (1980), 'Swaziland Country Development Strategy', Washington DC: USAID

USDA (1981), *Food Problems and Prospects in Sub-Saharan Africa: the decade of the 1980s*, summary report, International Economics Division, Washington DC: USDA

de Vletter, F. (1978), *The Rural Homestead as an Economic Unit*, Kwaluseni: University College of Swaziland

de Vletter, F. (1979), *Subsistence Farmer, Cash Cropper or Consumer?: A socio-economic profile of a sample of Swazi rural homesteads*, University College of Swaziland, Kwaluseni

de Vletter, F. (1983), *The Swazi Rural Homestead*, Kwaluseni: Social Science Research Unit, University of Swaziland

de Vletter, F. et al. (1981), 'Labour migration in Swaziland', in W.R. Bohning (ed.), *Black Migration to South Africa*, Geneva: ILO

Watson, V. (1983), *Farming Systems on Swazi Nation Land: Results of Extension Field Officer Survey September–November 1982*, mimeo, Cropping Systems Research and Extension Training Project, Malkerns, Swaziland

Westcott, G. (1977), 'Obstacles to agricultural development in the Transkei', in F. Wilson, A. Kooy and D. Hendrie (eds), *Farm Labour in South Africa*, Cape Town: David Philip

White, J. (1981), *The Estimation and Interpretation of Pastoralists' Price Responsiveness: Comment*, Pastoral Network Paper No. 11f, London: Overseas Development Institute

White, N.F. (1980), 'Rural household studies in anthropological perspective', in Binswanger, H.P. et al. (eds) (1980)

van der Wiel, A.C.A. (1977), *Migratory Wage Labour: Its Role in the Economy of Lesotho*, Mazenod, Lesotho

de Wilde, J.C. (1967), *Experiences with Agricultural Development in Tropical Africa*, Vol 1, Baltimore: Johns Hopkins University Press

Yudelman, M. (1964a), 'Some aspects of African agricultural development', in E.A.G. Robinson (ed.), 1964, pp. 554-87

Yudelman, M., (1964b), *Africans on the Land*, London: Oxford University Press

Yudelman, M. (1981), 'Africa in crisis: a banker's view', *International Agricultural Development*, October 1981

Index

adoption: of crops; 72, 136, 139; of technology, 7, 62, 63, 83, 85, **90-106**, 136, 137, 139, 142-149, 161, 167-168

Africa, sub-Saharan: 8; agricultural crisis in, 24-25, 179; cheap food policy, 158, 189; increasing food gap, 25, 53, 158-159, 189

agro climatic factors: drought, 1, 2, 50, 59; influence of, 4, 26, 48, **73-74**, 113-114, 167-168, 190

aid: food imports, 1, 25, 189; international, 1, 25, 137, 189, 190, 190n

Asia: 2, 21n, 29, 135, 181, 182, 183, 189, 190

Botswana: cattle sales rates, 114; development history of, 4, **48-53**; economic growth, 23-24; employment and wages, 26; extension programmes, 136; food deficits, 24, 25, 50; grazing land tenure, 115-116; migration patterns, 124, 126, 185; technology, appropriate for, 105; adoption of, 136

cattle: attributes of, 6, 17, 40, 111; costs of keeping, 40, 115; herd size, 76; by domestic development group, 82, 83, 171; influence on crop production, 170-171; investment in, 111, 115, 187; sales of, 40, 111-115; by domestic development group, 84, 85; for cash needs, 112-114; related to price, 113; reasons for, 114; slaughter/offtake, 112-114

Chayanov, A.V.: complex cooperation principle, 29, 34, 45, 127, 146, 188; domestic development cycle, 5, 32, 75-76, 85, 86, 87; peasant economics, 28-30, 75

children: numbers of, 17, 30, 81-82; value of, 16, 17, 21n, 29, 30, 151, 153n, 191n

colonial administrations: 49-53, 119, 121, 129, 136-137, 186

commercial farming: 23-24, 179; cash cropping, 4, 18-19, **40-44**, 70-73; variations in, 74-75, 83, 85; conflict with other roles of land, 5, 109; wage employment, effect on, 4, 5, 74-75, 77-78, 95-100, 142-147, 151

comparative advantage: between household members, 19, **36-37**, 42, 123, 126, 188; implications for agriculture, 127-129; in wage employment, 6, 94-97; model of migration, 123-126

complex cooperation principle: Chayanov's concept, 29, 34, 45, 127, 146, 188; evidence of, 30, 68, 181, 182

consumer goods: attributes of, 14, 20; cattle as, 6, 112, 116; introduction and purchase of, 4, 49, 115; relative cost of, 3, 17, 20, 32, 39, 40, 41, 110, 115

consumer/worker ratio: 5, 182; analysis by, 81-86, 88, 95-96;

213

Index

Chayanov's concept, 29, 32, 34, 77
consumption behaviour: consumption/production units, 2, 3, 18, 30, 31; luxury consumption, 6, 40, 111, 112, 114, 116, 180; minimise cost of consumption, 3, 15, 21n, 28, 35, 37, 90, 96–97, 175–176

data sources: 65–66
demographic differentiation: 86–88
development: strategies, 2, 151–152; patterns, 24–26, 48–53, 120; dualistic, 22–24, 54, 179; theory, **53–55**, 119, 179, 186
domestic development cycle; **75–86**, 180; analysis by, 81–86, 102; influence, on farm production, 5, 17, 29, 33, 34, 102, 170–171; on migration, 86–88, 124–126, 132n, 170–171, 187
domestic duties: 6, 104, 105, 110, 127, 171, 188; child care, 6, 15, 19, 104, 105, 110, 127, 132n, 171

economies, southern African: dualism, 22–24, 54; economic growth in, 1, 24–26, 84
education: development of human capital, 7, 16, 20, 151, 153n; facilities, 136, 137, 149–150; migration related to, 124, 151
Ethiopia: 106n, 171
extension: packages, 87, 136; services, 137, 149

family, farm: composition of, 17, 29, 32, 153n, 181–182, 191n; groupings, nuclear/extended, 79–81; motivations/objectives of, 168, 172, 180; welfare, 9, 14, 151, 168–169, 172, 177
farm-household: African model of, 3, 28, **35–46**, 92–96, 144–146, 190; conventional models of, 3, **30–35**, 68, 69, 123, 153n; labour allocation in, **35–39**, 72, 93–96, 144–146, 180, 181–183; size and composition of, 5, 15, 33–34, 135; related to wage income, 78–79, 83, 85; related to crop production, 78–79, 101, 126, 181; related to stage in domestic development cycle, 81–82; surplus/deficit producers, 34–35, **77–78, 95–101**
fertiliser uptake: 136, 137, 140, 142, 147
food production and utilisation, Africa: trends, 1, 50–52, 179; imports, 52, 158; surplus/deficit producers, 34–35, 43, 72, **77–78**, 95–101n
food crisis: Asia vs Africa, 2, 135, 190, 183; in sub-Saharan Africa, 24–25, 53, 54, 179

goods: desired, 20, 49, 111; input/time intensive, 15–16, **29**, 30, 44, 104, 110, 148, 184; demand for market, 49, 112, 115, 157

household economics: previous applications of, 1, 3, **15–16, 18–20**, 21n; relevance of, **16–18**, 19, 20, 28–30, 110, 180–183 *passim*, 188–190; theory of, 3, **13–15**
household production: technology of, 15, 104, 106, 110; importance of, 17, 181; income sources, 26, 27, 63, 74–75, 77, 130, 170–171
hybrid maize: adoption of, 5, 136, 190; theoretical, 91–98; observed, 98–104; introduction of, 137

indigenous economies: underdevelopment of, 2, 49–52, 119; social structure, **108–111**; influence of, 5, 54, 55n, 109–110, 127–129, 185
infrastructure: 7,

137–142 *passim*, 149–151, 152

Kenya: 46n; application of Chayanov's theory, 46n, 85; cattle holding, 116; land tenure, 116, 162; maize yields, 152n; migration, 55n, 186, 188; technology adoption, 100, 152n, 169

labour: allocation within households, **35–39**, 72, 93–96, 144–146, 180, 181–183; hiring, 18, 62, 129, 182, 183; landless, 164; lack of, 9, 19, 183; 189; markets, development of, 119–120; returns to, 32, 41, 52, **66–69**, 105, 127, 132n, 181; in cropping, 70–71; opportunity cost of, 52, 53, 97
land: distribution of, 23, 162; fixed vs flexible holdings, 32, 46n, 67, 76; traditional use of, 108–110; under-utilization of, 118, 121–122, shortage of, 119–122, 127, 129
land tenure: 135, **162–165**, 189; allocation of, 19, 61, 129; constraint to development, 107, 162, 166; change in, 115–116, 133n, 162, 164, 165; freehold, 162–165; policy, 8, 162–165; roles of land, 5, 39, **108–110**; use rights, 5, 8, 39, 53, **108**, 163; security of tenure, 108, 162–163
leisure: 15, 19, 30, 40, 44–45, 85, 103–104, 105, 131, 182
Lesotho: development cycle of households, 34, 76; development history of, 4, **48–53**, 136; employment and wages, 26, 130–131; extension programmes, 136; food deficits, 24, 25, 50; investment of wage income, 111, 129; land use, 122, 130, 164; maize yields, 120, 122, **132**; migration patterns, 124, 130–131, 185; rural development, 137, 140–142

maize: dominance of, 23, 62; imports and utilisation, 158; production costs and returns, 70–72, 91–93; yields per hectare and per hour, 90–92, 132, 147, 170–171
Malawi: agricultural performance, 8, 161–162; employment and wages, 26, 34, 162; farm-household behaviour, 3, **18–20**; land use, 122, 129; rural population, 22; technology adoption, 136, 149, 169, 174
market, marketing: 71, 135, 184; informal, 71; infrastructure, 2, 142, 157, 184; marketed production, 23, 40–41, 71, 86, 87, 98, 100–102, 157, 189, 190
Marxist development theories: 53, 54, 86, 87, 118–119, 185, 186
migration: effect on agricultural production, 52, 87, 88; causes of, 6, 119, 180, 185, 186; comparative advantage model of, **123–126**, 188; conventional models of, 119, 123, 186; oscillating, 4, 180, 184–186; rural-urban, 8, 159; 160–162, 165n, 172, 180; to the mines, 24, 49–52, 72, 184–185
modern sector: development, in southern Africa, 3, 22–26, 49–52, 54, 184; elsewhere, 54, 160, 161, 179–181, 184

neo-classical development theory: 54, 119, 121
Nigeria: household life cycles, 88; food production decline, 161
non-market activities: production 3, 4, 17, 54, 104, 105, 158;

216 *Index*

production and consumption, 28, 39–40, 110, 180; importance of in African development, 18, 54, 135

opportunity cost: of purchase, 6, **37**, 38, 41, 71, 72, **93–96**; of time, 4, 97, 112, 128, 131, 163, 171, 174–175

overgrazing: 6, 51–52, 107, 115–116

Peru: cheap food policy, 158; development pattern, 179–181; peasant agriculture, 158, 180; urbanisation, 160

policy: food prices, 8, 157–160, 189, 190; subsidies, 157, 159; land tenure, 8, 115–116, 162–165; urban wage, 8, 160–162

population: distribution rural 22; pressure, 1, 4, 5, 7, 50, 52, 55n, 104–105, 118, 119, 128–129

prices: producer, 8, 157; gold, 30; cattle, 113; maize, 71, 92; food, 32, 41, 159; consumer/retail, food, 4, 8, 32, 38, 41, 53, 157–160, 189; maize, 71, 92; consumer goods, 3, 20, 39–40, 110

research: farming-systems: 8, 167–171; need for and characteristics of, 167–168; traditional, 167, 168

resource endowments: variations in, 82, 83, 85, 86, 101–102, 170–171, 173–174

risk: 41–42, 72, 168, 173, 177, 184

rural development: definition of, 134; evaluation of, 7, 134, 137–142, 151, 161; social accounting, 152n; implementation and results, 2, 25, 134–135, **137–142**, 161; integrated, 160–162; past initiatives, 136–137; urbanisation and, 160–162, 189

rural home base: attraction of, 3, 4, 9, 110, 187; maintenance of, 53, 110, 163, 186, 187, 188, 189

social security: through land tenure, 9, 39–40, 109, 164, 166n, 189; through cattle, 40, 111, 119

South Africa: economic structure of, 22; homelands, employment and wages, 26, 34; land use, 121, 122, 164; migration patterns, 24, 52, 124–126, 185; technology adoption in, 136; extension programmes, 137; mine, earnings, 144; recruitment, 49, 52, 63, 184, 185

subjective equilibrium theory: 28; limitations of, **31–35**, 68, 69, 153n; Nakajima model, 30–31, 123, 153n;

subsistence production: 4, 31–32; economics of, **70–75**, 92–98; effect of wage employment on, 77–78, 92–100, 127–129, 130–132, 142–149, 160–162; model of, **35–46**

Swaziland: 4, **59–63**; economic growth, 24; employment and wages, 26, 34, 63, 120, 143–144; food deficits, 24, 25; geography and climate, 59–60; history, 60–62; migration patterns, 120, 124–125, 185–187; rural sector, 62–63; population, 22; agriculture, 62, 63; income, 63; rural development, 137–140; surplus/deficit producers, 35, 77–78, 100–101; technology adoption, 136

target income concept: 112

technology: appropriate 5, 8, 104–106; green revolution, 9, 106n, 190; labour saving,

5, 26, 92–104, 131, 132n, 144–149, 161, 162, 169–170, 174–176, 181–183, 189
time, human, 15, 20, 128; allocation within households, 18–19, **35–39**, 181–183; economize on, 15–16, 131, 159, 189; opportunity cost of, 4, 53, 85, 112, 128, 131; purchase, of, 15, 104; returns to, 4, 32, **66–69**, 105, 127, 161; value of, 16, 17, 19, 85, 127, 142–146, 149, 151, 159, 160, 170, 176

Uganda: land tenure, 162; migration and farm production, 75, 133n, 187
urbanisation: cost of urban living, 110, 159; effect on, peasant agriculture, 158; rural development, 160–162; food subsidies related to, 159; premature, 9, 9n, 189; rate of, 159, 188, 189
utility: maximisation of, 13, 15, 21n, 30–31, 131; by cost minimisation, 21n, 28, 35–36, 96–97, 172

veld, rangelands: ranching, fencing, 6, 39, 115, 150–151; ownership of, 6; 115
vent for surplus development pattern: 49, 53

wage employment: effect on crop production, 26, 52, 74–75, 77–78, 95–100, 118, 133n, 142–149, 160–162; effect on investment, in cattle, 111; in farming, 151, 153n opportunities in southern Africa, 3, 4, 24, 26, 125, 144; relationship with household size and composition, 78, 83, 85, 170–171; variable opportunities for houehold members, 32, 96–97, 124–126
wage rate: increases in southern Africa, 24, 26, 143–144, 189; variability within households, 16, 19, 32, 34, 126
West Africa: food production, 1, 159; food imports and utilisation, 158; migration, 186, 188; modern sector development, 159, 184; technology adoption, 169, 175
wheat: production of, 50; imports and utilisation, 158
women: headed households, 81–86 *passim*, 171; labour force participation, 16, 127; roles of, 18, 117n, 132n, 171

Z goods: 14, 19, **35–40**, 71, 72, 103, 144
Zambia: demographic differentiation, 86–88; economic growth, 24; employment and wages, 26, 34; food deficits, 24, 25; land use, 122; migration, 122, 186, 187; rural population, 22; surplus/deficit producers, 35; technology adoption, 136, 177
Zimbabwe: cattle, influence of, 170–171; economic growth, 24; employment and wages, 26, 34; extension programmes, 136; land use, 122; land tenure, 108–109, 165; maize marketing, 165, 166n; migration, 27, 182; patterns of 124, 126, 148; rural population, 22; surplus/deficit producers, 35, 126; technology adoption, 136, 148–149, 169, 170, 177